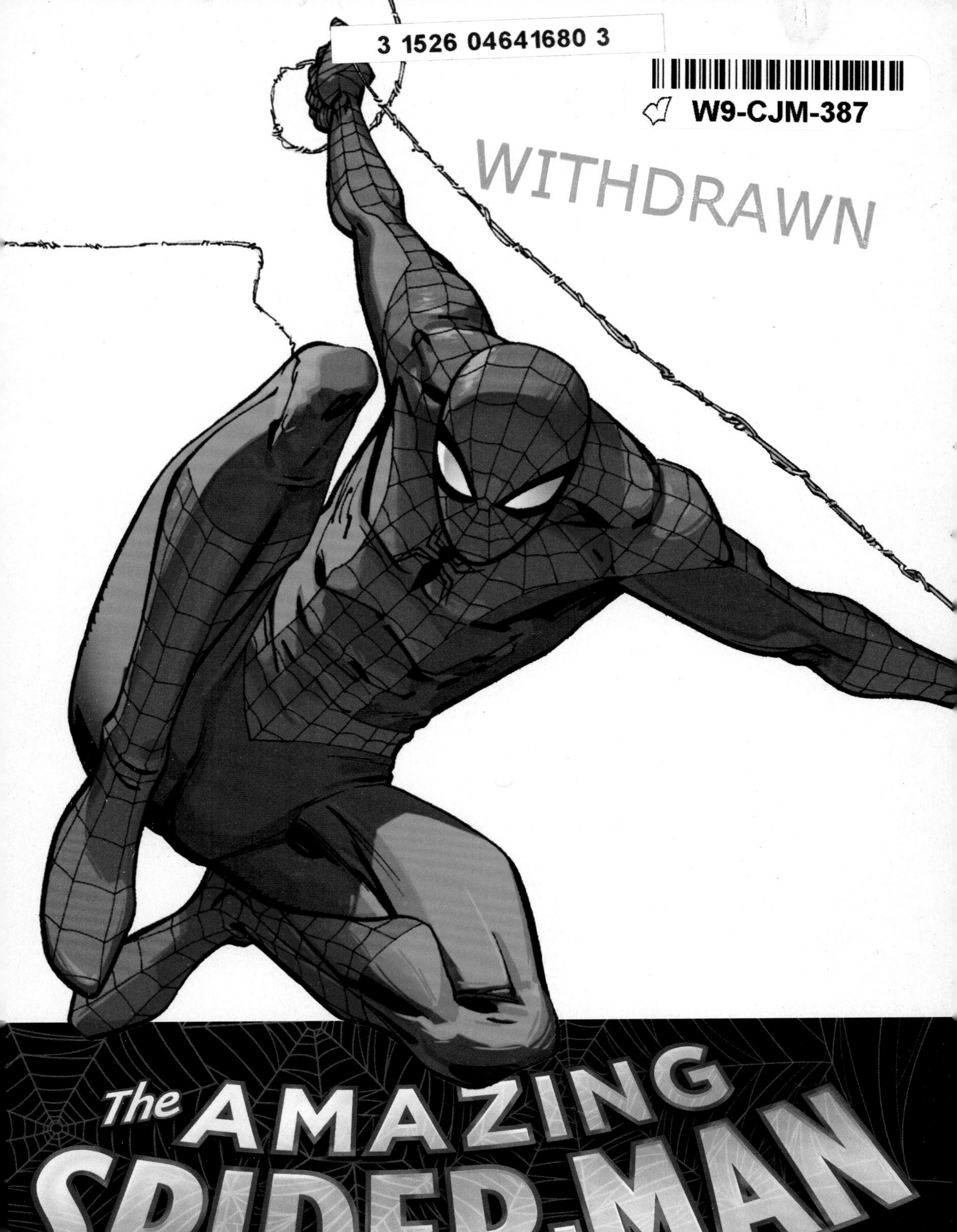

The AMAZING SPIDER-MAN

SPIDER-VERSE PRELUDE

Collection Editor: **Jennifer Grünwald**
Assistant Editor: **Sarah Brunstad**
Associate Managing Editor: **Alex Starbuck**
Editor, Special Projects: **Mark D. Beazley**
Senior Editor, Special Projects: **Jeff Youngquist**
SVP Print, Sales & Marketing: **David Gabriel**
Book Designer: **Rodolfo Muraguchi**

Editor in Chief: **Axel Alonso**
Chief Creative Officer: **Joe Quesada**
Publisher: **Dan Buckley**
Executive Producer: **Alan Fine**

AMAZING SPIDER-MAN VOL. 2: SPIDER-VERSE PRELUDE. Contains material originally published in magazine form as AMAZING SPIDER-MAN #7-8, SUPERIOR SPIDER-MAN #32-33 and FREE C BOOK DAY 2014 (GUARDIANS OF THE GALAXY) #1. First printing 2015. ISBN# 978-0-7851-8798-1. Published by MARVEL WORLDWIDE, INC., a subsidiary of MARVEL ENTERTAINMENT, LLC. OFFIC PUBLICATION: 135 West 50th Street, New York, NY 10020. **Printed in Canada.** ALAN FINE, EVP - Office of the President, Marvel Worldwide, Inc EVP & CMO Marvel Characters B.V.; DAN BUCKLEY, Publisher & President - Print, Animation & Digital Divisions; JOE QUESADA, Chief Creative Officer; TOM BREVOORT, SVP of Publishing; DAVID BO SVP of Operations & Procurement, Publishing; C.B. CEBULSKI, SVP of Creator & Content Development; DAVID GABRIEL, SVP Print, Sales & Marketing; JIM O'KEEFE, VP of Operations & Logistics; CARR, Executive Director of Publishing Technology; SUSAN CRESPI, Editorial Operations Manager; ALEX MORALES, Publishing Operations Manager; STAN LEE, Chairman Emeritus. For inform regarding advertising in Marvel Comics or on Marvel.com, please contact Niza Disla, Director of Marvel Partnerships, at ndisla@marvel.com. For Marvel subscription inquiries, please call 800-217-
Manufactured between 11/7/2014 and 12/15/2014 by SOLISCO PRINTERS, SCOTT, QC, CANADA.

10 9 8 7 6 5 4 3 2 1

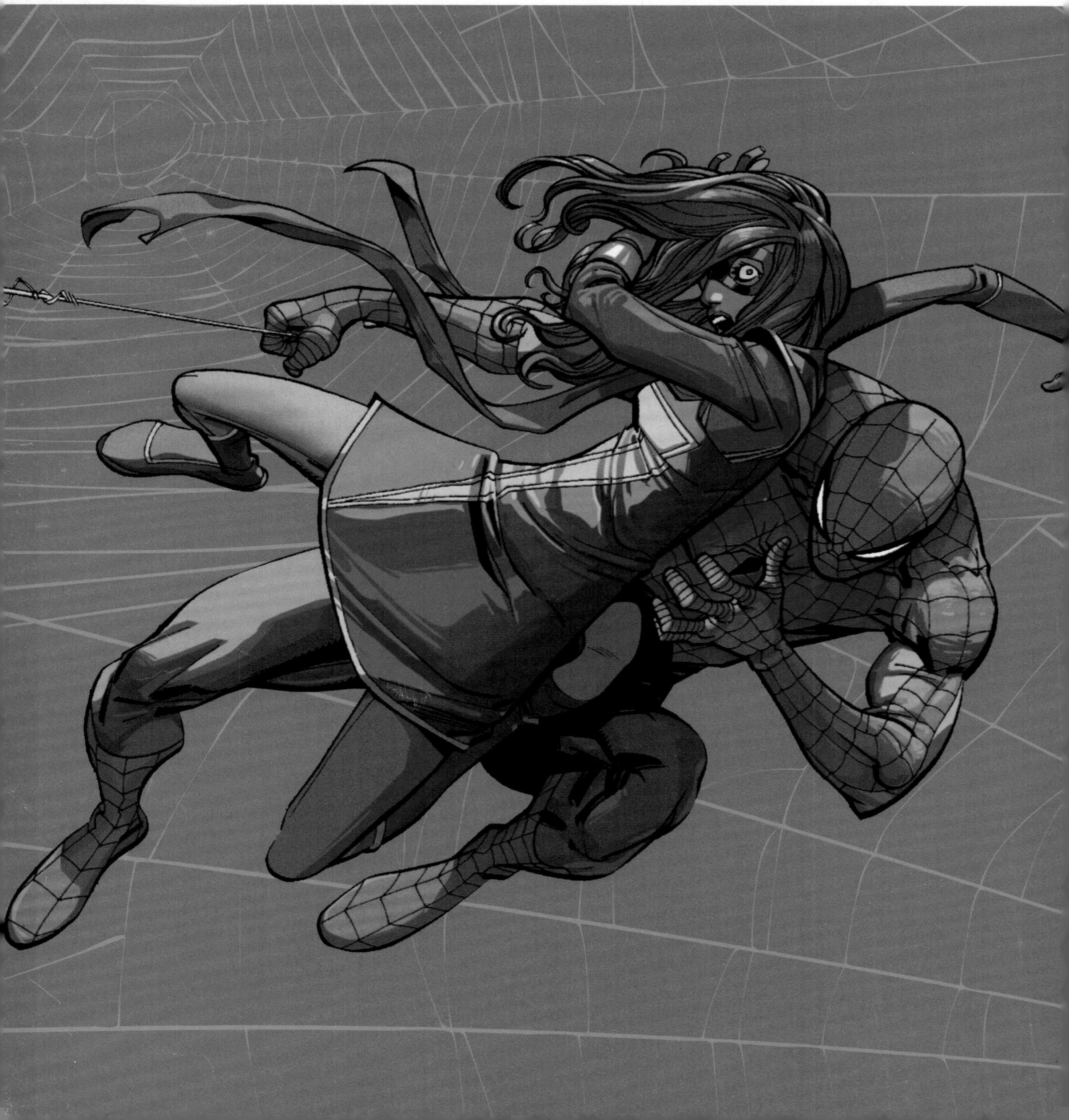

The AMAZING SPIDER-MAN

SPIDER-VERSE PRELUDE

FREE COMIC BOOK DAY 2014
"STAGING GROUND"
WRITER: **DAN SLOTT**
PENCILER: **GIUSEPPE CAMUNCOLI**
INKER: **JOHN DELL**
COLORIST: **EDGAR DELGADO**
LETTERER: **VC'S CORY PETIT**
EDITORS: **STEPHEN WACKER**
& ELLIE PYLE

"EDGE OF SPIDER-VERSE:
WEB OF FEAR"
WRITER: **DAN SLOTT**
PENCILER: **GIUSEPPE CAMUNCOLI**
INKER: **CAM SMITH**
COLORIST: **ANTONIO FABELA**

"EDGE OF SPIDER-VERSE:
MY BROTHER'S KEEPER"
WRITER: **DAN SLOTT**
PENCILER: **HUMBERTO RAMOS**
INKER: **VICTOR OLAZABA**
COLORIST: **EDGAR DELGADO**

"THE SPIDER-SANCTION"
WRITER: **CHRISTOS GAGE**
ARTIST: **ADAM KUBERT**
COLORIST: **RAIN BEREDO**

"BLACK SHEEP"
WRITER: **CHRISTOS GAGE**
ARTIST: **M.A. SEPULVEDA**
COLORIST: **RICHARD ISANOVE**

AMAZING SPIDER-MAN #7-8
& SUPERIOR SPIDER-MAN #32-33

PLOT:
DAN SLOTT
WITH **CHRISTOS GAGE**
(SUPERIOR SPIDER-MAN #33)

SCRIPT:
CHRISTOS GAGE

PENCILER:
GIUSEPPE CAMUNCOLI

INKERS:
CAM SMITH
(AMAZING SPIDER-MAN #7-8)

& JOHN DELL
(SUPERIOR SPIDER-MAN #32-33)

COLORIST:
ANTONIO FABELA

LETTERERS: **CHRIS ELIOPOULOS**
WITH **VC'S JOE CARAMAGNA**
(SUPERIOR SPIDER-MAN #33)
COVER ART: **GIUSEPPE CAMUNCOLI,
CAM SMITH & ANTONIO FABELA**
ASSOCIATE EDITOR: **ELLIE PYLE**
EDITOR: **NICK LOWE**

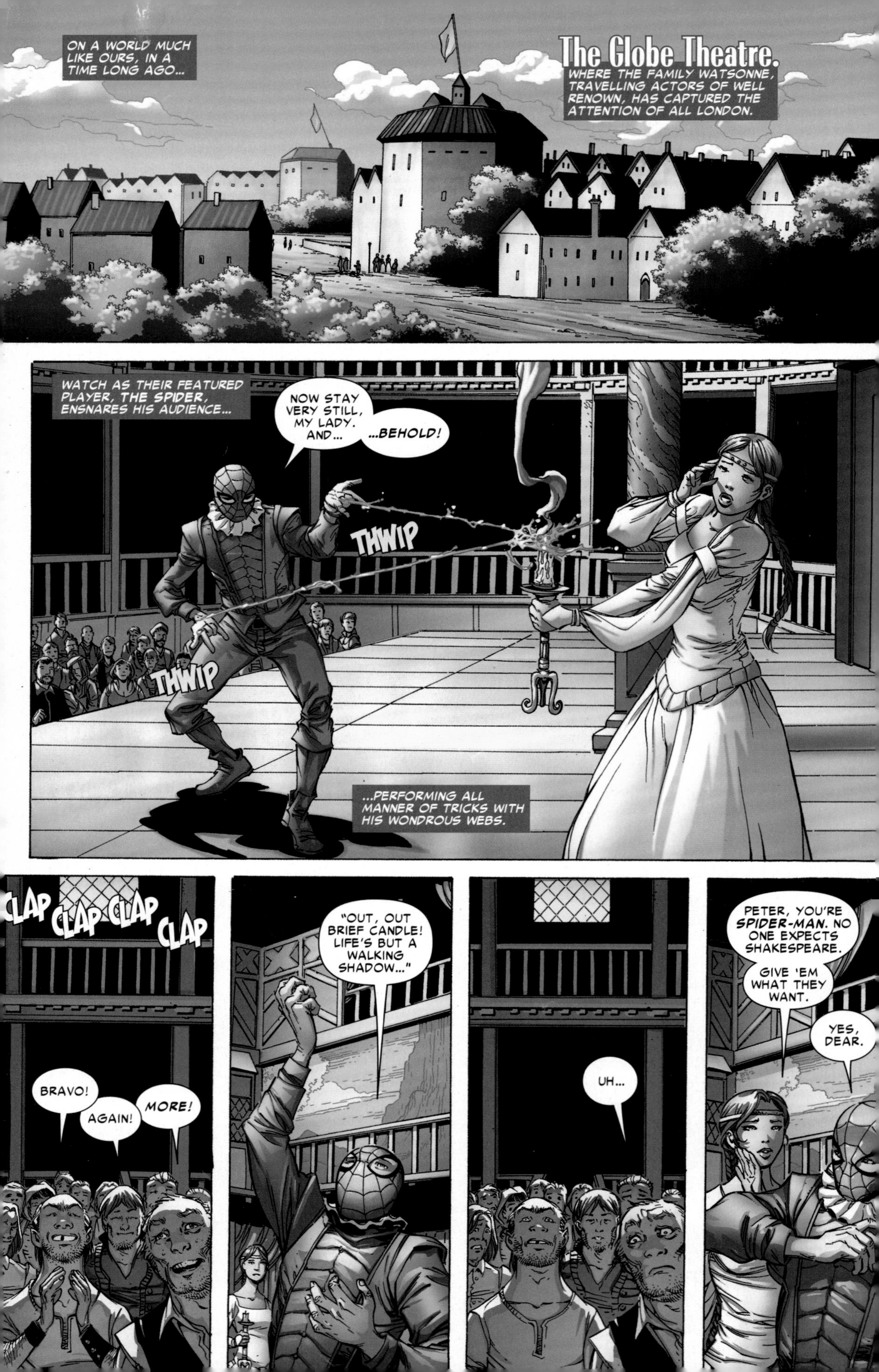
ON A WORLD MUCH LIKE OURS, IN A TIME LONG AGO...
The Globe Theatre.
WHERE THE FAMILY WATSONNE, TRAVELLING ACTORS OF WELL RENOWN, HAS CAPTURED THE ATTENTION OF ALL LONDON.
WATCH AS THEIR FEATURED PLAYER, THE SPIDER, ENSNARES HIS AUDIENCE...
NOW STAY VERY STILL, MY LADY. AND...
...BEHOLD!
THWIP
THWIP
...PERFORMING ALL MANNER OF TRICKS WITH HIS WONDROUS WEBS.
CLAP CLAP CLAP CLAP
BRAVO!
AGAIN!
MORE!
"OUT, OUT BRIEF CANDLE! LIFE'S BUT A WALKING SHADOW..."
UH...
PETER, YOU'RE SPIDER-MAN. NO ONE EXPECTS SHAKESPEARE.
GIVE 'EM WHAT THEY WANT.
YES, DEAR.

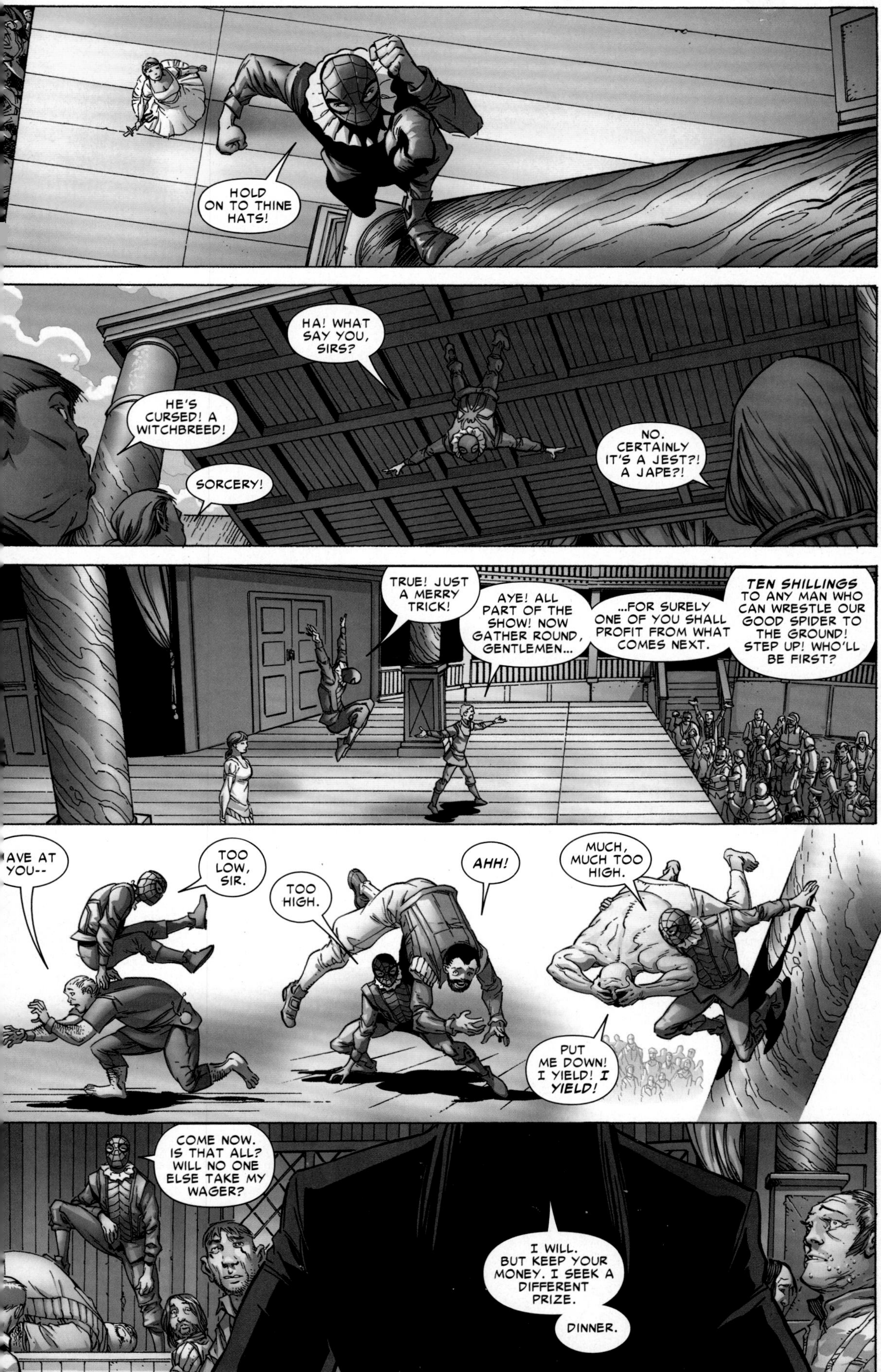
HOLD ON TO THINE HATS!
HA! WHAT SAY YOU, SIRS?
HE'S CURSED! A WITCHBREED!
SORCERY!
NO. CERTAINLY IT'S A JEST?! A JAPE?!
TRUE! JUST A MERRY TRICK!
AYE! ALL PART OF THE SHOW! NOW GATHER ROUND, GENTLEMEN...
...FOR SURELY ONE OF YOU SHALL PROFIT FROM WHAT COMES NEXT.
TEN SHILLINGS TO ANY MAN WHO CAN WRESTLE OUR GOOD SPIDER TO THE GROUND! STEP UP! WHO'LL BE FIRST?
AVE AT YOU--
TOO LOW, SIR.
TOO HIGH.
AHH!
MUCH, MUCH TOO HIGH.
PUT ME DOWN! I YIELD! I YIELD!
COME NOW. IS THAT ALL? WILL NO ONE ELSE TAKE MY WAGER?
I WILL. BUT KEEP YOUR MONEY. I SEEK A DIFFERENT PRIZE.
DINNER.

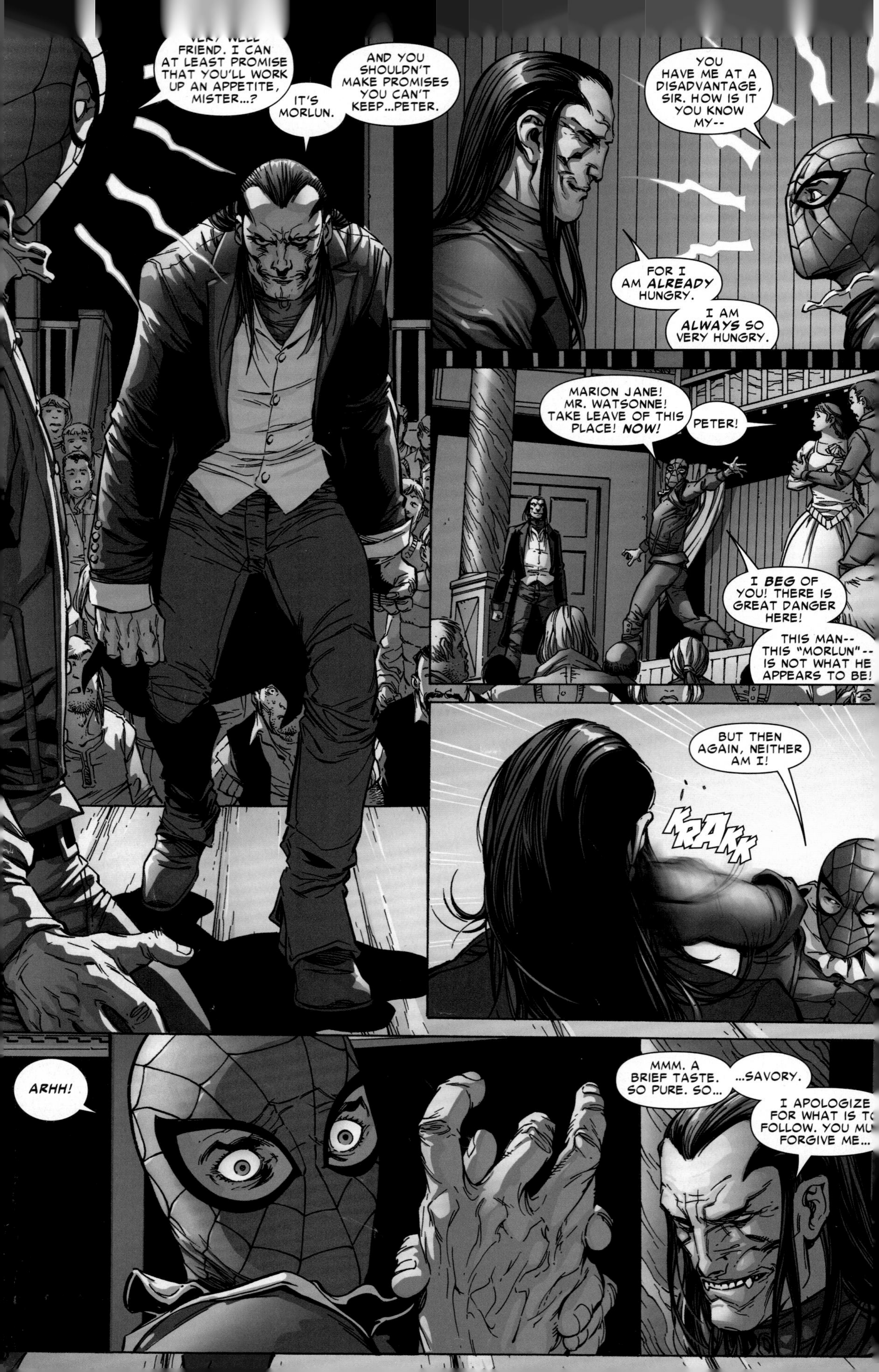
FRIEND. I CAN AT LEAST PROMISE THAT YOU'LL WORK UP AN APPETITE, MISTER...?
IT'S MORLUN.
AND YOU SHOULDN'T MAKE PROMISES YOU CAN'T KEEP...PETER.
YOU HAVE ME AT A DISADVANTAGE, SIR. HOW IS IT YOU KNOW MY--
FOR I AM ALREADY HUNGRY.
I AM ALWAYS SO VERY HUNGRY.
MARION JANE! MR. WATSONNE! TAKE LEAVE OF THIS PLACE! NOW!
PETER!
I BEG OF YOU! THERE IS GREAT DANGER HERE!
THIS MAN-- THIS "MORLUN"-- IS NOT WHAT HE APPEARS TO BE!
BUT THEN AGAIN, NEITHER AM I!
KRAKK
ARHH!
MMM. A BRIEF TASTE. SO PURE. SO...
...SAVORY.
I APOLOGIZE FOR WHAT IS T FOLLOW. YOU MU FORGIVE ME...

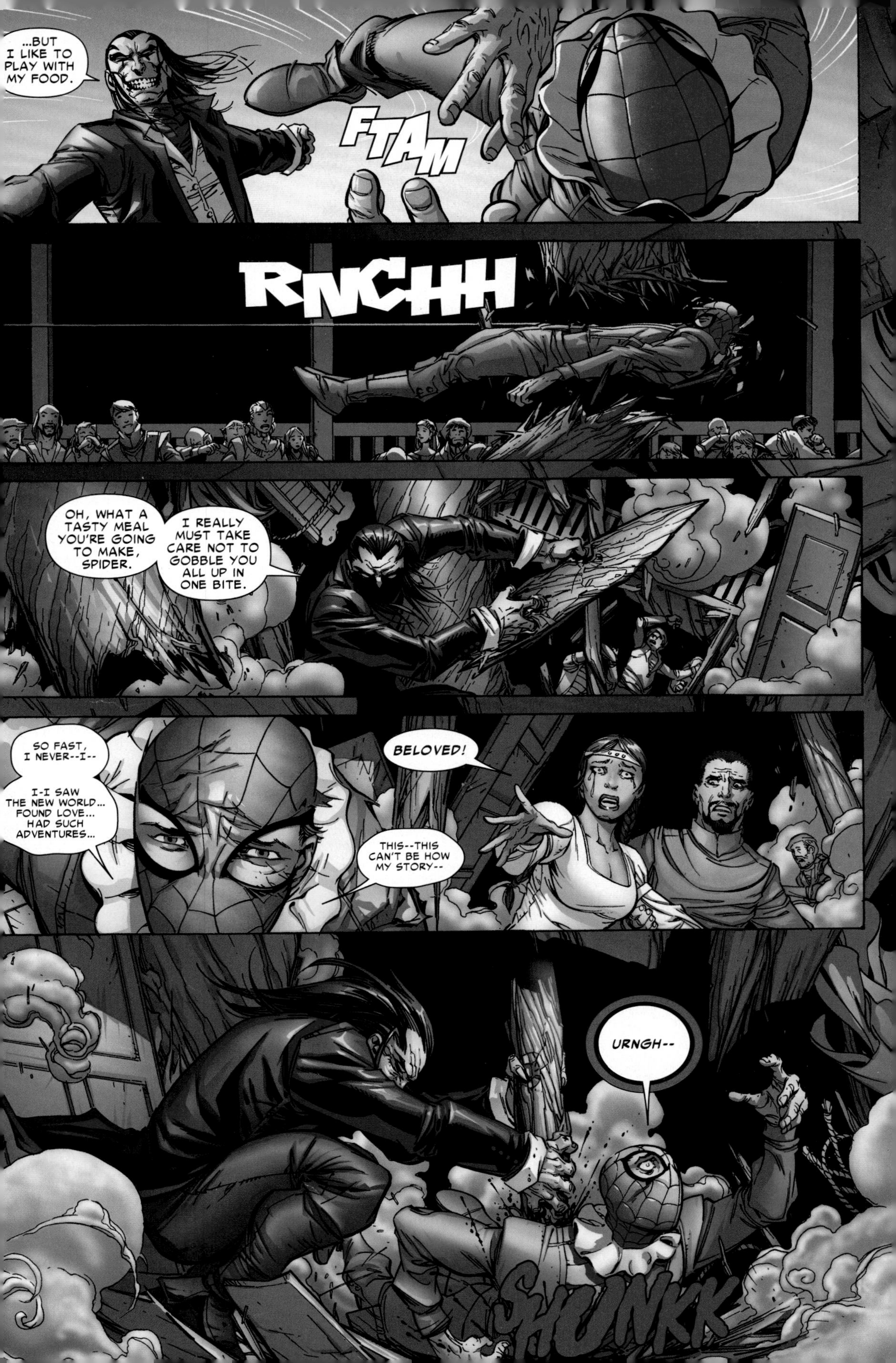
...BUT I LIKE TO PLAY WITH MY FOOD.
FTAM
RNCHH
OH, WHAT A TASTY MEAL YOU'RE GOING TO MAKE, SPIDER.
I REALLY MUST TAKE CARE NOT TO GOBBLE YOU ALL UP IN ONE BITE.
SO FAST, I NEVER--I--
I-I SAW THE NEW WORLD... FOUND LOVE... HAD SUCH ADVENTURES...
BELOVED!
THIS--THIS CAN'T BE HOW MY STORY--
URNGH--
SHUNKK

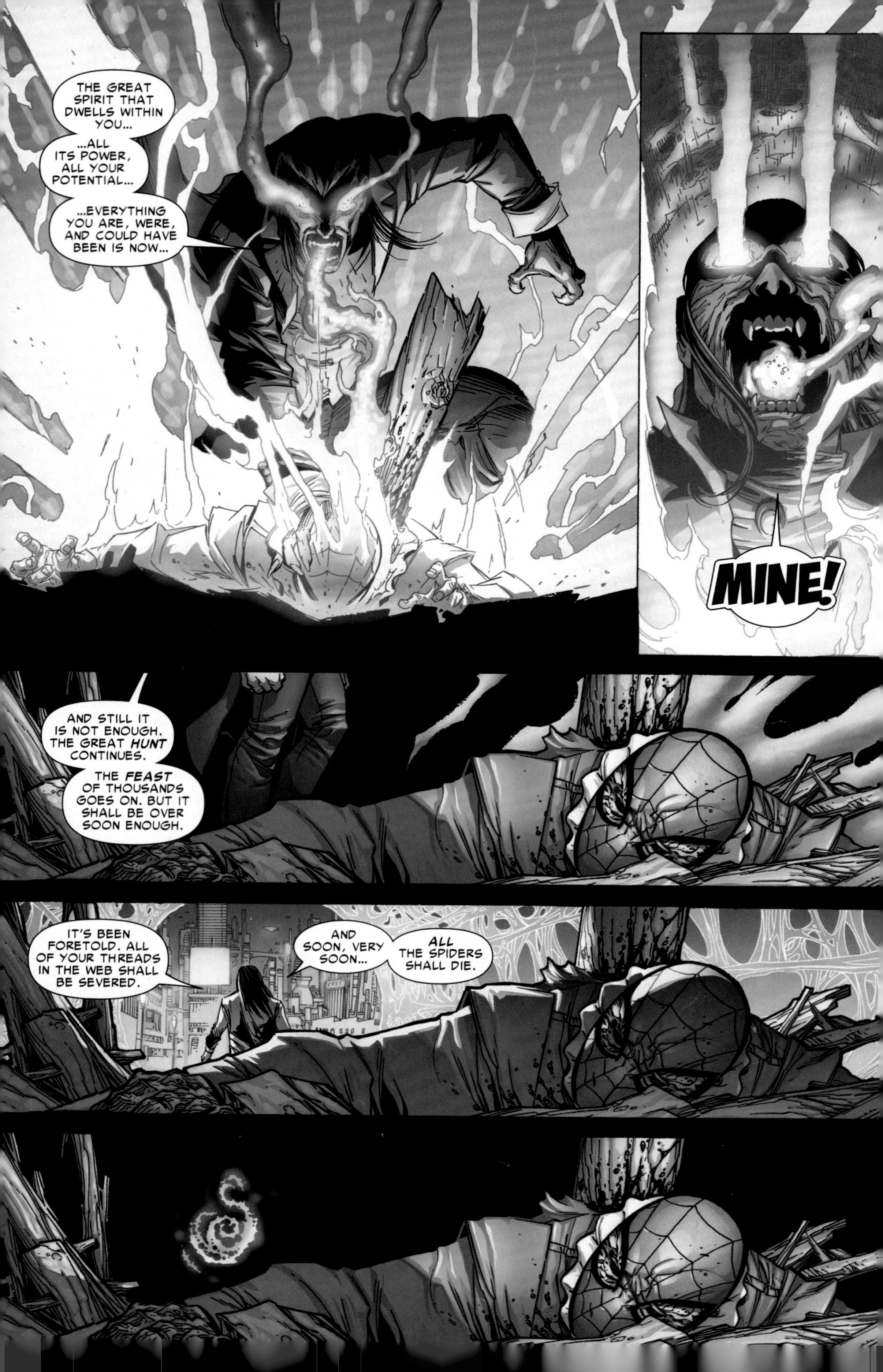
THE GREAT SPIRIT THAT DWELLS WITHIN YOU...
...ALL ITS POWER, ALL YOUR POTENTIAL...
...EVERYTHING YOU ARE, WERE, AND COULD HAVE BEEN IS NOW...
MINE!
AND STILL IT IS NOT ENOUGH. THE GREAT *HUNT* CONTINUES.
THE *FEAST* OF THOUSANDS GOES ON. BUT IT SHALL BE OVER SOON ENOUGH.
IT'S BEEN FORETOLD. ALL OF YOUR THREADS IN THE WEB SHALL BE SEVERED.
AND SOON, VERY SOON...
ALL THE SPIDERS SHALL DIE.

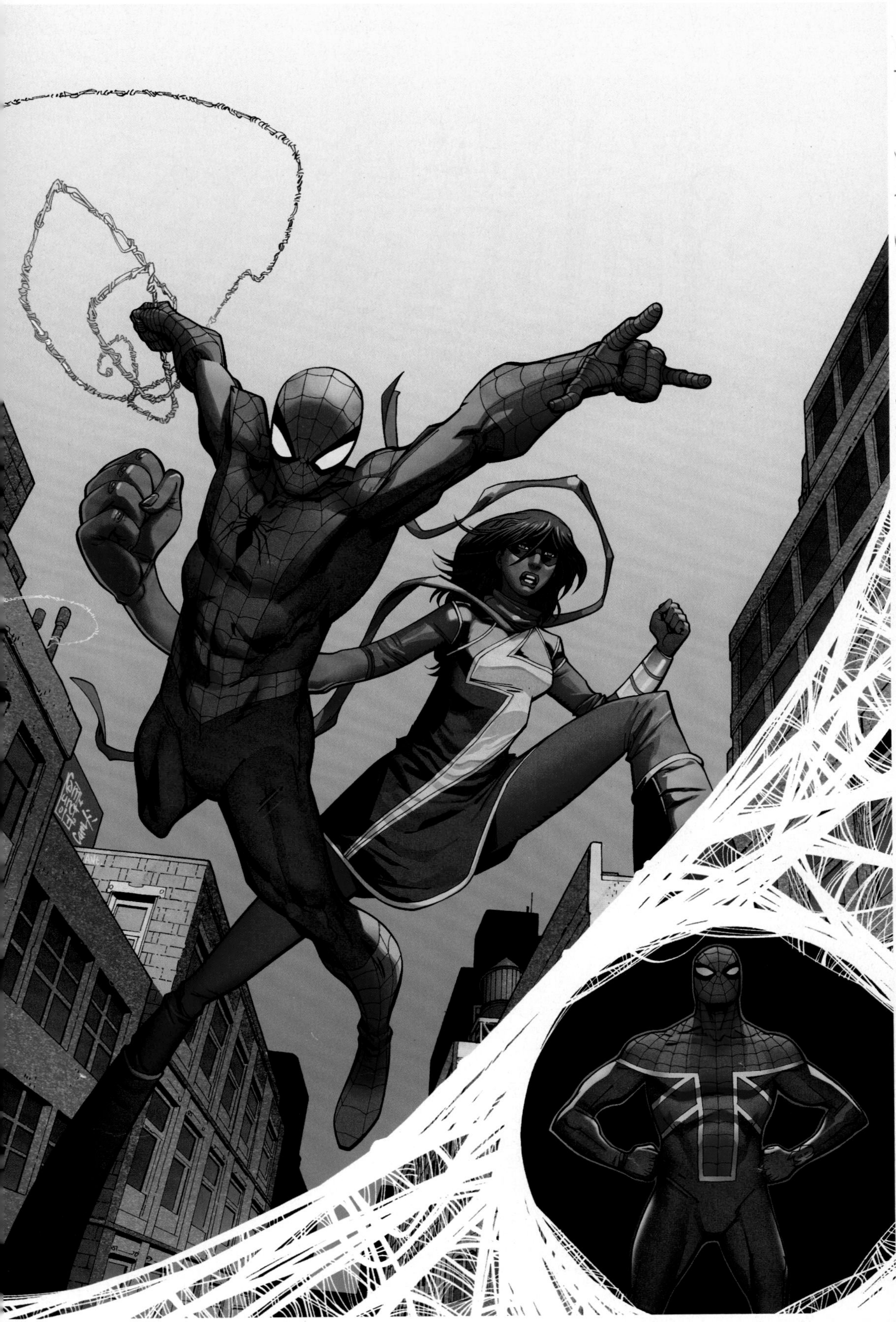

AMAZING SPIDER-MAN 7

Years ago, high school student PETER PARKER was bitten by a radioactive spider and gained the speed, agility, a proportional strength of a spider as well as the ability to stick to walls and a spider-sense that warned him of immin danger. After learning that with great power there must also come great responsibility, he became the crime-fight super hero...

the AMAZING SPIDER-MAN

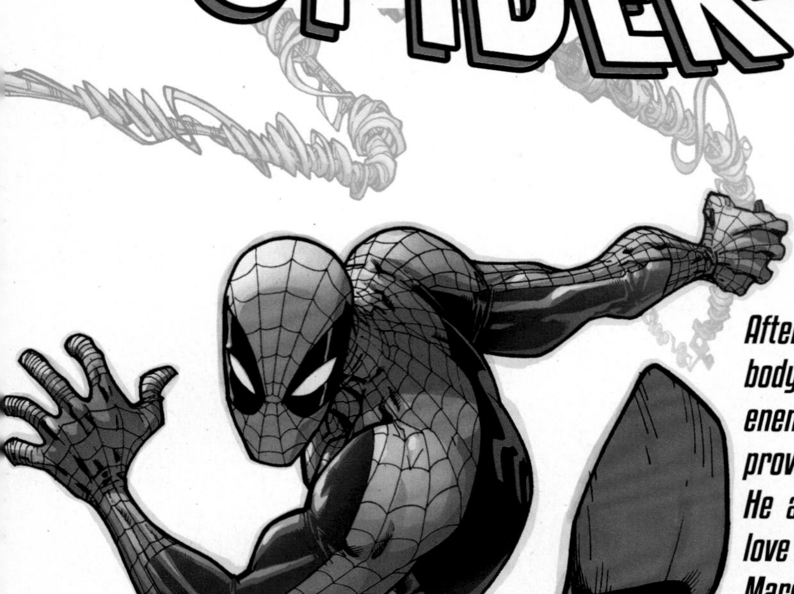

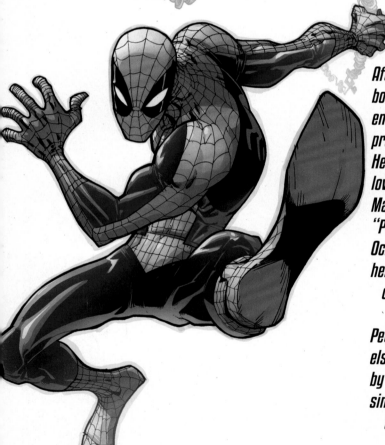

After swapping his mind into Peter' body, one of Spider-Man's greates enemies, DOCTOR OCTOPUS, set out t prove himself the SUPERIOR SPIDER-MAN He also completed Peter's PhD, fell i love with a woman named Anna Mari Marconi, and started his own company "Parker Industries." But in the end Do Ock realized that in order to be a tru hero, he had to sacrifice himself and giv control of Peter's body back to Peter.

Peter recently found out that someon else, Cindy Moon A.K.A. SILK, was bitte by his radioactive spider giving he similar powers to Peter. And that's no the only thing they have in common.

When you see this: AR, open up the MARVEL AR APP (available on applicable Apple ® iOS or Android TM devices) and use your camera-enabled device to unlock extra-special exclusive features!*

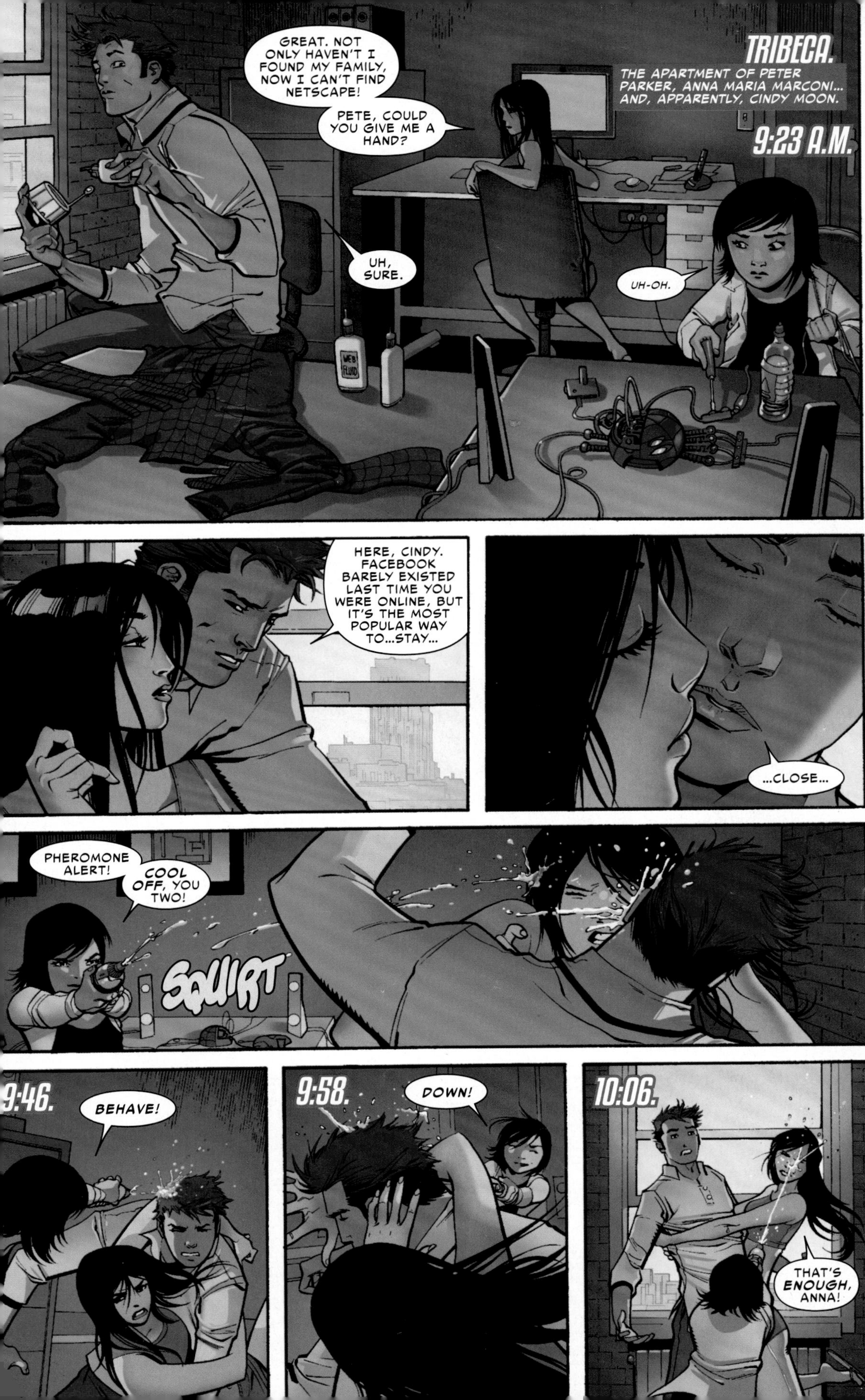
TRIBECA.
THE APARTMENT OF PETER PARKER, ANNA MARIA MARCONI... AND, APPARENTLY, CINDY MOON.
9:23 A.M.
GREAT. NOT ONLY HAVEN'T I FOUND MY FAMILY, NOW I CAN'T FIND NETSCAPE!
PETE, COULD YOU GIVE ME A HAND?
UH, SURE.
UH-OH.
WEB FLUID
HERE, CINDY. FACEBOOK BARELY EXISTED LAST TIME YOU WERE ONLINE, BUT IT'S THE MOST POPULAR WAY TO...STAY...
...CLOSE...
PHEROMONE ALERT!
COOL OFF, YOU TWO!
SQUIRT
9:46.
BEHAVE!
9:58.
DOWN!
10:06.
THAT'S ENOUGH, ANNA!

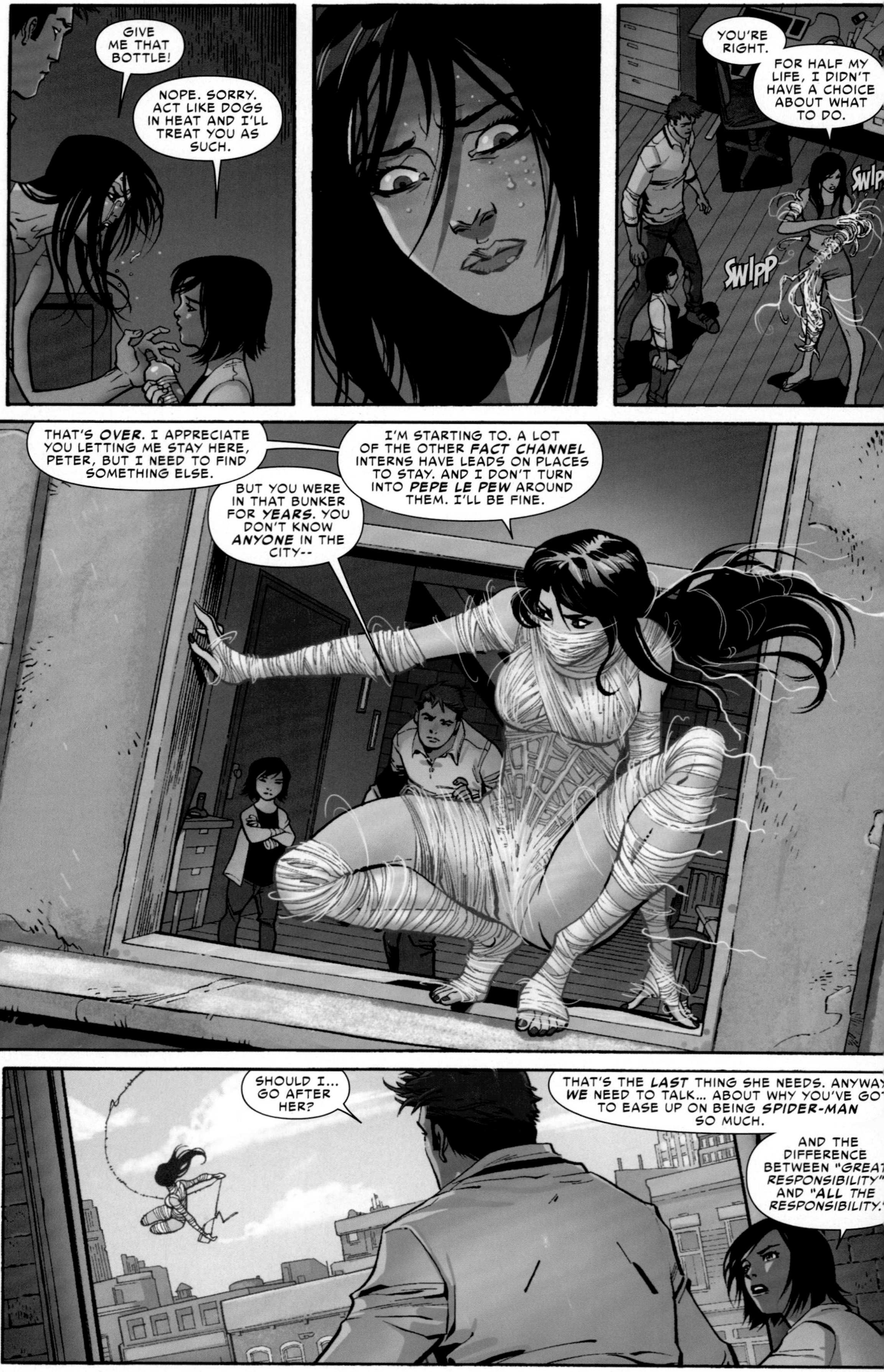

GIVE ME THAT BOTTLE!
NOPE. SORRY. ACT LIKE DOGS IN HEAT AND I'LL TREAT YOU AS SUCH.
YOU'RE RIGHT.
FOR HALF MY LIFE, I DIDN'T HAVE A CHOICE ABOUT WHAT TO DO.
SWIP
SWIPP
THAT'S OVER. I APPRECIATE YOU LETTING ME STAY HERE, PETER, BUT I NEED TO FIND SOMETHING ELSE.
BUT YOU WERE IN THAT BUNKER FOR YEARS. YOU DON'T KNOW ANYONE IN THE CITY--
I'M STARTING TO. A LOT OF THE OTHER FACT CHANNEL INTERNS HAVE LEADS ON PLACES TO STAY. AND I DON'T TURN INTO PEPE LE PEW AROUND THEM. I'LL BE FINE.
SHOULD I... GO AFTER HER?
THAT'S THE LAST THING SHE NEEDS. ANYWAY WE NEED TO TALK... ABOUT WHY YOU'VE GOT TO EASE UP ON BEING SPIDER-MAN SO MUCH.
AND THE DIFFERENCE BETWEEN "GREAT RESPONSIBILITY" AND "ALL THE RESPONSIBILITY."

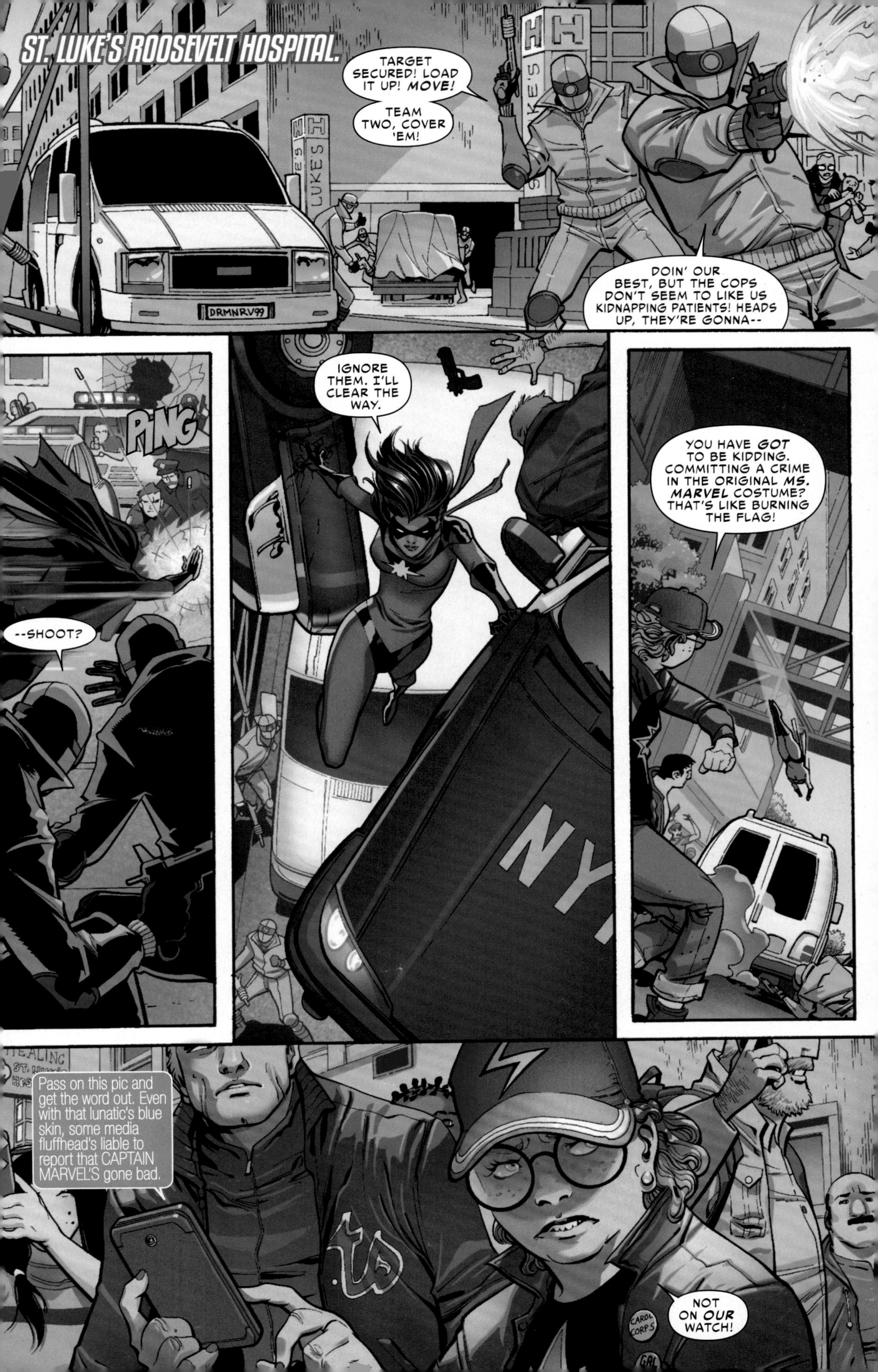
ST. LUKE'S ROOSEVELT HOSPITAL.
TARGET SECURED! LOAD IT UP! MOVE!
TEAM TWO, COVER 'EM!
DOIN' OUR BEST, BUT THE COPS DON'T SEEM TO LIKE US KIDNAPPING PATIENTS! HEADS UP, THEY'RE GONNA--
PING
--SHOOT?
IGNORE THEM. I'LL CLEAR THE WAY.
YOU HAVE GOT TO BE KIDDING. COMMITTING A CRIME IN THE ORIGINAL MS. MARVEL COSTUME? THAT'S LIKE BURNING THE FLAG!
Pass on this pic and get the word out. Even with that lunatic's blue skin, some media fluffhead's liable to report that CAPTAIN MARVEL'S gone bad.
NOT ON OUR WATCH!

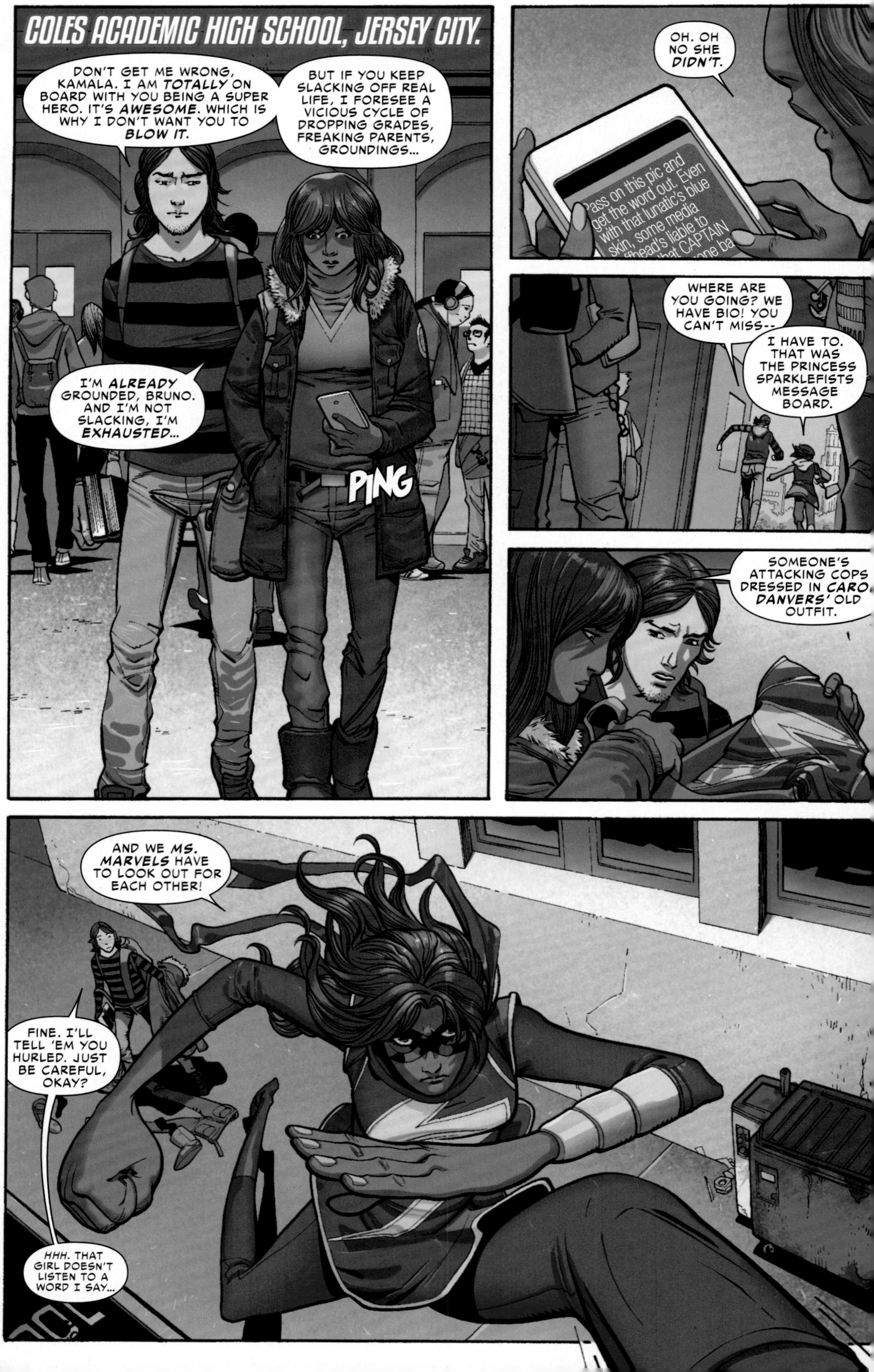
COLES ACADEMIC HIGH SCHOOL, JERSEY CITY.
DON'T GET ME WRONG, KAMALA. I AM TOTALLY ON BOARD WITH YOU BEING A SUPER HERO. IT'S AWESOME. WHICH IS WHY I DON'T WANT YOU TO BLOW IT.
BUT IF YOU KEEP SLACKING OFF REAL LIFE, I FORESEE A VICIOUS CYCLE OF DROPPING GRADES, FREAKING PARENTS, GROUNDINGS...
I'M ALREADY GROUNDED, BRUNO. AND I'M NOT SLACKING, I'M EXHAUSTED...
PING
OH. OH NO SHE DIDN'T.
Pass on this pic and get the word out. Even with that lunatic's blue skin, some media
WHERE ARE YOU GOING? WE HAVE BIO! YOU CAN'T MISS--
I HAVE TO. THAT WAS THE PRINCESS SPARKLEFISTS MESSAGE BOARD.
SOMEONE'S ATTACKING COPS DRESSED IN CARO DANVERS' OLD OUTFIT.
AND WE MS. MARVELS HAVE TO LOOK OUT FOR EACH OTHER!
FINE. I'LL TELL 'EM YOU HURLED. JUST BE CAREFUL, OKAY?
HHH. THAT GIRL DOESN'T LISTEN TO A WORD I SAY...

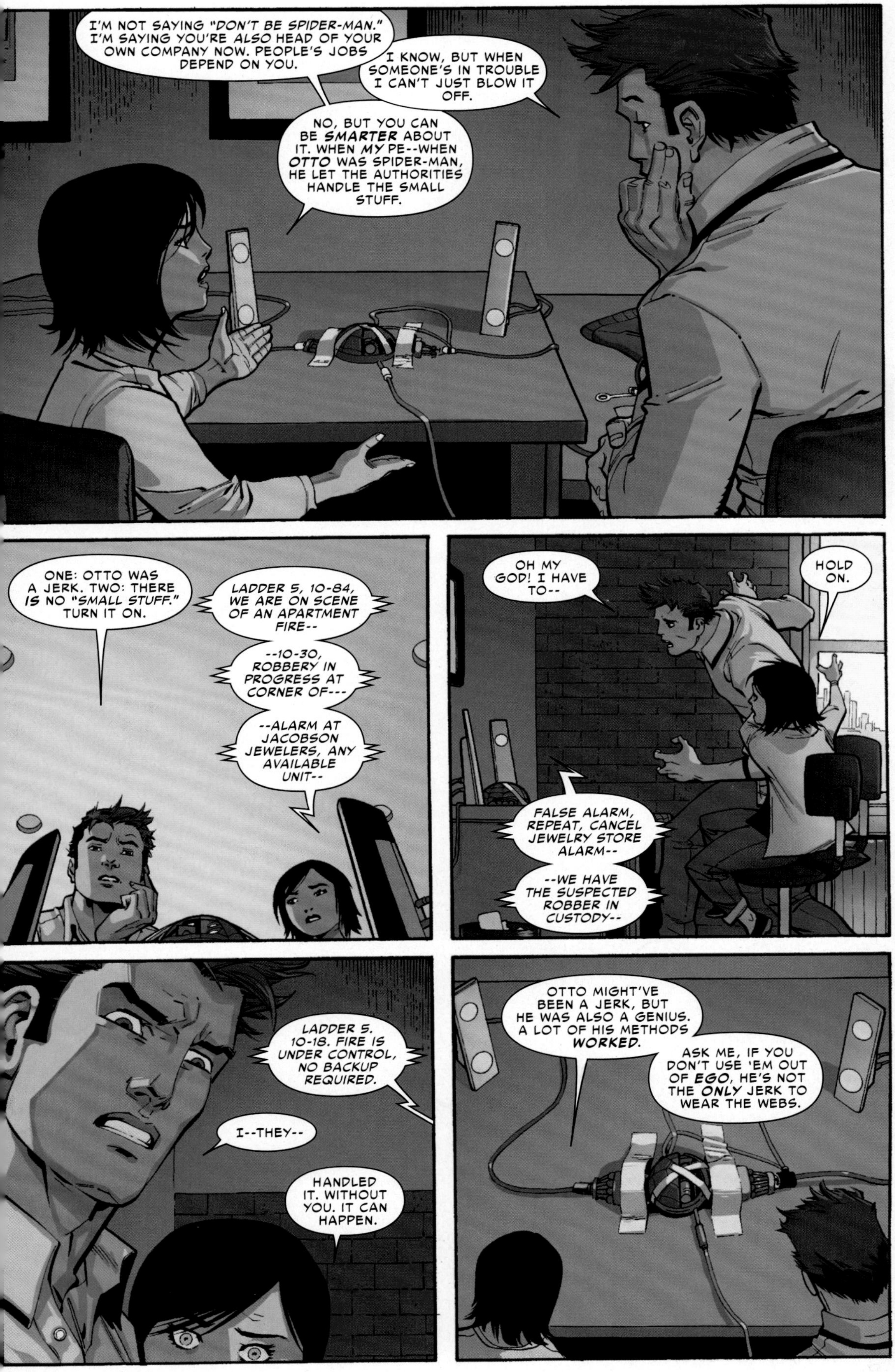
I'M NOT SAYING "DON'T BE SPIDER-MAN." I'M SAYING YOU'RE ALSO HEAD OF YOUR OWN COMPANY NOW. PEOPLE'S JOBS DEPEND ON YOU.
I KNOW, BUT WHEN SOMEONE'S IN TROUBLE I CAN'T JUST BLOW IT OFF.
NO, BUT YOU CAN BE SMARTER ABOUT IT. WHEN MY PE--WHEN OTTO WAS SPIDER-MAN, HE LET THE AUTHORITIES HANDLE THE SMALL STUFF.
ONE: OTTO WAS A JERK. TWO: THERE IS NO "SMALL STUFF." TURN IT ON.
LADDER 5, 10-84, WE ARE ON SCENE OF AN APARTMENT FIRE--
--10-30, ROBBERY IN PROGRESS AT CORNER OF---
--ALARM AT JACOBSON JEWELERS, ANY AVAILABLE UNIT--
OH MY GOD! I HAVE TO--
HOLD ON.
FALSE ALARM, REPEAT, CANCEL JEWELRY STORE ALARM--
--WE HAVE THE SUSPECTED ROBBER IN CUSTODY--
LADDER 5. 10-18. FIRE IS UNDER CONTROL, NO BACKUP REQUIRED.
I--THEY--
HANDLED IT. WITHOUT YOU. IT CAN HAPPEN.
OTTO MIGHT'VE BEEN A JERK, BUT HE WAS ALSO A GENIUS. A LOT OF HIS METHODS WORKED.
ASK ME, IF YOU DON'T USE 'EM OUT OF EGO, HE'S NOT THE ONLY JERK TO WEAR THE WEBS.

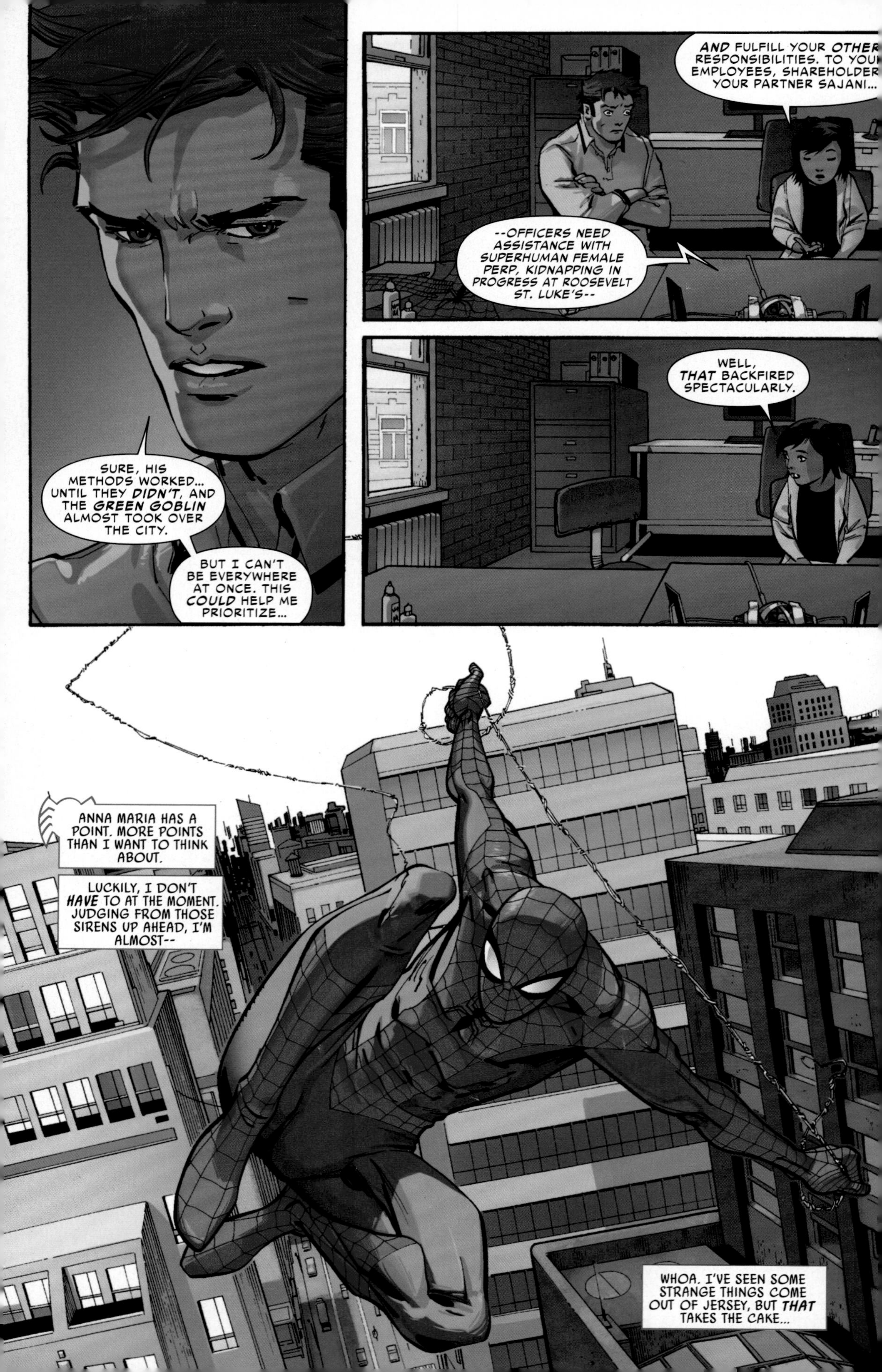
SURE, HIS METHODS WORKED... UNTIL THEY DIDN'T, AND THE GREEN GOBLIN ALMOST TOOK OVER THE CITY.
BUT I CAN'T BE EVERYWHERE AT ONCE. THIS COULD HELP ME PRIORITIZE...
AND FULFILL YOUR OTHER RESPONSIBILITIES. TO YOUR EMPLOYEES, SHAREHOLDERS, YOUR PARTNER SAJANI...
--OFFICERS NEED ASSISTANCE WITH SUPERHUMAN FEMALE PERP, KIDNAPPING IN PROGRESS AT ROOSEVELT ST. LUKE'S--
WELL, THAT BACKFIRED SPECTACULARLY.
ANNA MARIA HAS A POINT. MORE POINTS THAN I WANT TO THINK ABOUT.
LUCKILY, I DON'T HAVE TO AT THE MOMENT. JUDGING FROM THOSE SIRENS UP AHEAD, I'M ALMOST--
WHOA. I'VE SEEN SOME STRANGE THINGS COME OUT OF JERSEY, BUT THAT TAKES THE CAKE...

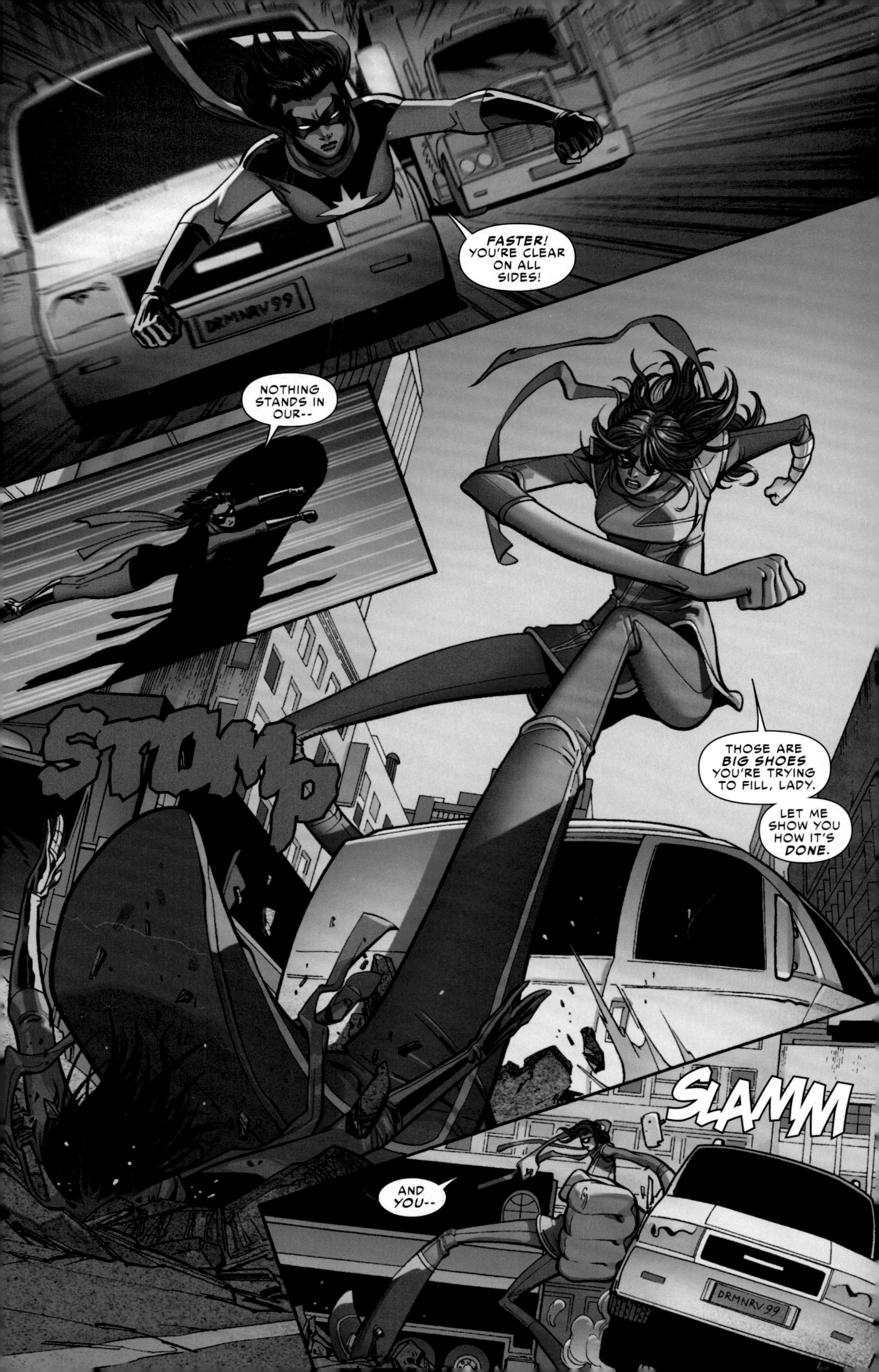
DRMNRV99
FASTER! YOU'RE CLEAR ON ALL SIDES!
NOTHING STANDS IN OUR--
STOMP
THOSE ARE BIG SHOES YOU'RE TRYING TO FILL, LADY.
LET ME SHOW YOU HOW IT'S DONE.
SLAMM
AND YOU--
DRMNRV99

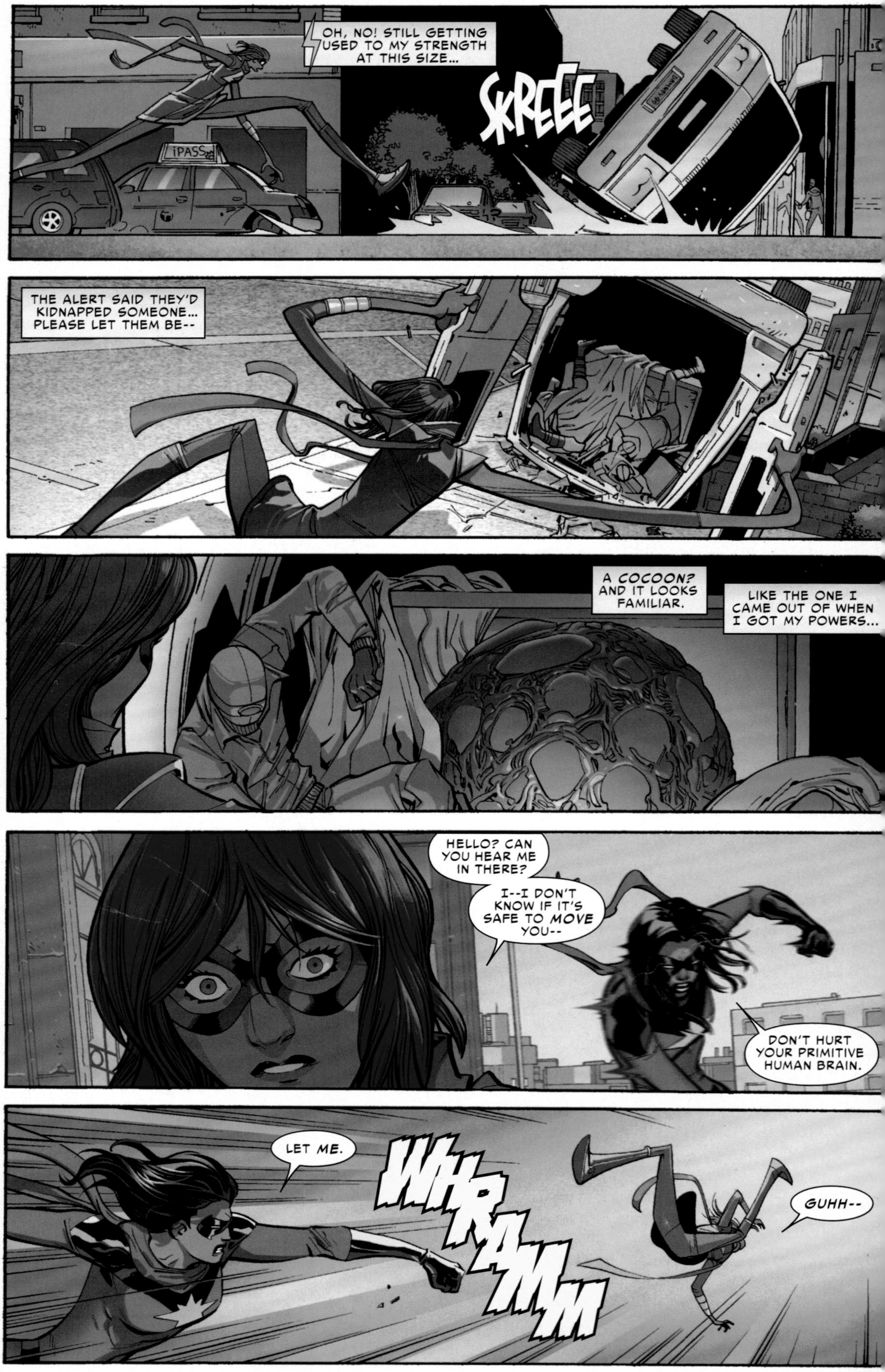
OH, NO! STILL GETTING USED TO MY STRENGTH AT THIS SIZE...
SKREEE
THE ALERT SAID THEY'D KIDNAPPED SOMEONE... PLEASE LET THEM BE--
A COCOON? AND IT LOOKS FAMILIAR.
LIKE THE ONE I CAME OUT OF WHEN I GOT MY POWERS...
HELLO? CAN YOU HEAR ME IN THERE?
I--I DON'T KNOW IF IT'S SAFE TO MOVE YOU--
DON'T HURT YOUR PRIMITIVE HUMAN BRAIN.
LET ME.
WHRAMM
GUHH--

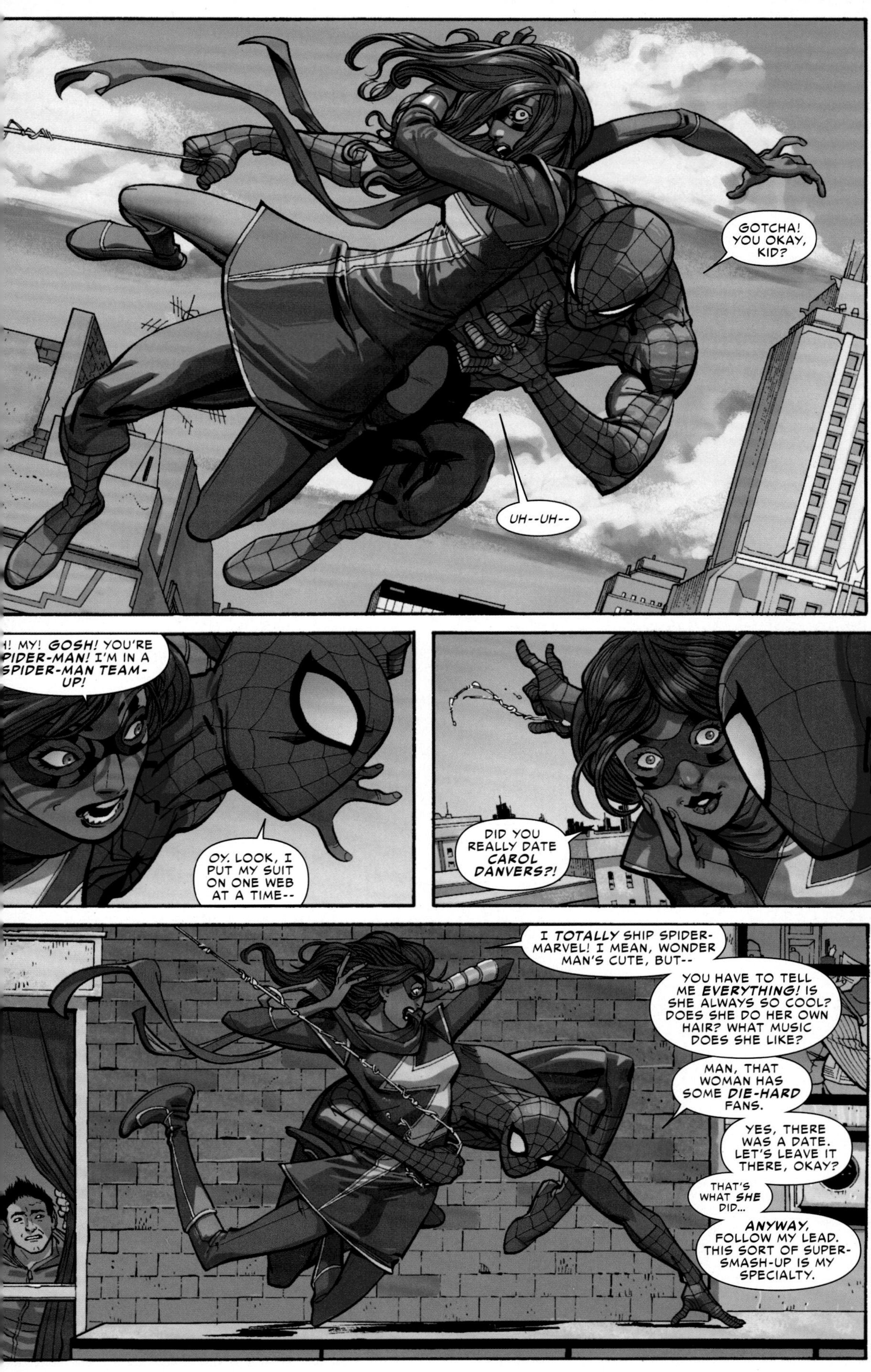
GOTCHA! YOU OKAY, KID?
UH--UH--
H! MY! GOSH! YOU'RE SPIDER-MAN! I'M IN A SPIDER-MAN TEAM-UP!
OY. LOOK, I PUT MY SUIT ON ONE WEB AT A TIME--
DID YOU REALLY DATE CAROL DANVERS?!
I TOTALLY SHIP SPIDER-MARVEL! I MEAN, WONDER MAN'S CUTE, BUT--
YOU HAVE TO TELL ME EVERYTHING! IS SHE ALWAYS SO COOL? DOES SHE DO HER OWN HAIR? WHAT MUSIC DOES SHE LIKE?
MAN, THAT WOMAN HAS SOME DIE-HARD FANS.
YES, THERE WAS A DATE. LET'S LEAVE IT THERE, OKAY?
THAT'S WHAT SHE DID...
ANYWAY, FOLLOW MY LEAD. THIS SORT OF SUPER-SMASH-UP IS MY SPECIALTY.

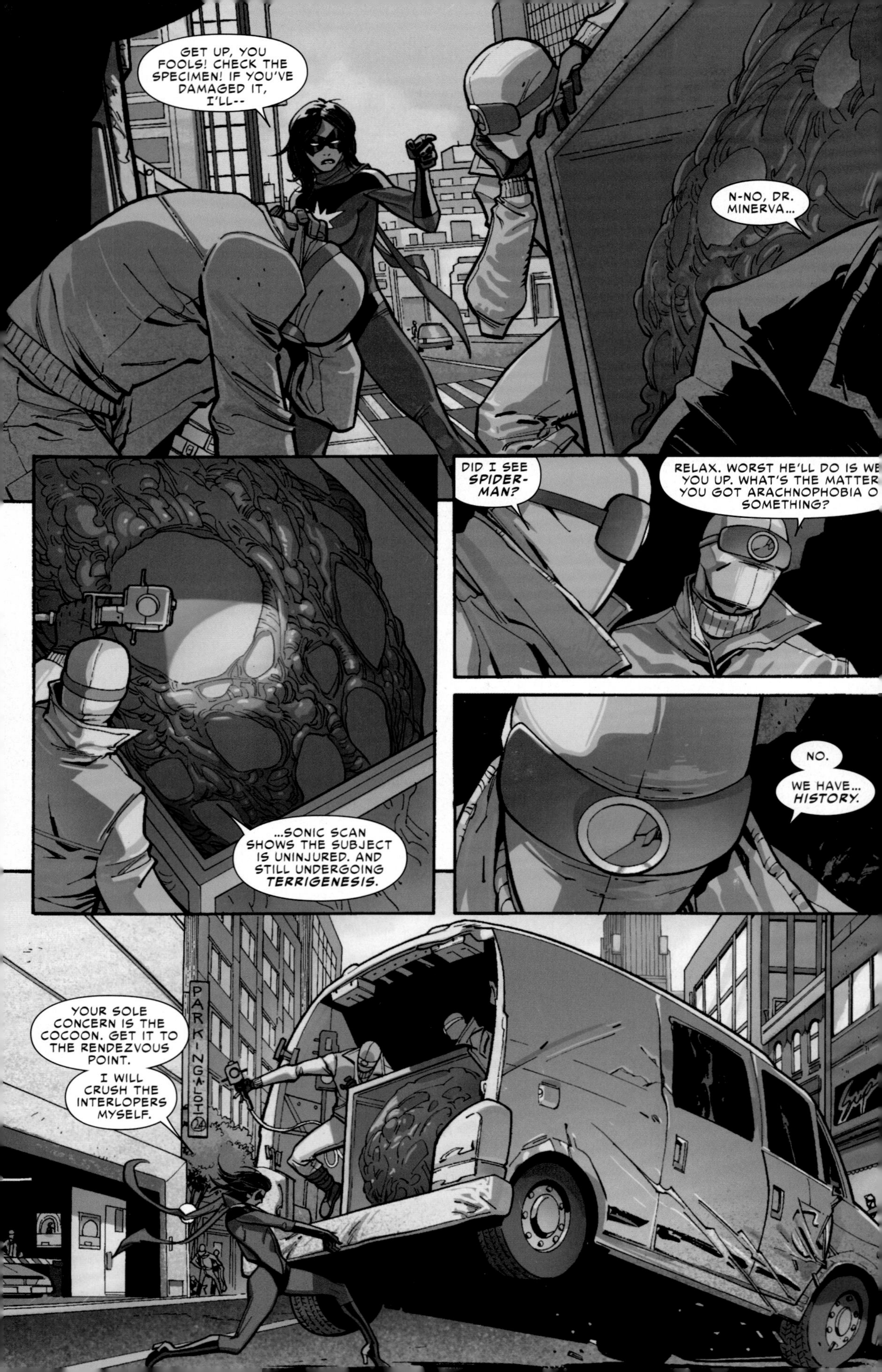
GET UP, YOU FOOLS! CHECK THE SPECIMEN! IF YOU'VE DAMAGED IT, I'LL--
N-NO, DR. MINERVA...
...SONIC SCAN SHOWS THE SUBJECT IS UNINJURED. AND STILL UNDERGOING TERRIGENESIS.
DID I SEE SPIDER-MAN?
RELAX. WORST HE'LL DO IS WE YOU UP. WHAT'S THE MATTER YOU GOT ARACHNOPHOBIA O SOMETHING?
NO.
WE HAVE... HISTORY.
YOUR SOLE CONCERN IS THE COCOON. GET IT TO THE RENDEZVOUS POINT.
I WILL CRUSH THE INTERLOPERS MYSELF.
PARKING LOT 24

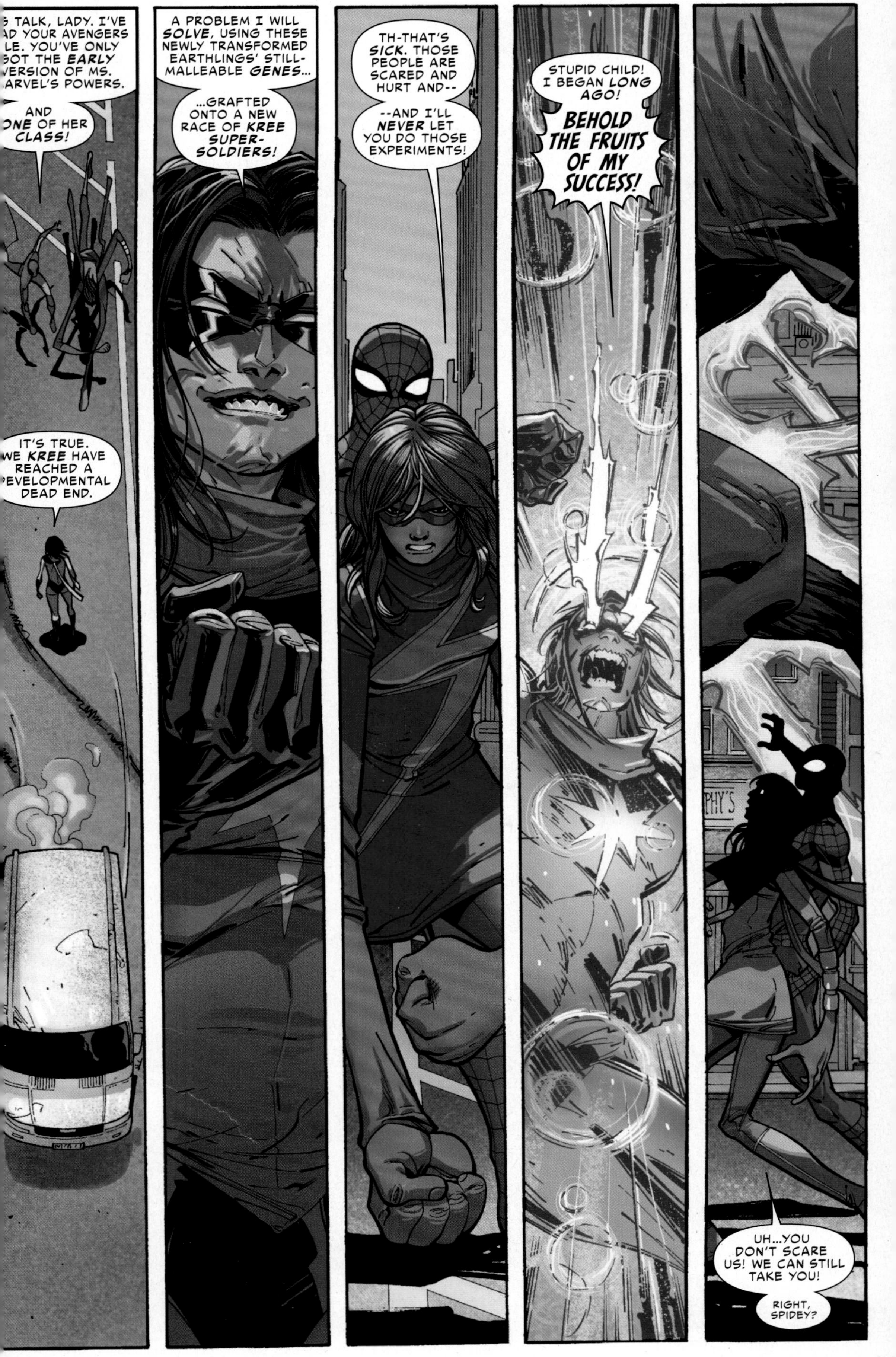

G TALK, LADY. I'VE
AD YOUR AVENGERS
LE. YOU'VE ONLY
GOT THE EARLY
VERSION OF MS.
ARVEL'S POWERS.
AND
ONE OF HER
CLASS!
IT'S TRUE.
WE KREE HAVE
REACHED A
DEVELOPMENTAL
DEAD END.
A PROBLEM I WILL SOLVE, USING THESE NEWLY TRANSFORMED EARTHLINGS' STILL-MALLEABLE GENES...
...GRAFTED ONTO A NEW RACE OF KREE SUPER-SOLDIERS!
TH-THAT'S SICK. THOSE PEOPLE ARE SCARED AND HURT AND--
--AND I'LL NEVER LET YOU DO THOSE EXPERIMENTS!
STUPID CHILD! I BEGAN LONG AGO!
BEHOLD THE FRUITS OF MY SUCCESS!
UH...YOU DON'T SCARE US! WE CAN STILL TAKE YOU!
RIGHT, SPIDEY?

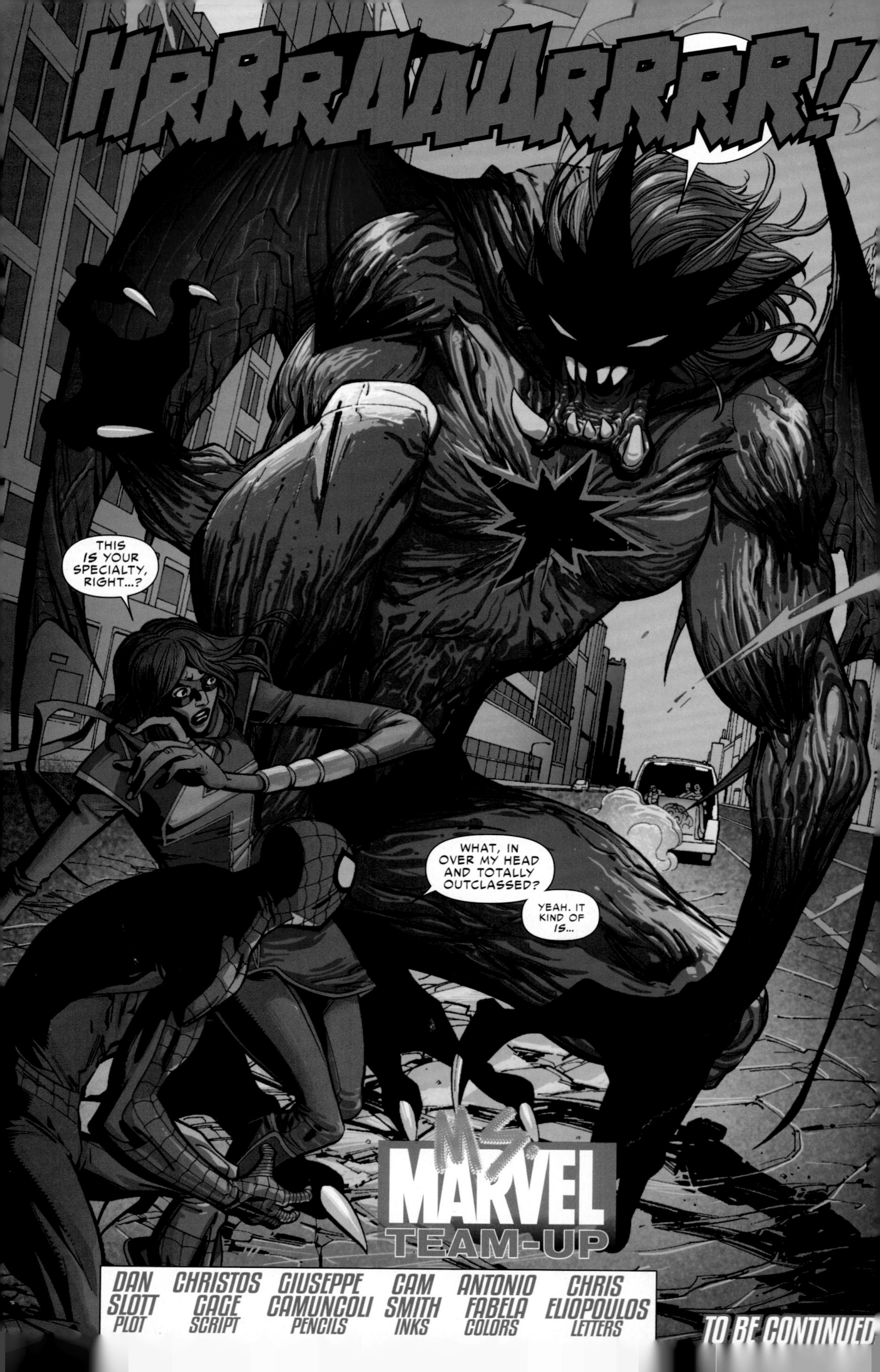
HRRRAWARRRR!
THIS IS YOUR SPECIALTY, RIGHT...?
WHAT, IN OVER MY HEAD AND TOTALLY OUTCLASSED?
YEAH. IT KIND OF IS...
MS. MARVEL TEAM-UP
DAN SLOTT PLOT
CHRISTOS GAGE SCRIPT
GIUSEPPE CAMUNCOLI PENCILS
CAM SMITH INKS
ANTONIO FABELA COLORS
CHRIS ELIOPOULOS LETTERS
TO BE CONTINUED

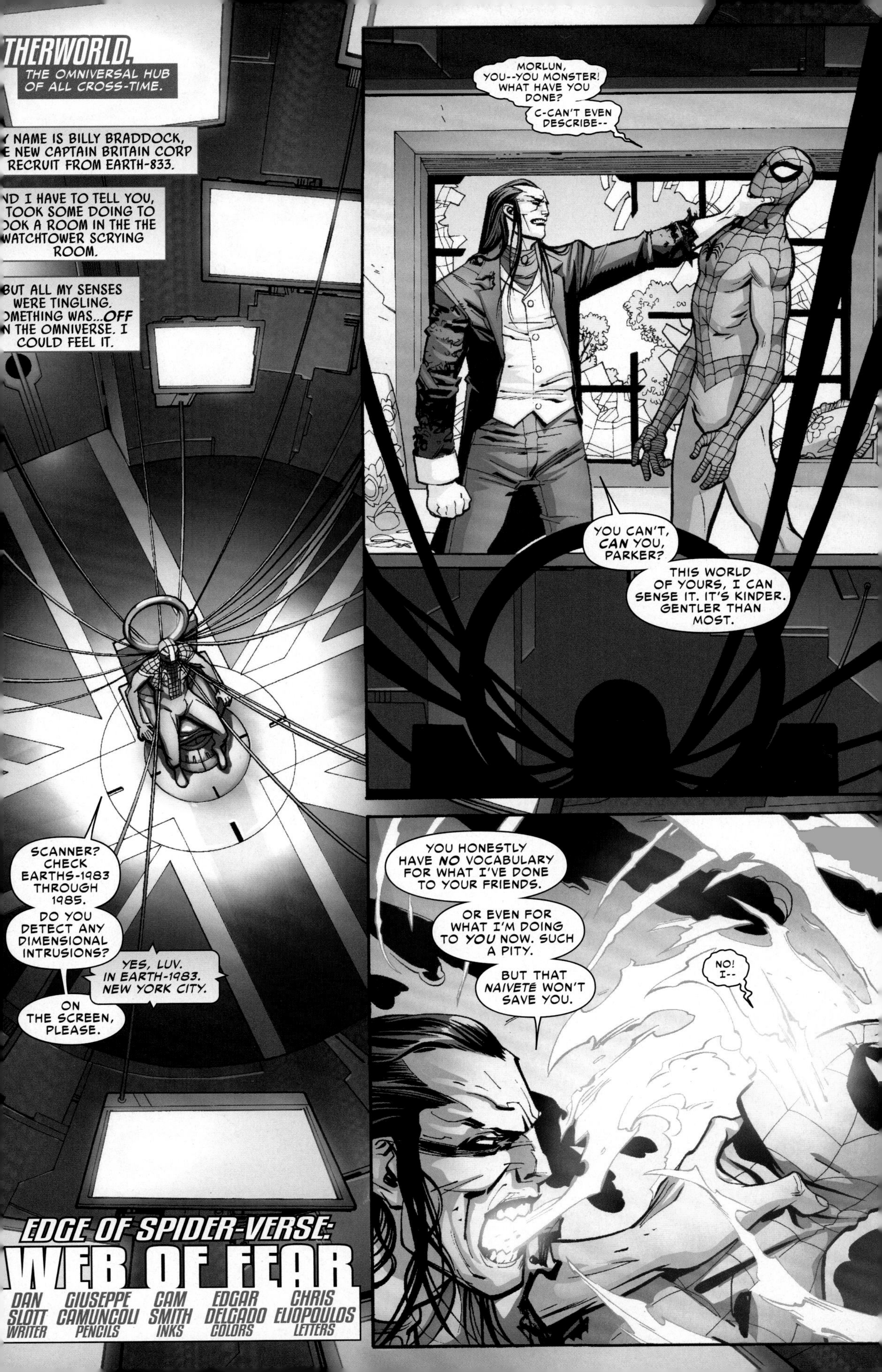
THERWORLD.
THE OMNIVERSAL HUB OF ALL CROSS-TIME.
NAME IS BILLY BRADDOCK, E NEW CAPTAIN BRITAIN CORP RECRUIT FROM EARTH-833.
ND I HAVE TO TELL YOU, TOOK SOME DOING TO OOK A ROOM IN THE THE WATCHTOWER SCRYING ROOM.
BUT ALL MY SENSES WERE TINGLING. OMETHING WAS...OFF N THE OMNIVERSE. I COULD FEEL IT.
SCANNER? CHECK EARTHS-1983 THROUGH 1985.
DO YOU DETECT ANY DIMENSIONAL INTRUSIONS?
YES, LUV. IN EARTH-1983. NEW YORK CITY.
ON THE SCREEN, PLEASE.
MORLUN, YOU--YOU MONSTER! WHAT HAVE YOU DONE?
C-CAN'T EVEN DESCRIBE--
YOU CAN'T, CAN YOU, PARKER?
THIS WORLD OF YOURS, I CAN SENSE IT. IT'S KINDER. GENTLER THAN MOST.
YOU HONESTLY HAVE NO VOCABULARY FOR WHAT I'VE DONE TO YOUR FRIENDS.
OR EVEN FOR WHAT I'M DOING TO YOU NOW. SUCH A PITY.
BUT THAT NAIVETÉ WON'T SAVE YOU.
NO! I--
EDGE OF SPIDER-VERSE:
WEB OF FEAR
DAN SLOTT WRITER
GIUSEPPE CAMUNCOLI PENCILS
CAM SMITH INKS
EDGAR DELGADO COLORS
CHRIS ELIOPOULOS LETTERS

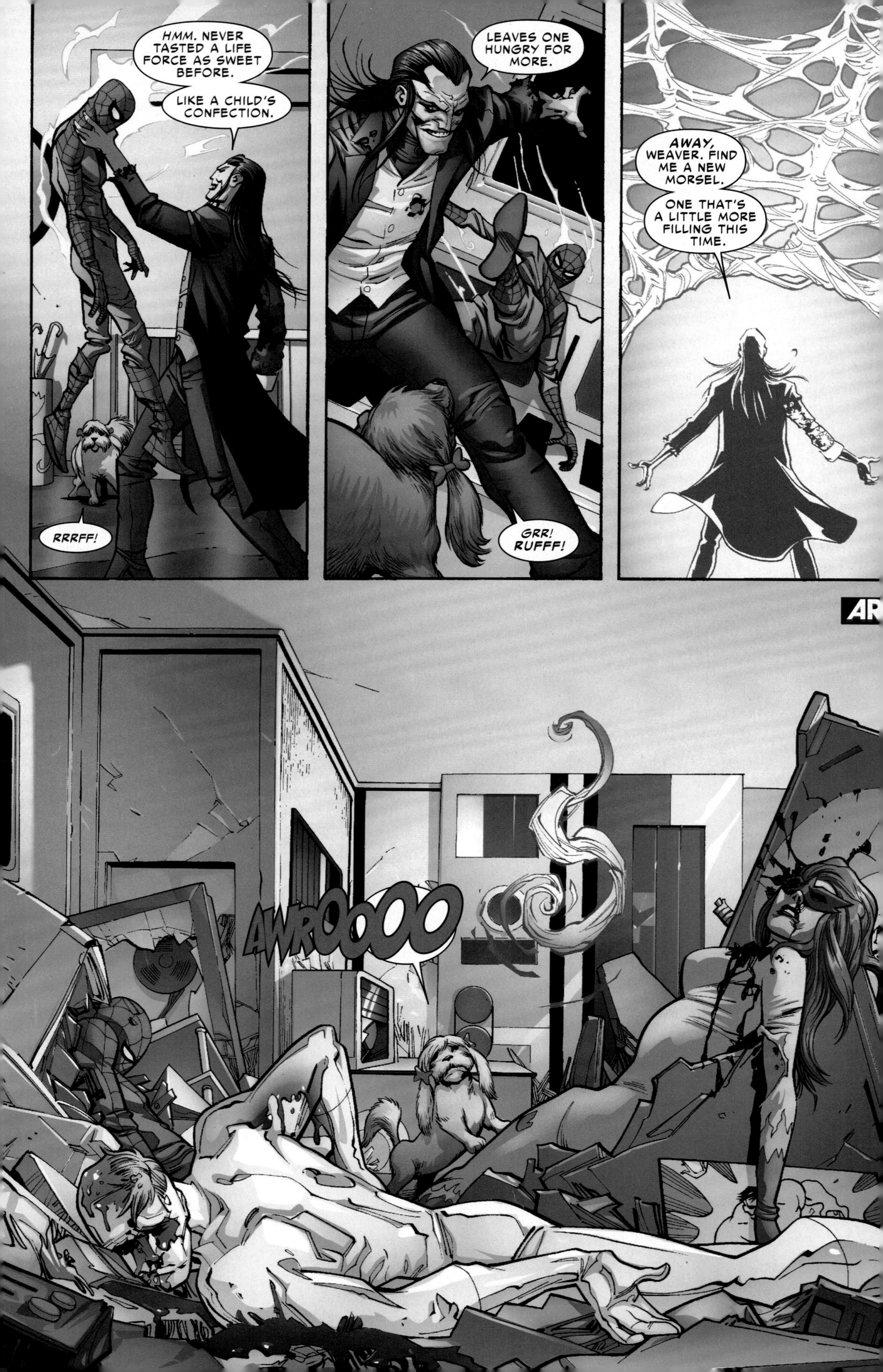
HMM. NEVER TASTED A LIFE FORCE AS SWEET BEFORE.
LIKE A CHILD'S CONFECTION.
RRRFF!
LEAVES ONE HUNGRY FOR MORE.
GRR! RUFFF!
AWAY, WEAVER. FIND ME A NEW MORSEL.
ONE THAT'S A LITTLE MORE FILLING THIS TIME.
AWROOOO

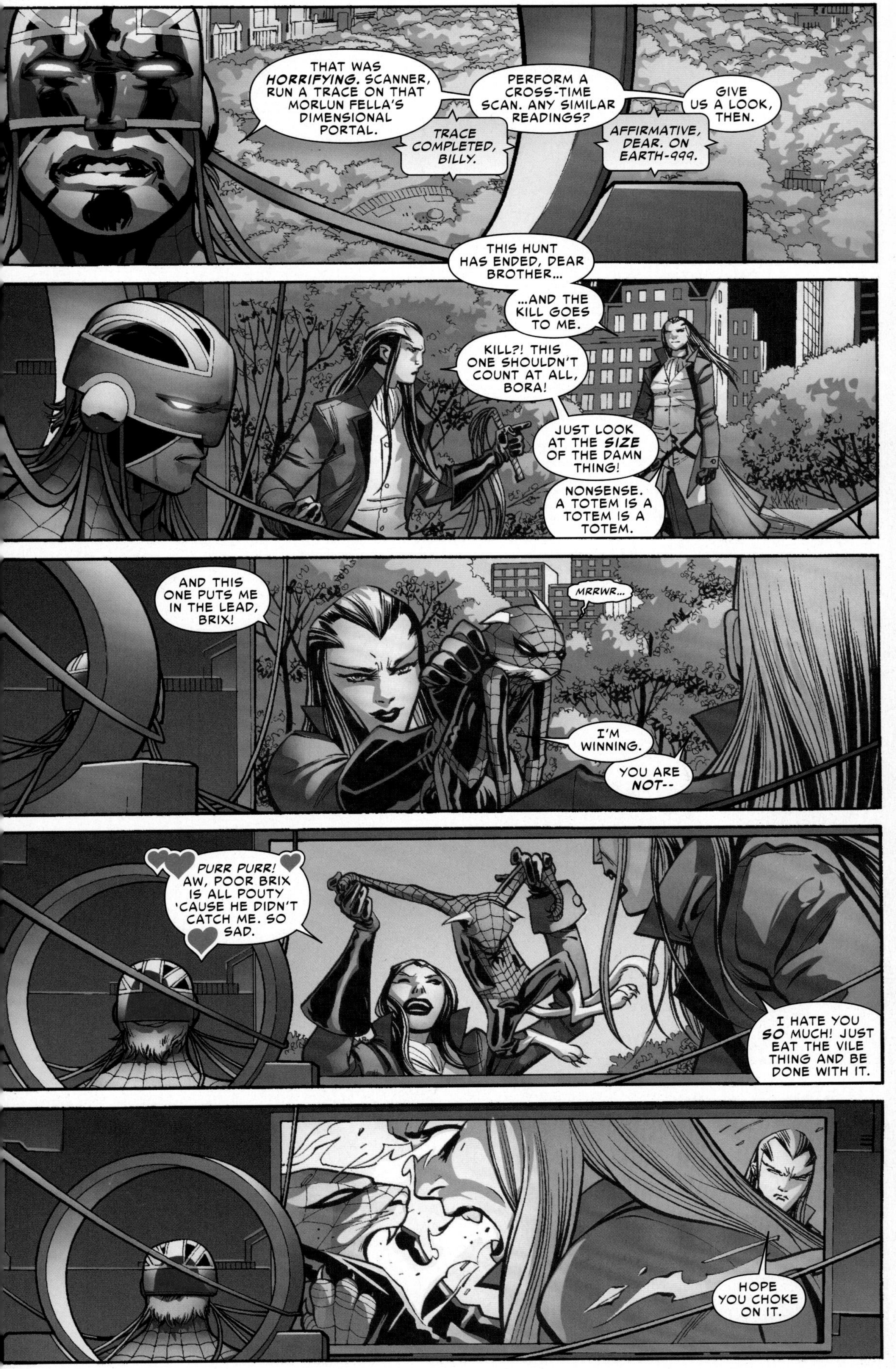

THAT WAS *HORRIFYING.* SCANNER, RUN A TRACE ON THAT MORLUN FELLA'S DIMENSIONAL PORTAL.
TRACE COMPLETED, BILLY.
PERFORM A CROSS-TIME SCAN. ANY SIMILAR READINGS?
AFFIRMATIVE, DEAR. ON EARTH-999.
GIVE US A LOOK, THEN.
THIS HUNT HAS ENDED, DEAR BROTHER...
...AND THE KILL GOES TO ME.
KILL?! THIS ONE SHOULDN'T COUNT AT ALL, BORA!
JUST LOOK AT THE *SIZE* OF THE DAMN THING!
NONSENSE. A TOTEM IS A TOTEM IS A TOTEM.
AND THIS ONE PUTS ME IN THE LEAD, BRIX!
MRRWR...
I'M WINNING.
YOU ARE *NOT*--
PURR PURR! AW, POOR BRIX IS ALL POUTY 'CAUSE HE DIDN'T CATCH ME. SO SAD.
I HATE YOU *SO* MUCH! JUST EAT THE VILE THING AND BE DONE WITH IT.
HOPE YOU CHOKE ON IT.

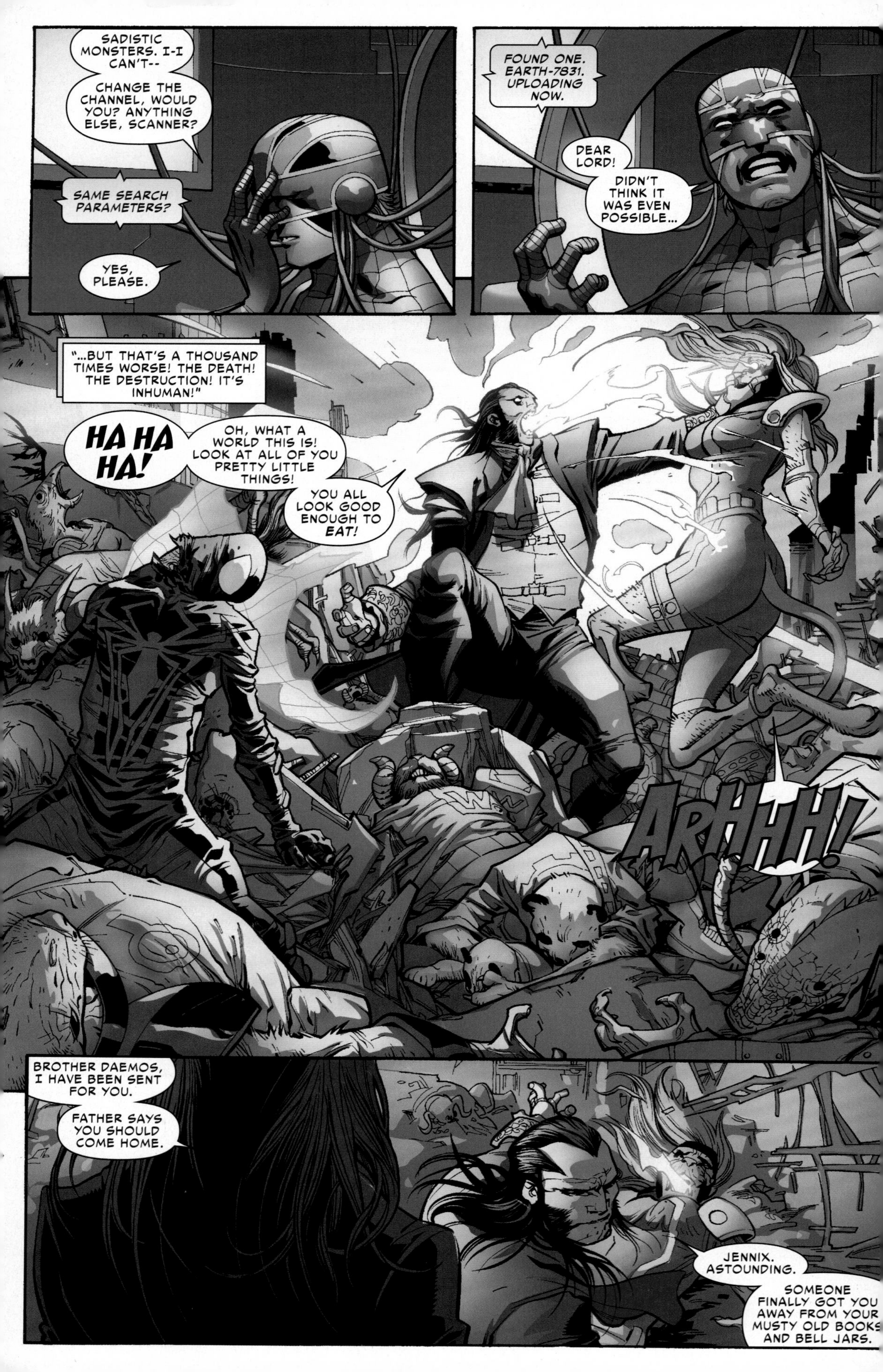
SADISTIC MONSTERS. I-I CAN'T--
CHANGE THE CHANNEL, WOULD YOU? ANYTHING ELSE, SCANNER?
SAME SEARCH PARAMETERS?
YES, PLEASE.
FOUND ONE. EARTH-7831. UPLOADING NOW.
DEAR LORD!
DIDN'T THINK IT WAS EVEN POSSIBLE...
"...BUT THAT'S A THOUSAND TIMES WORSE! THE DEATH! THE DESTRUCTION! IT'S INHUMAN!"
HA HA HA!
OH, WHAT A WORLD THIS IS! LOOK AT ALL OF YOU PRETTY LITTLE THINGS!
YOU ALL LOOK GOOD ENOUGH TO EAT!
ARHHH!
BROTHER DAEMOS, I HAVE BEEN SENT FOR YOU.
FATHER SAYS YOU SHOULD COME HOME.
JENNIX. ASTOUNDING.
SOMEONE FINALLY GOT YOU AWAY FROM YOUR MUSTY OLD BOOKS AND BELL JARS.

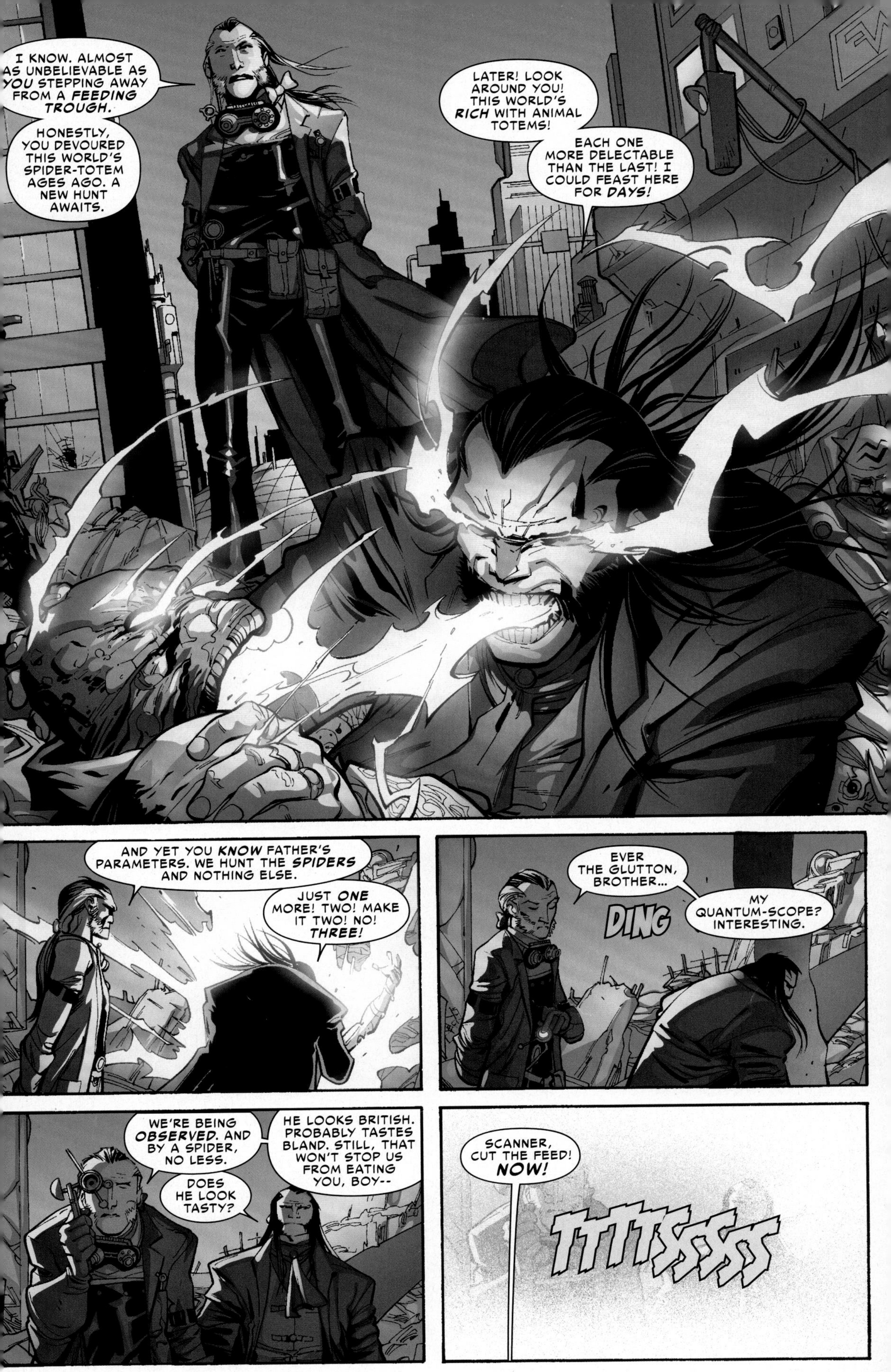
I KNOW. ALMOST AS UNBELIEVABLE AS YOU STEPPING AWAY FROM A FEEDING TROUGH.
HONESTLY, YOU DEVOURED THIS WORLD'S SPIDER-TOTEM AGES AGO. A NEW HUNT AWAITS.
LATER! LOOK AROUND YOU! THIS WORLD'S RICH WITH ANIMAL TOTEMS!
EACH ONE MORE DELECTABLE THAN THE LAST! I COULD FEAST HERE FOR DAYS!
AND YET YOU KNOW FATHER'S PARAMETERS. WE HUNT THE SPIDERS AND NOTHING ELSE.
JUST ONE MORE! TWO! MAKE IT TWO! NO! THREE!
EVER THE GLUTTON, BROTHER...
DING
MY QUANTUM-SCOPE? INTERESTING.
WE'RE BEING OBSERVED. AND BY A SPIDER, NO LESS.
DOES HE LOOK TASTY?
HE LOOKS BRITISH. PROBABLY TASTES BLAND. STILL, THAT WON'T STOP US FROM EATING YOU, BOY--
SCANNER, CUT THE FEED! NOW!
TTTTSSSSS

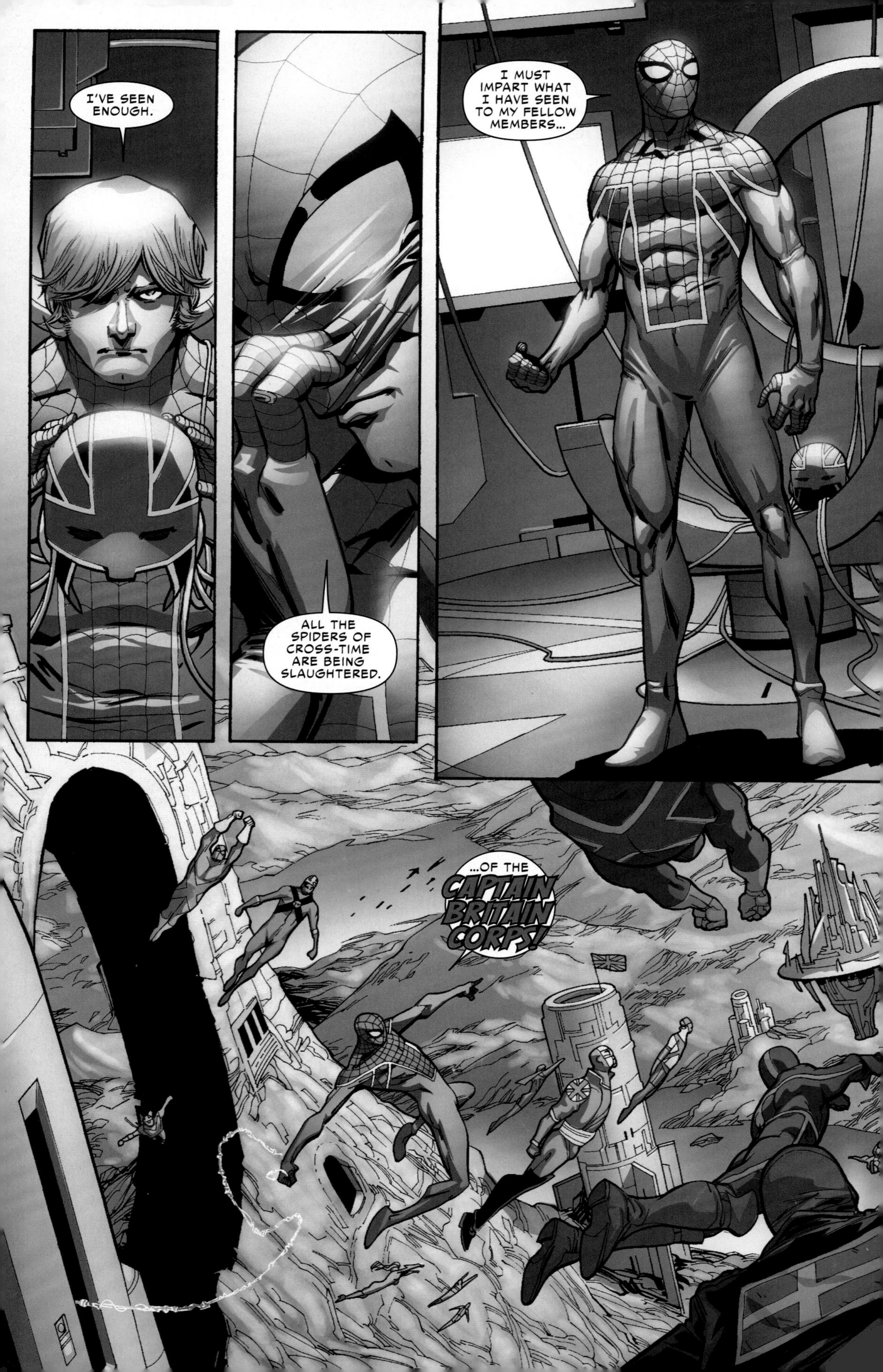
I'VE SEEN ENOUGH.
ALL THE SPIDERS OF CROSS-TIME ARE BEING SLAUGHTERED.
I MUST IMPART WHAT I HAVE SEEN TO MY FELLOW MEMBERS...
...OF THE CAPTAIN BRITAIN CORPS!

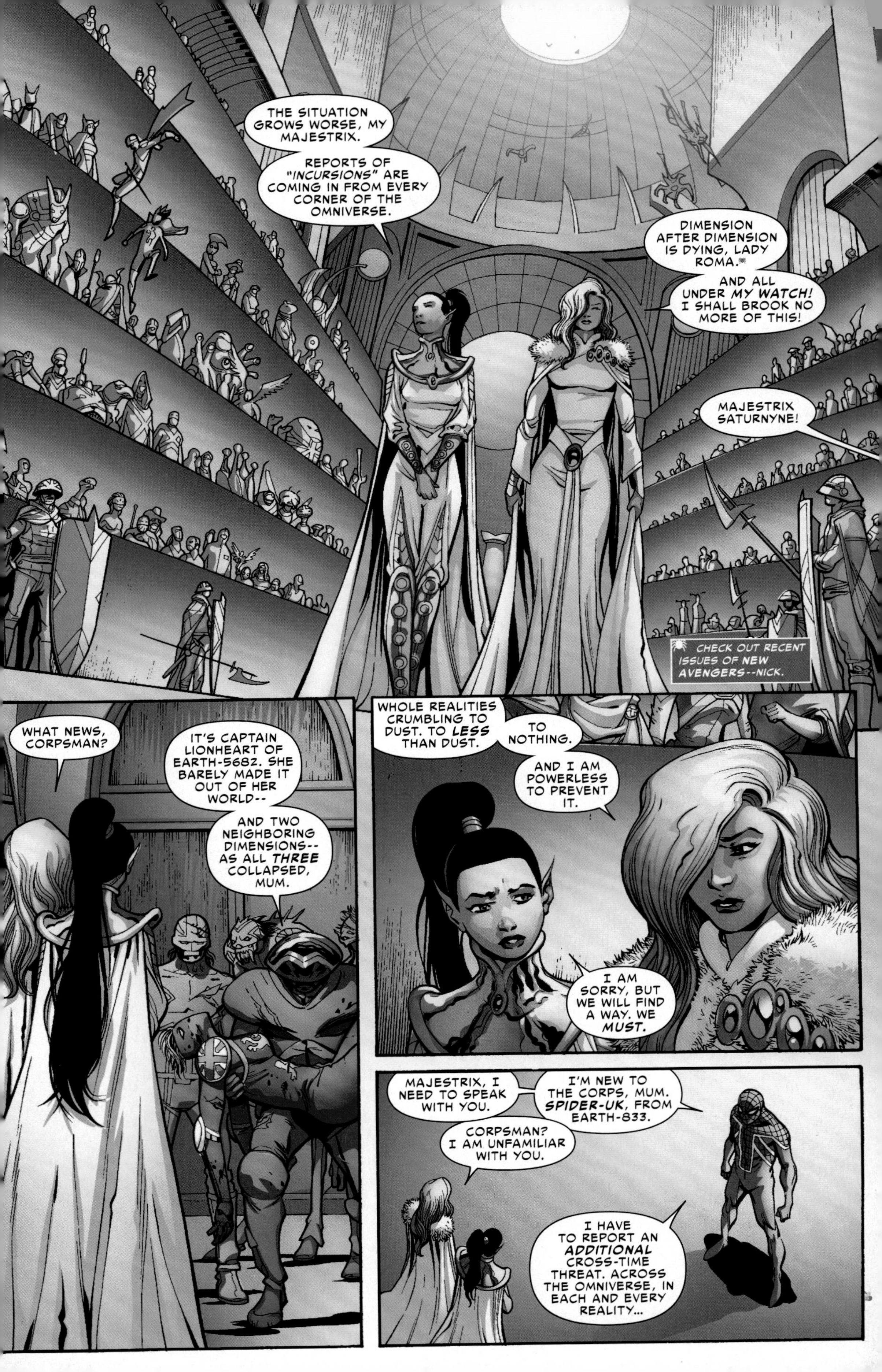
THE SITUATION GROWS WORSE, MY MAJESTRIX.
REPORTS OF "INCURSIONS" ARE COMING IN FROM EVERY CORNER OF THE OMNIVERSE.
DIMENSION AFTER DIMENSION IS DYING, LADY ROMA.*
AND ALL UNDER MY WATCH! I SHALL BROOK NO MORE OF THIS!
MAJESTRIX SATURNYNE!
*CHECK OUT RECENT ISSUES OF NEW AVENGERS--NICK.
WHAT NEWS, CORPSMAN?
IT'S CAPTAIN LIONHEART OF EARTH-5682. SHE BARELY MADE IT OUT OF HER WORLD--
AND TWO NEIGHBORING DIMENSIONS--AS ALL THREE COLLAPSED, MUM.
WHOLE REALITIES CRUMBLING TO DUST. TO LESS THAN DUST.
TO NOTHING.
AND I AM POWERLESS TO PREVENT IT.
I AM SORRY, BUT WE WILL FIND A WAY. WE MUST.
MAJESTRIX, I NEED TO SPEAK WITH YOU.
I'M NEW TO THE CORPS, MUM. SPIDER-UK, FROM EARTH-833.
CORPSMAN? I AM UNFAMILIAR WITH YOU.
I HAVE TO REPORT AN ADDITIONAL CROSS-TIME THREAT. ACROSS THE OMNIVERSE, IN EACH AND EVERY REALITY...

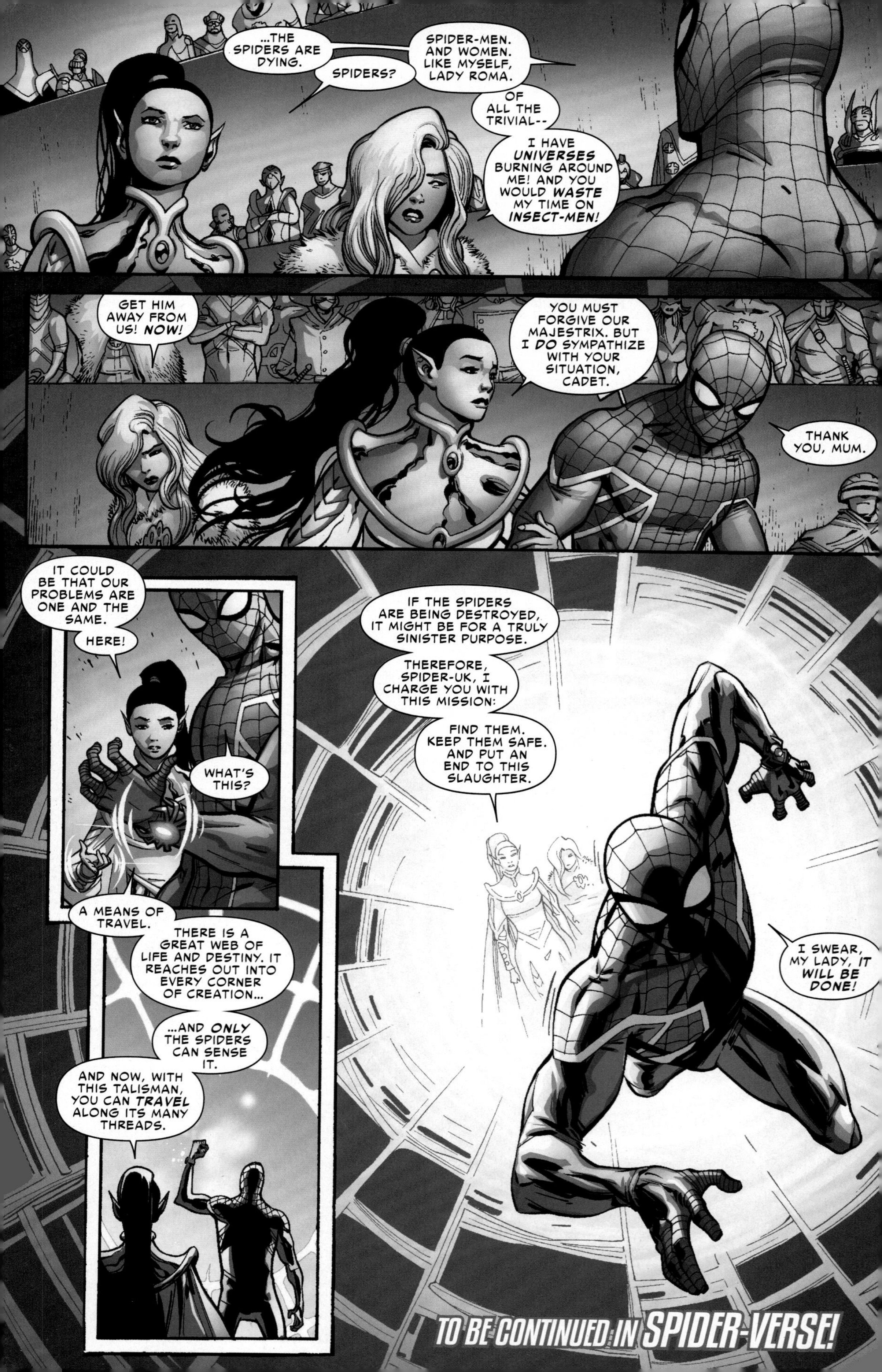

...THE SPIDERS ARE DYING.
SPIDERS?
SPIDER-MEN. AND WOMEN. LIKE MYSELF, LADY ROMA.
OF ALL THE TRIVIAL--
I HAVE UNIVERSES BURNING AROUND ME! AND YOU WOULD WASTE MY TIME ON INSECT-MEN!
GET HIM AWAY FROM US! NOW!
YOU MUST FORGIVE OUR MAJESTRIX. BUT I DO SYMPATHIZE WITH YOUR SITUATION, CADET.
THANK YOU, MUM.
IT COULD BE THAT OUR PROBLEMS ARE ONE AND THE SAME.
HERE!
WHAT'S THIS?
A MEANS OF TRAVEL.
THERE IS A GREAT WEB OF LIFE AND DESTINY. IT REACHES OUT INTO EVERY CORNER OF CREATION...
...AND ONLY THE SPIDERS CAN SENSE IT.
AND NOW, WITH THIS TALISMAN, YOU CAN TRAVEL ALONG ITS MANY THREADS.
IF THE SPIDERS ARE BEING DESTROYED, IT MIGHT BE FOR A TRULY SINISTER PURPOSE.
THEREFORE, SPIDER-UK, I CHARGE YOU WITH THIS MISSION:
FIND THEM. KEEP THEM SAFE. AND PUT AN END TO THIS SLAUGHTER.
I SWEAR, MY LADY, IT WILL BE DONE!
TO BE CONTINUED IN SPIDER-VERSE!

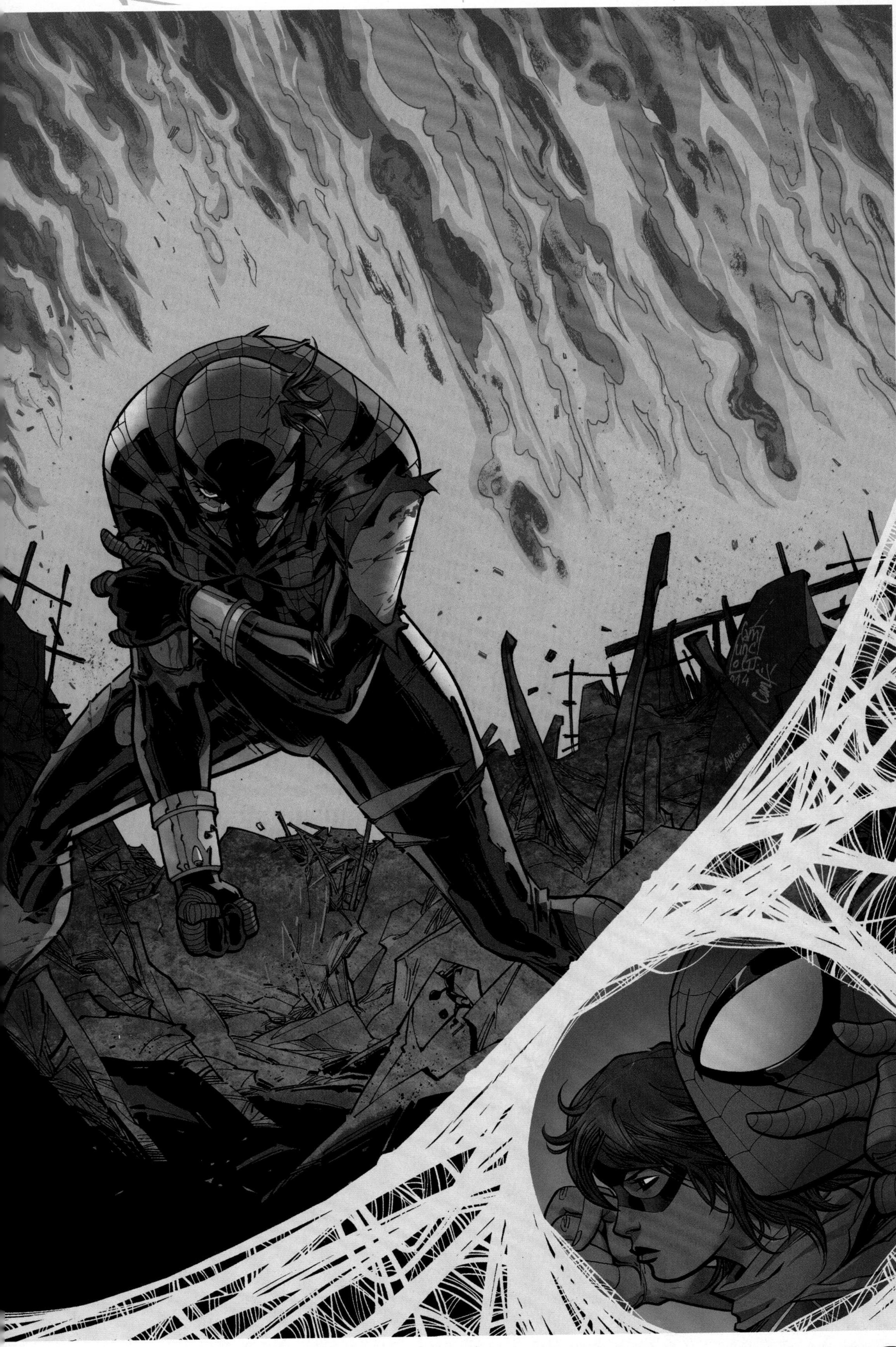

AMAZING SPIDER-MAN 8

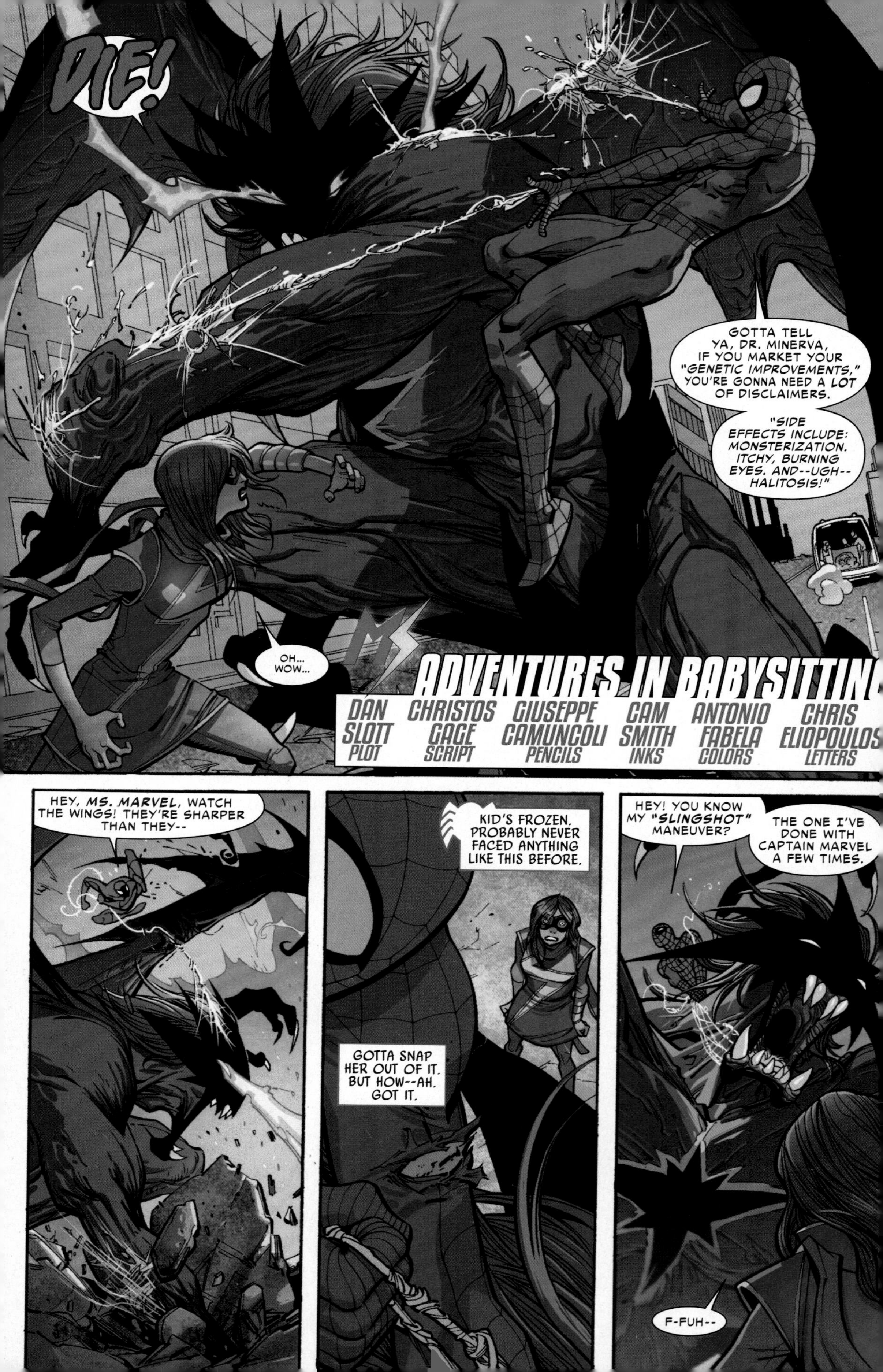
DIE!
GOTTA TELL YA, DR. MINERVA, IF YOU MARKET YOUR "GENETIC IMPROVEMENTS," YOU'RE GONNA NEED A LOT OF DISCLAIMERS.
"SIDE EFFECTS INCLUDE: MONSTERIZATION. ITCHY, BURNING EYES. AND--UGH--HALITOSIS!"
OH... WOW...
ADVENTURES IN BABYSITTING
DAN SLOTT PLOT
CHRISTOS GAGE SCRIPT
GIUSEPPE CAMUNCOLI PENCILS
CAM SMITH INKS
ANTONIO FABELA COLORS
CHRIS ELIOPOULOS LETTERS
HEY, MS. MARVEL, WATCH THE WINGS! THEY'RE SHARPER THAN THEY--
KID'S FROZEN. PROBABLY NEVER FACED ANYTHING LIKE THIS BEFORE.
GOTTA SNAP HER OUT OF IT. BUT HOW--AH. GOT IT.
HEY! YOU KNOW MY "SLINGSHOT" MANEUVER?
THE ONE I'VE DONE WITH CAPTAIN MARVEL A FEW TIMES.
F-FUH--

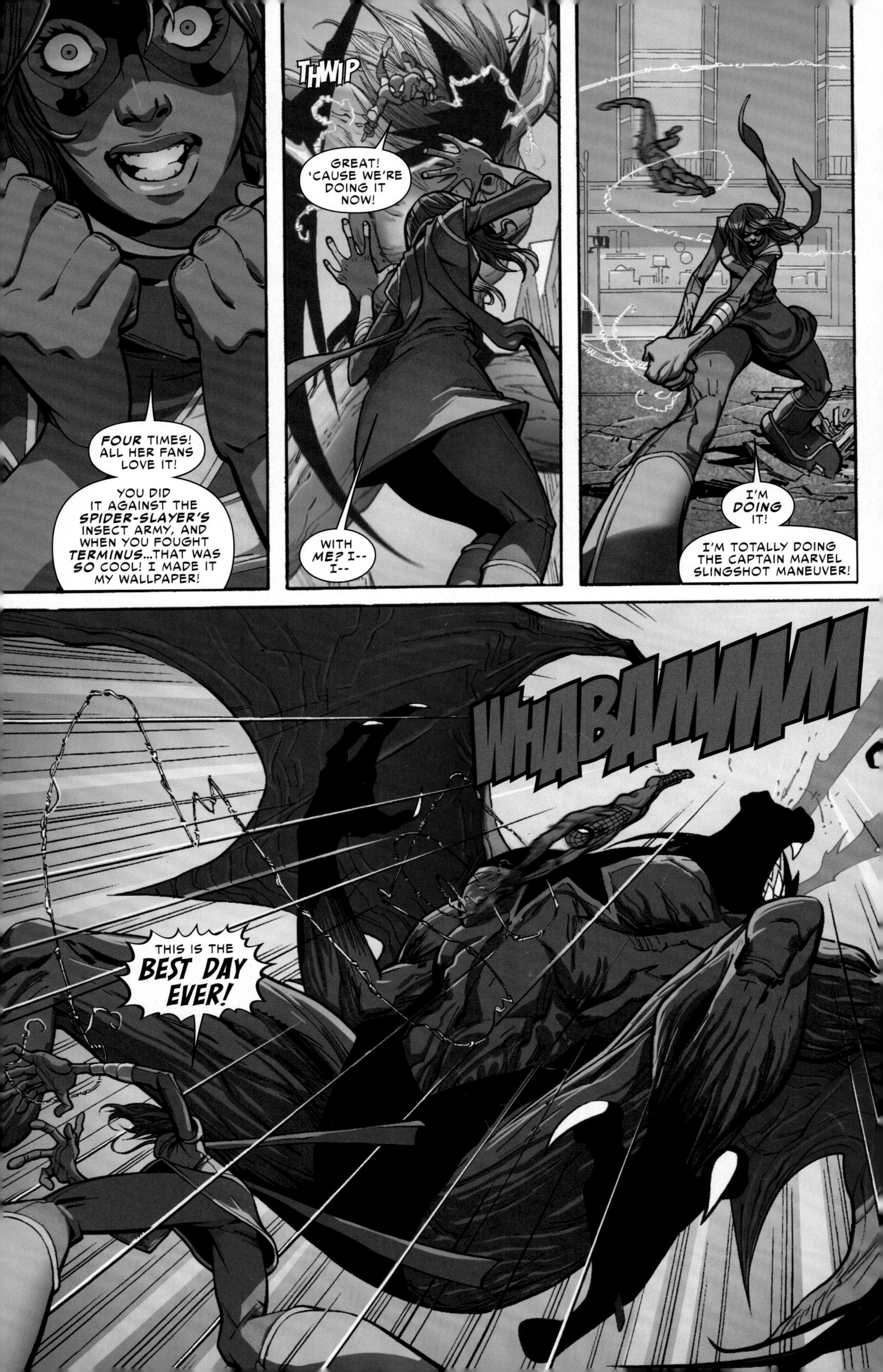
FOUR TIMES! ALL HER FANS LOVE IT!
YOU DID IT AGAINST THE SPIDER-SLAYER'S INSECT ARMY, AND WHEN YOU FOUGHT TERMINUS...THAT WAS SO COOL! I MADE IT MY WALLPAPER!
THWIP
GREAT! 'CAUSE WE'RE DOING IT NOW!
WITH ME? I-- I--
I'M DOING IT!
I'M TOTALLY DOING THE CAPTAIN MARVEL SLINGSHOT MANEUVER!
WHABAMMMM
THIS IS THE BEST DAY EVER!

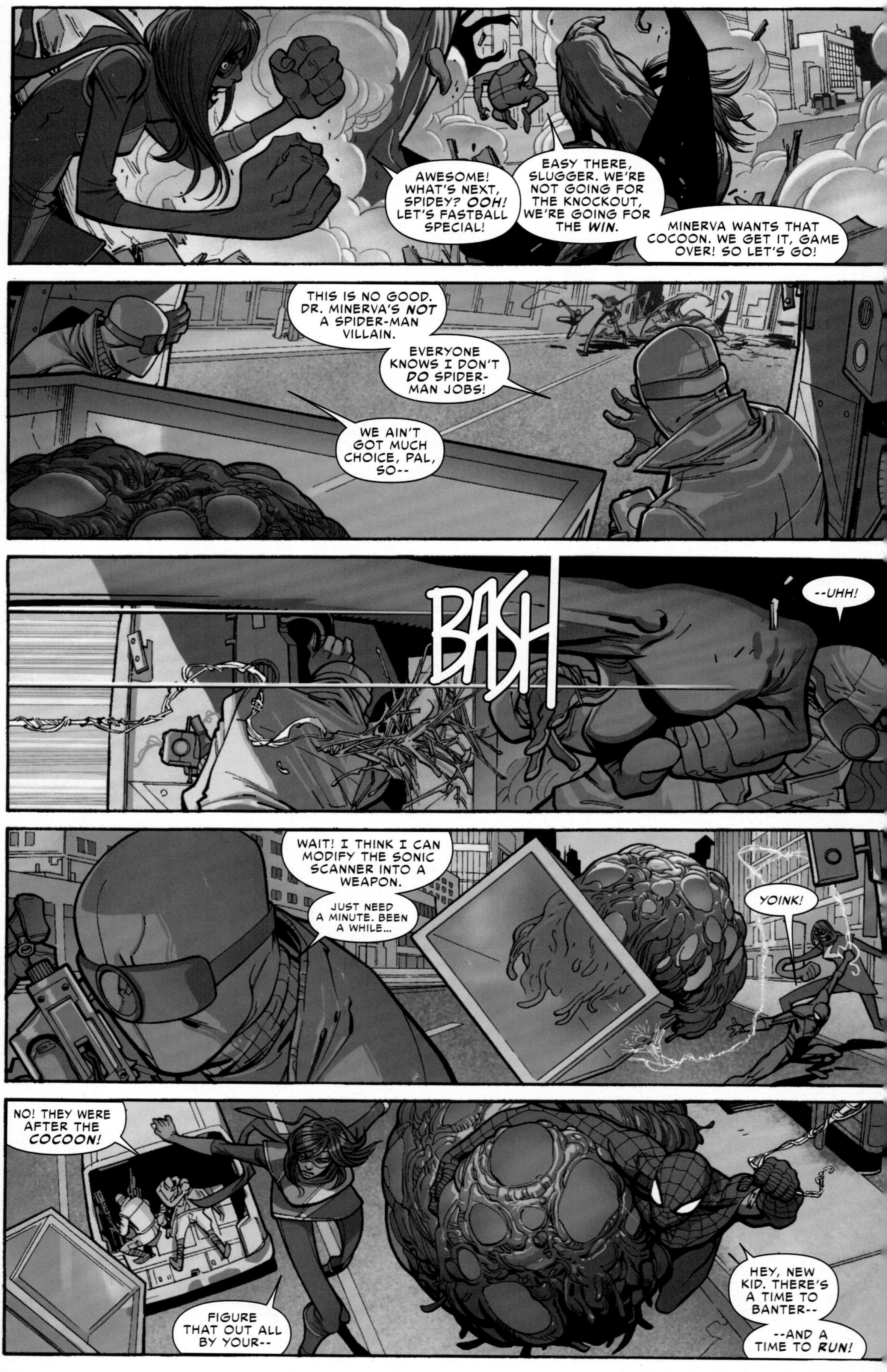
AWESOME! WHAT'S NEXT, SPIDEY? OOH! LET'S FASTBALL SPECIAL!
EASY THERE, SLUGGER. WE'RE NOT GOING FOR THE KNOCKOUT, WE'RE GOING FOR THE WIN.
MINERVA WANTS THAT COCOON. WE GET IT, GAME OVER! SO LET'S GO!
THIS IS NO GOOD. DR. MINERVA'S NOT A SPIDER-MAN VILLAIN.
EVERYONE KNOWS I DON'T DO SPIDER-MAN JOBS!
WE AIN'T GOT MUCH CHOICE, PAL, SO--
BASH
--UHH!
WAIT! I THINK I CAN MODIFY THE SONIC SCANNER INTO A WEAPON.
JUST NEED A MINUTE. BEEN A WHILE...
YOINK!
NO! THEY WERE AFTER THE COCOON!
FIGURE THAT OUT ALL BY YOUR--
HEY, NEW KID. THERE'S A TIME TO BANTER--
--AND A TIME TO RUN!

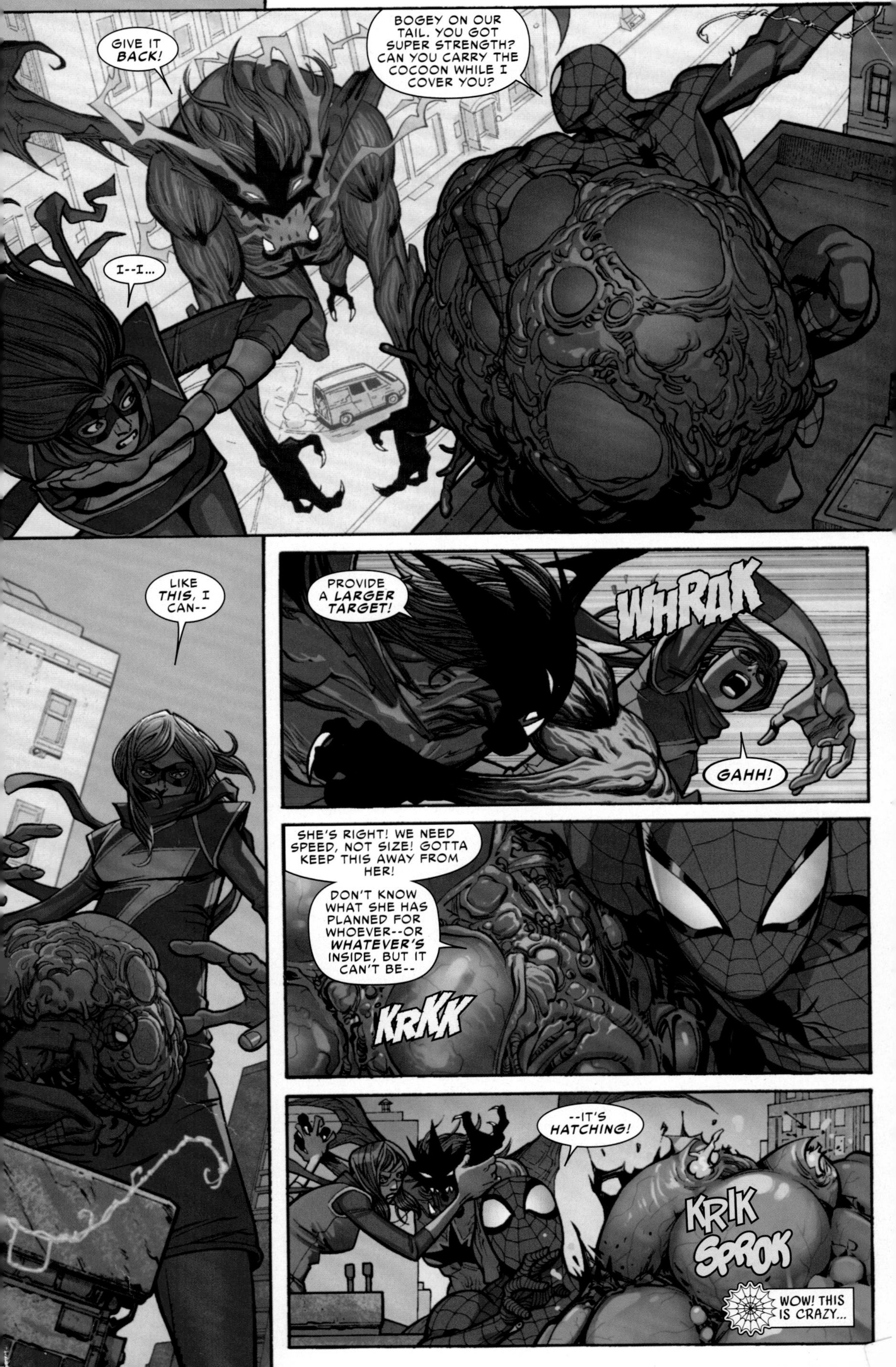
GIVE IT BACK!
BOGEY ON OUR TAIL. YOU GOT SUPER STRENGTH? CAN YOU CARRY THE COCOON WHILE I COVER YOU?
I--I...
LIKE THIS, I CAN--
PROVIDE A LARGER TARGET!
WHRAK
GAHH!
SHE'S RIGHT! WE NEED SPEED, NOT SIZE! GOTTA KEEP THIS AWAY FROM HER!
DON'T KNOW WHAT SHE HAS PLANNED FOR WHOEVER--OR WHATEVER'S INSIDE, BUT IT CAN'T BE--
KRKK
--IT'S HATCHING!
KRIK
SPROK
WOW! THIS IS CRAZY...

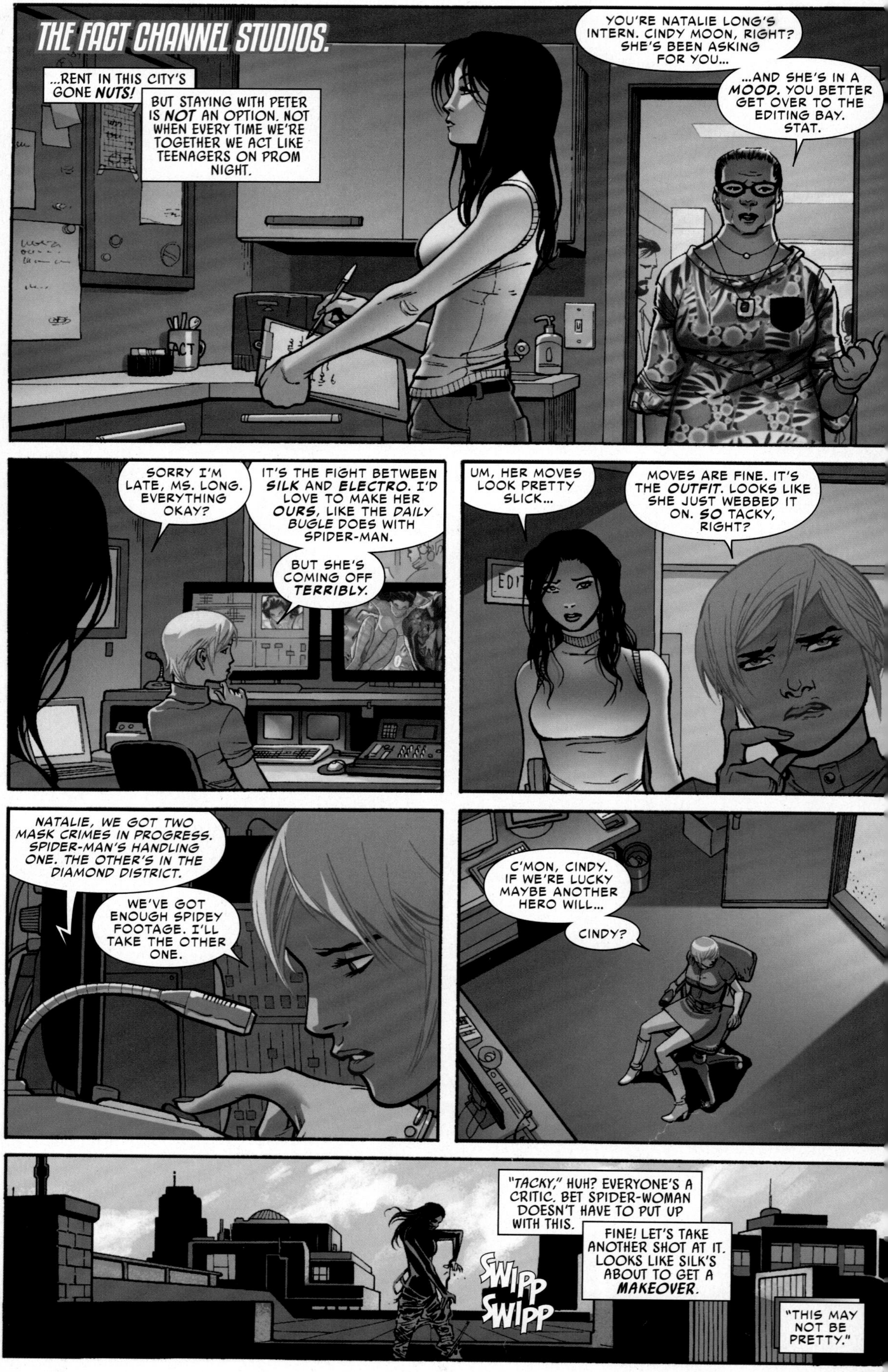
THE FACT CHANNEL STUDIOS.
...RENT IN THIS CITY'S GONE NUTS!
BUT STAYING WITH PETER IS NOT AN OPTION. NOT WHEN EVERY TIME WE'RE TOGETHER WE ACT LIKE TEENAGERS ON PROM NIGHT.
YOU'RE NATALIE LONG'S INTERN. CINDY MOON, RIGHT? SHE'S BEEN ASKING FOR YOU...
...AND SHE'S IN A MOOD. YOU BETTER GET OVER TO THE EDITING BAY. STAT.
SORRY I'M LATE, MS. LONG. EVERYTHING OKAY?
IT'S THE FIGHT BETWEEN SILK AND ELECTRO. I'D LOVE TO MAKE HER OURS, LIKE THE DAILY BUGLE DOES WITH SPIDER-MAN.
BUT SHE'S COMING OFF TERRIBLY.
UM, HER MOVES LOOK PRETTY SLICK...
MOVES ARE FINE. IT'S THE OUTFIT. LOOKS LIKE SHE JUST WEBBED IT ON. SO TACKY, RIGHT?
NATALIE, WE GOT TWO MASK CRIMES IN PROGRESS. SPIDER-MAN'S HANDLING ONE. THE OTHER'S IN THE DIAMOND DISTRICT.
WE'VE GOT ENOUGH SPIDEY FOOTAGE. I'LL TAKE THE OTHER ONE.
C'MON, CINDY. IF WE'RE LUCKY MAYBE ANOTHER HERO WILL...
CINDY?
"TACKY," HUH? EVERYONE'S A CRITIC. BET SPIDER-WOMAN DOESN'T HAVE TO PUT UP WITH THIS.
FINE! LET'S TAKE ANOTHER SHOT AT IT. LOOKS LIKE SILK'S ABOUT TO GET A MAKEOVER.
SWIPP
SWIPP
"THIS MAY NOT BE PRETTY."

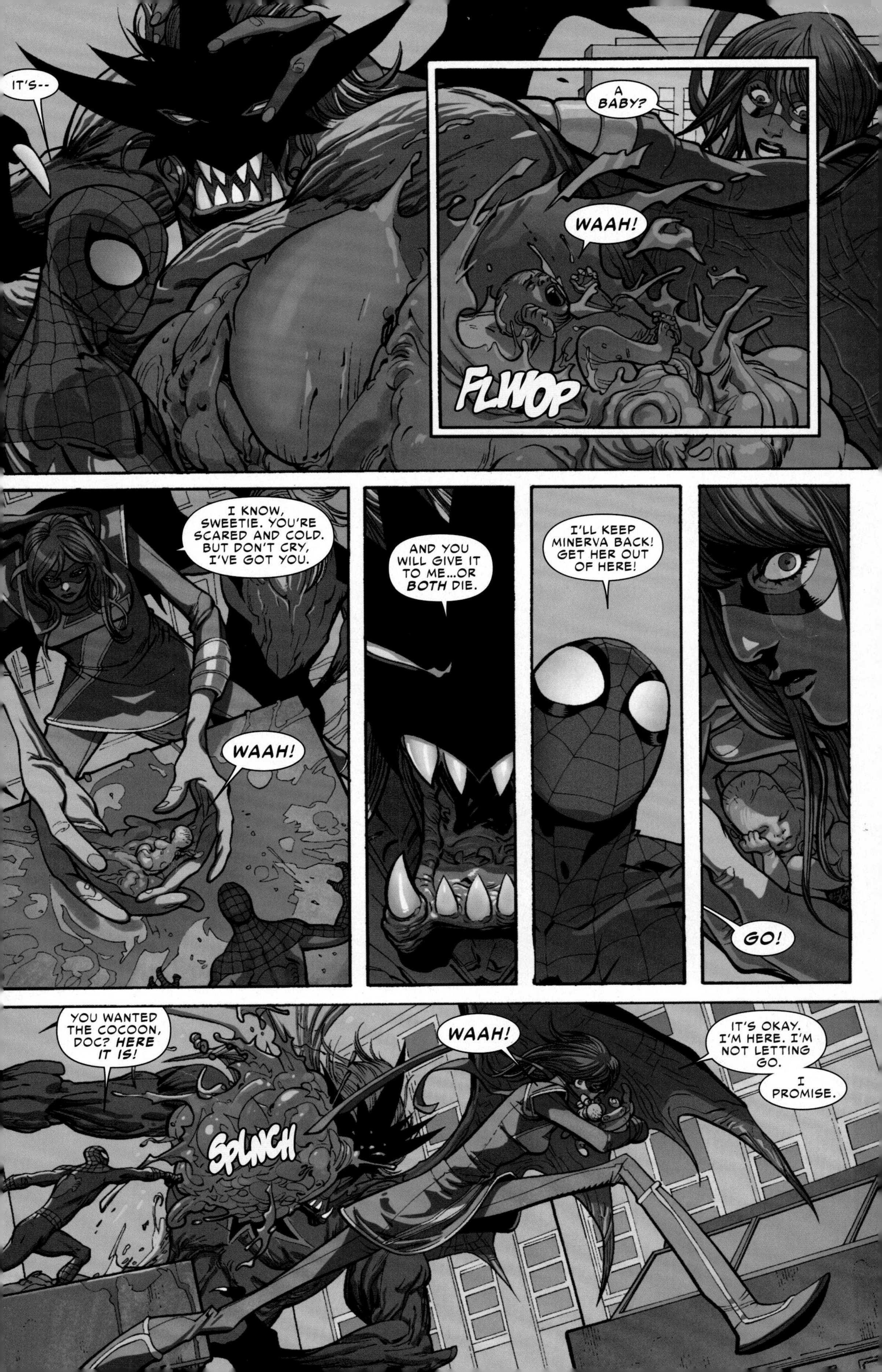
IT'S--
A BABY?
WAAH!
FLWOP
I KNOW, SWEETIE. YOU'RE SCARED AND COLD. BUT DON'T CRY, I'VE GOT YOU.
WAAH!
AND YOU WILL GIVE IT TO ME...OR BOTH DIE.
I'LL KEEP MINERVA BACK! GET HER OUT OF HERE!
GO!
YOU WANTED THE COCOON, DOC? HERE IT IS!
SPLNCH
WAAH!
IT'S OKAY. I'M HERE. I'M NOT LETTING GO.
I PROMISE.

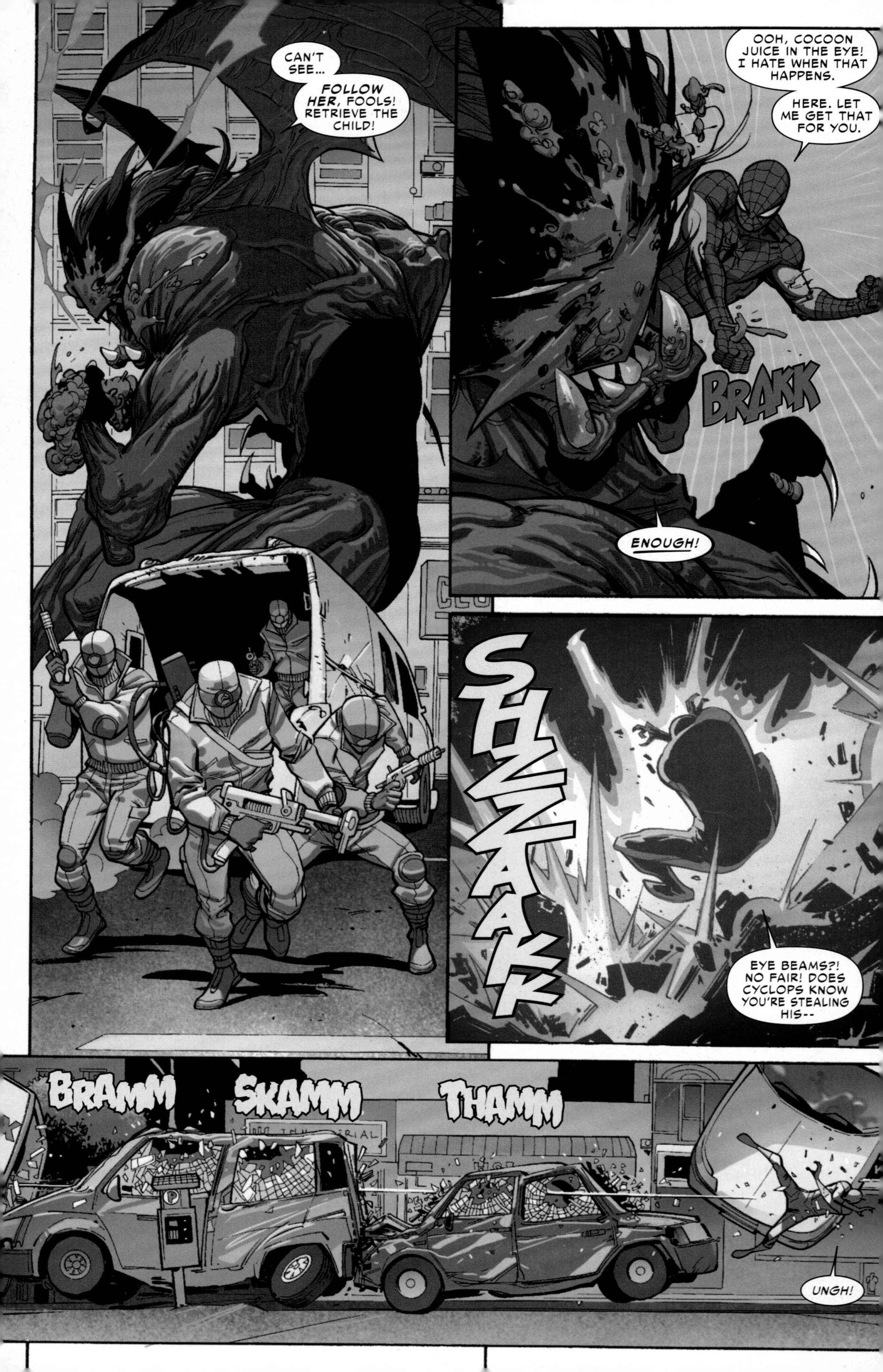
CAN'T SEE... FOLLOW HER, FOOLS! RETRIEVE THE CHILD!
OOH, COCOON JUICE IN THE EYE! I HATE WHEN THAT HAPPENS.
HERE. LET ME GET THAT FOR YOU.
BRAKK
ENOUGH!
SHZZAKK
EYE BEAMS?! NO FAIR! DOES CYCLOPS KNOW YOU'RE STEALING HIS--
BRAMM
SKAMM
THAMM
UNGH!

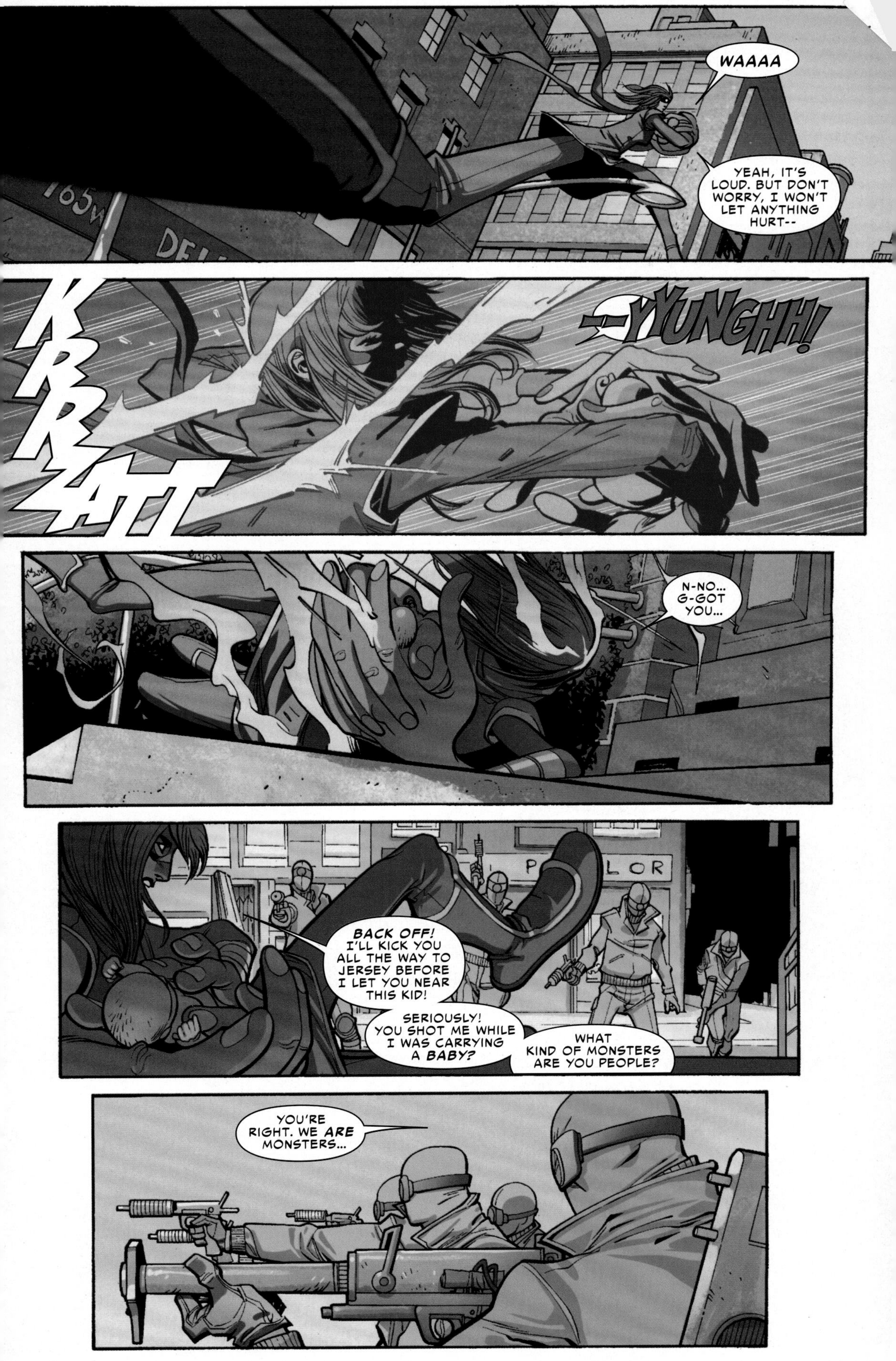

WAAAA
YEAH, IT'S LOUD. BUT DON'T WORRY, I WON'T LET ANYTHING HURT--
KRRZATT
--YYUNGHH!
N-NO... G-GOT YOU...
PARLOR
BACK OFF! I'LL KICK YOU ALL THE WAY TO JERSEY BEFORE I LET YOU NEAR THIS KID!
SERIOUSLY! YOU SHOT ME WHILE I WAS CARRYING A BABY?
WHAT KIND OF MONSTERS ARE YOU PEOPLE?
YOU'RE RIGHT. WE ARE MONSTERS...

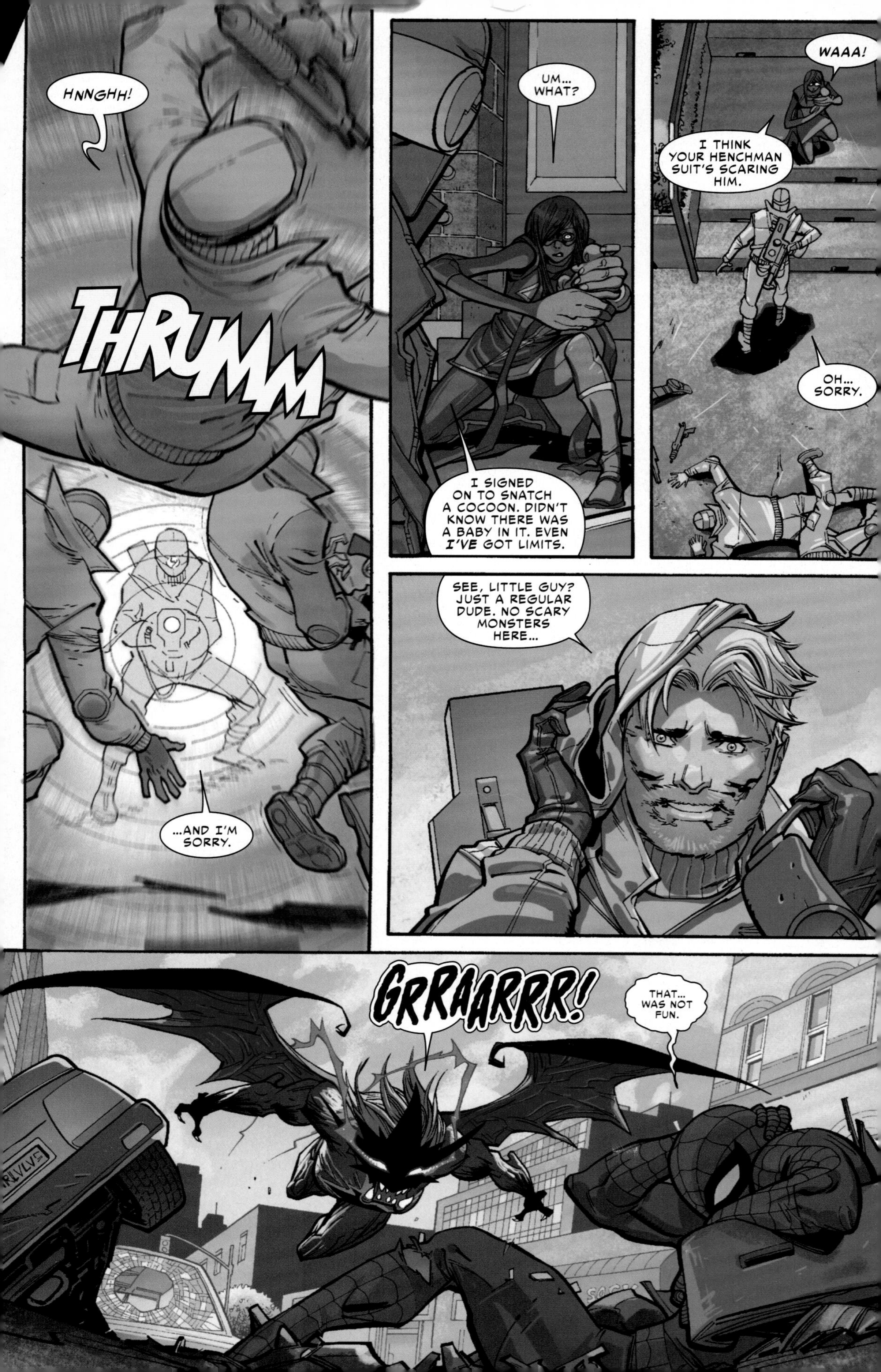
HNNGHH!
THRUMM
...AND I'M SORRY.
UM... WHAT?
I SIGNED ON TO SNATCH A COCOON. DIDN'T KNOW THERE WAS A BABY IN IT. EVEN I'VE GOT LIMITS.
WAAA!
I THINK YOUR HENCHMAN SUIT'S SCARING HIM.
OH... SORRY.
SEE, LITTLE GUY? JUST A REGULAR DUDE. NO SCARY MONSTERS HERE...
GRRAARRR!
THAT... WAS NOT FUN.

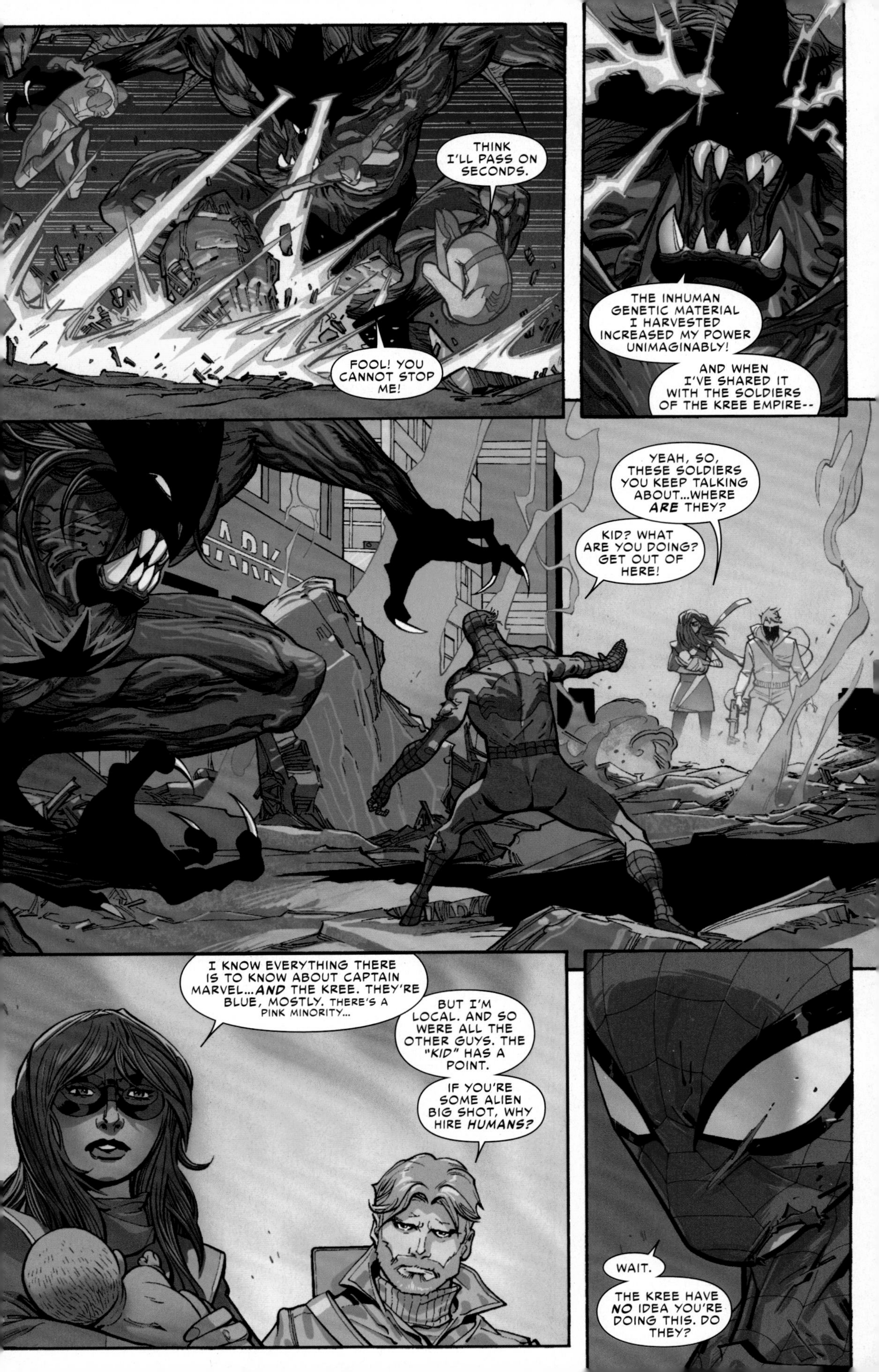
THINK I'LL PASS ON SECONDS.
FOOL! YOU CANNOT STOP ME!
THE INHUMAN GENETIC MATERIAL I HARVESTED INCREASED MY POWER UNIMAGINABLY!
AND WHEN I'VE SHARED IT WITH THE SOLDIERS OF THE KREE EMPIRE--
YEAH, SO, THESE SOLDIERS YOU KEEP TALKING ABOUT...WHERE *ARE* THEY?
KID? WHAT ARE YOU DOING? GET OUT OF HERE!
I KNOW EVERYTHING THERE IS TO KNOW ABOUT CAPTAIN MARVEL...*AND* THE KREE. THEY'RE BLUE, MOSTLY. THERE'S A PINK MINORITY...
BUT I'M LOCAL. AND SO WERE ALL THE OTHER GUYS. THE "*KID*" HAS A POINT.
IF YOU'RE SOME ALIEN BIG SHOT, WHY HIRE *HUMANS?*
WAIT.
THE KREE HAVE *NO* IDEA YOU'RE DOING THIS. DO THEY?

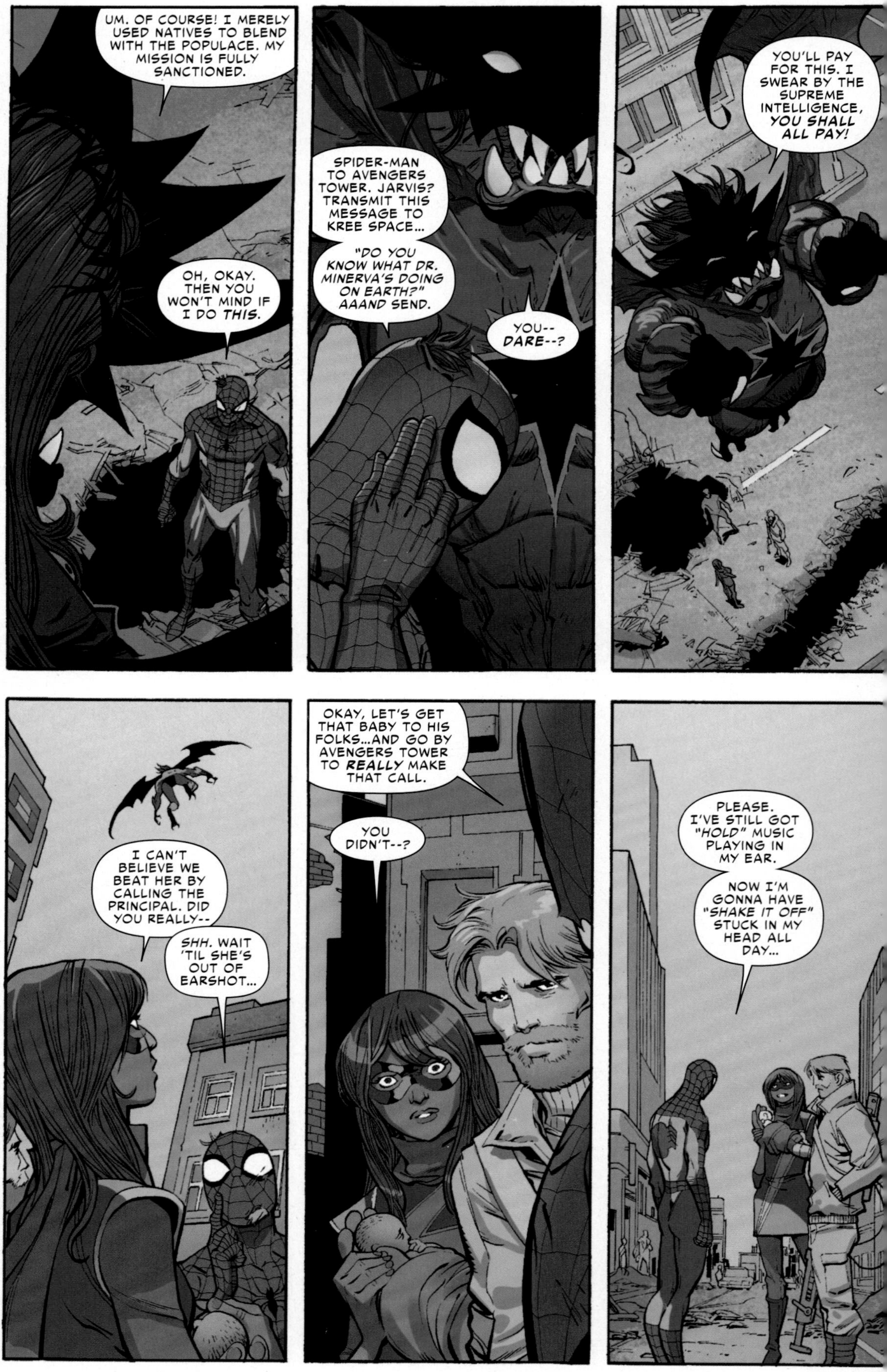
UM. OF COURSE! I MERELY USED NATIVES TO BLEND WITH THE POPULACE. MY MISSION IS FULLY SANCTIONED.
OH, OKAY. THEN YOU WON'T MIND IF I DO *THIS*.
SPIDER-MAN TO AVENGERS TOWER. JARVIS? TRANSMIT THIS MESSAGE TO KREE SPACE...
"DO YOU KNOW WHAT DR. MINERVA'S DOING ON EARTH?" AAAND SEND.
YOU-- *DARE*--?
YOU'LL PAY FOR THIS. I SWEAR BY THE SUPREME INTELLIGENCE, ***YOU SHALL ALL PAY!***
I CAN'T BELIEVE WE BEAT HER BY CALLING THE PRINCIPAL. DID YOU REALLY--
SHH. WAIT 'TIL SHE'S OUT OF EARSHOT...
OKAY, LET'S GET THAT BABY TO HIS FOLKS...AND GO BY AVENGERS TOWER TO ***REALLY*** MAKE THAT CALL.
YOU DIDN'T--?
PLEASE. I'VE STILL GOT *"HOLD"* MUSIC PLAYING IN MY EAR.
NOW I'M GONNA HAVE *"SHAKE IT OFF"* STUCK IN MY HEAD ALL DAY...

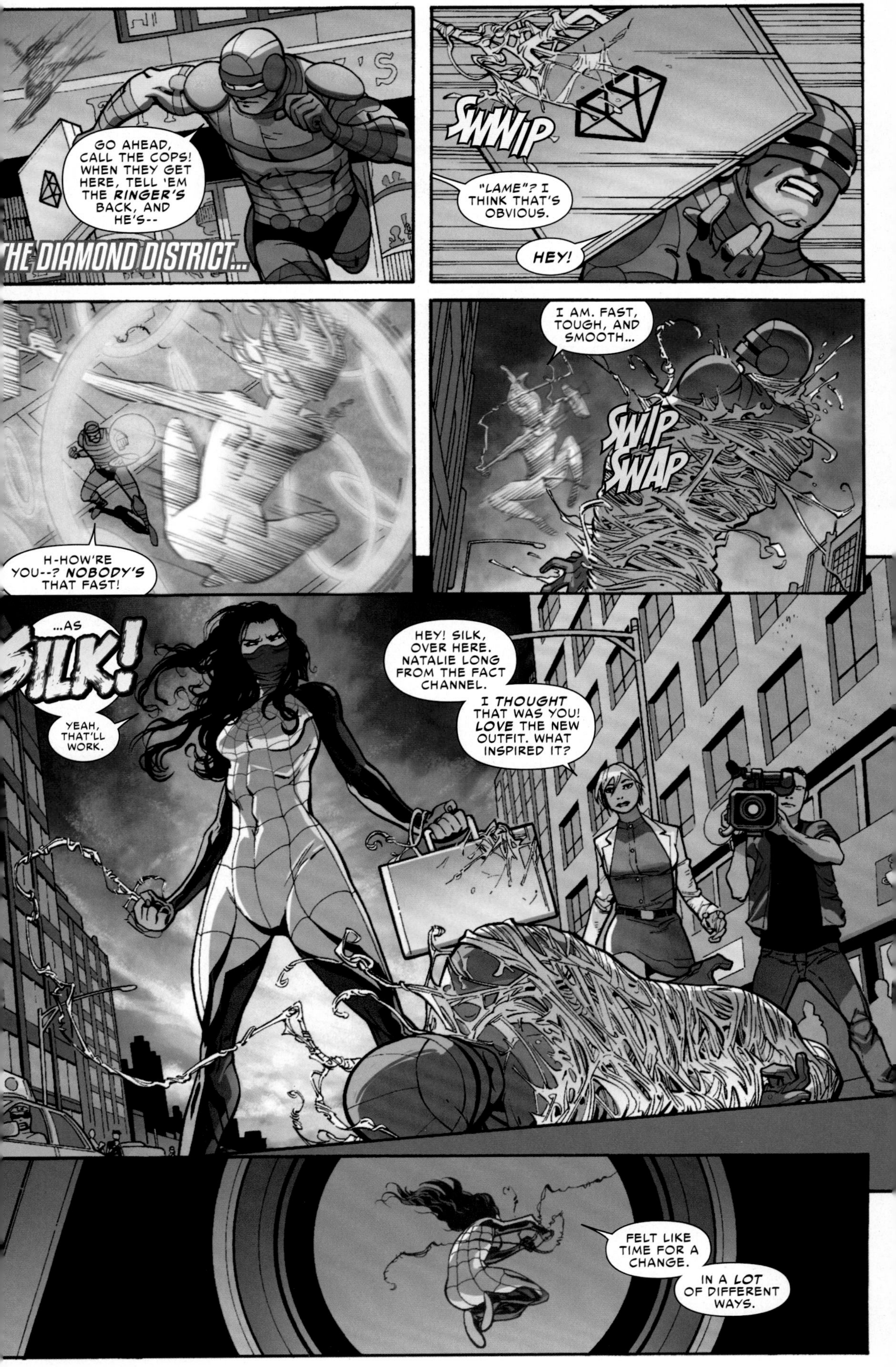
THE DIAMOND DISTRICT...
GO AHEAD, CALL THE COPS! WHEN THEY GET HERE, TELL 'EM THE RINGER'S BACK, AND HE'S--
SWWIP
"LAME"? I THINK THAT'S OBVIOUS.
HEY!
H-HOW'RE YOU--? NOBODY'S THAT FAST!
I AM. FAST, TOUGH, AND SMOOTH...
SWIP SWAP
...AS SILK!
YEAH, THAT'LL WORK.
HEY! SILK, OVER HERE. NATALIE LONG FROM THE FACT CHANNEL.
I THOUGHT THAT WAS YOU! LOVE THE NEW OUTFIT. WHAT INSPIRED IT?
FELT LIKE TIME FOR A CHANGE.
IN A LOT OF DIFFERENT WAYS.

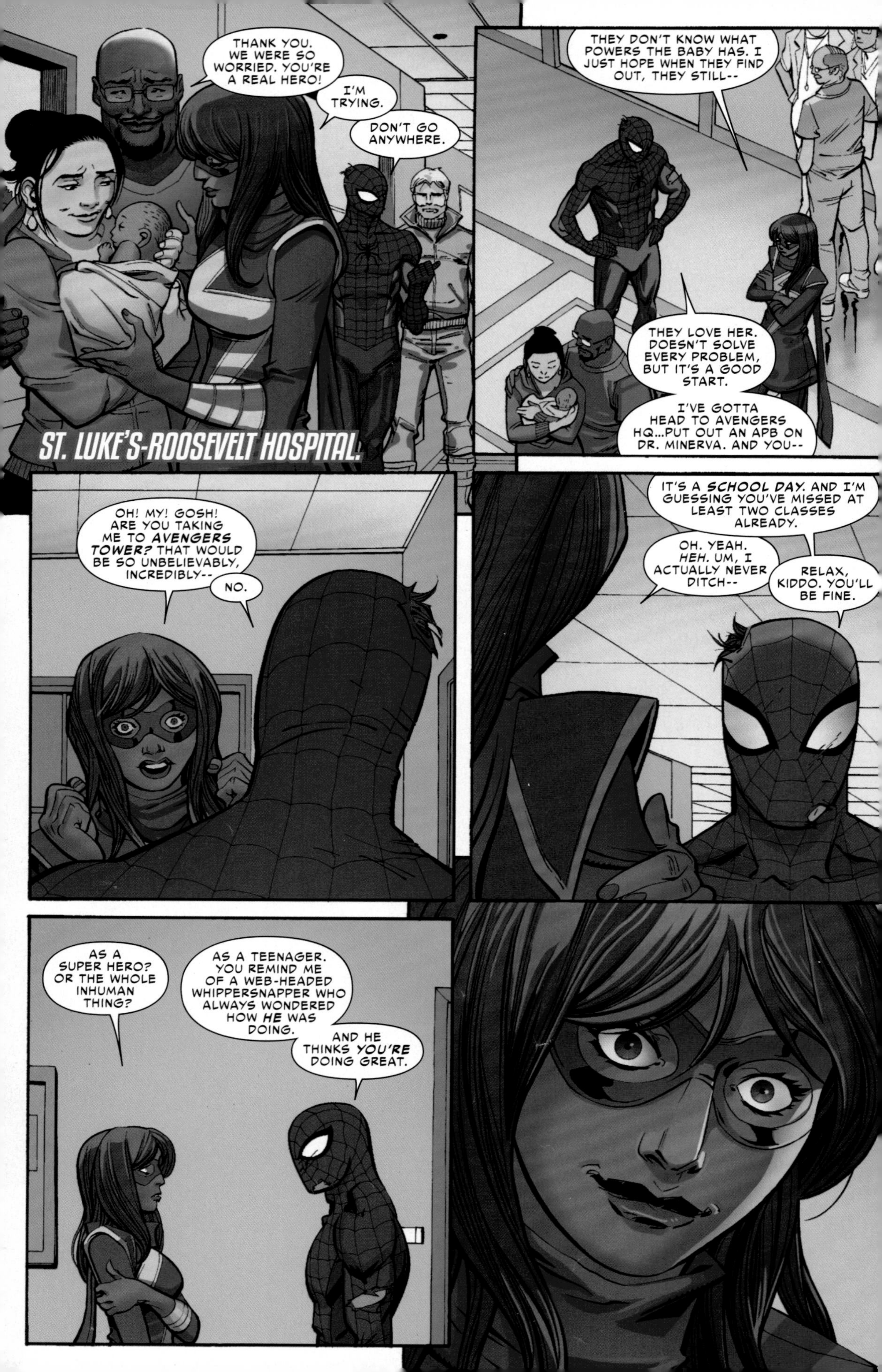
THANK YOU. WE WERE SO WORRIED. YOU'RE A REAL HERO!
I'M TRYING.
DON'T GO ANYWHERE.
ST. LUKE'S-ROOSEVELT HOSPITAL.
THEY DON'T KNOW WHAT POWERS THE BABY HAS. I JUST HOPE WHEN THEY FIND OUT, THEY STILL--
THEY LOVE HER. DOESN'T SOLVE EVERY PROBLEM, BUT IT'S A GOOD START.
I'VE GOTTA HEAD TO AVENGERS HQ...PUT OUT AN APB ON DR. MINERVA. AND YOU--
OH! MY! GOSH! ARE YOU TAKING ME TO AVENGERS TOWER? THAT WOULD BE SO UNBELIEVABLY, INCREDIBLY--
NO.
IT'S A SCHOOL DAY. AND I'M GUESSING YOU'VE MISSED AT LEAST TWO CLASSES ALREADY.
OH. YEAH. HEH. UM, I ACTUALLY NEVER DITCH--
RELAX, KIDDO. YOU'LL BE FINE.
AS A SUPER HERO? OR THE WHOLE INHUMAN THING?
AS A TEENAGER. YOU REMIND ME OF A WEB-HEADED WHIPPERSNAPPER WHO ALWAYS WONDERED HOW HE WAS DOING.
AND HE THINKS YOU'RE DOING GREAT.

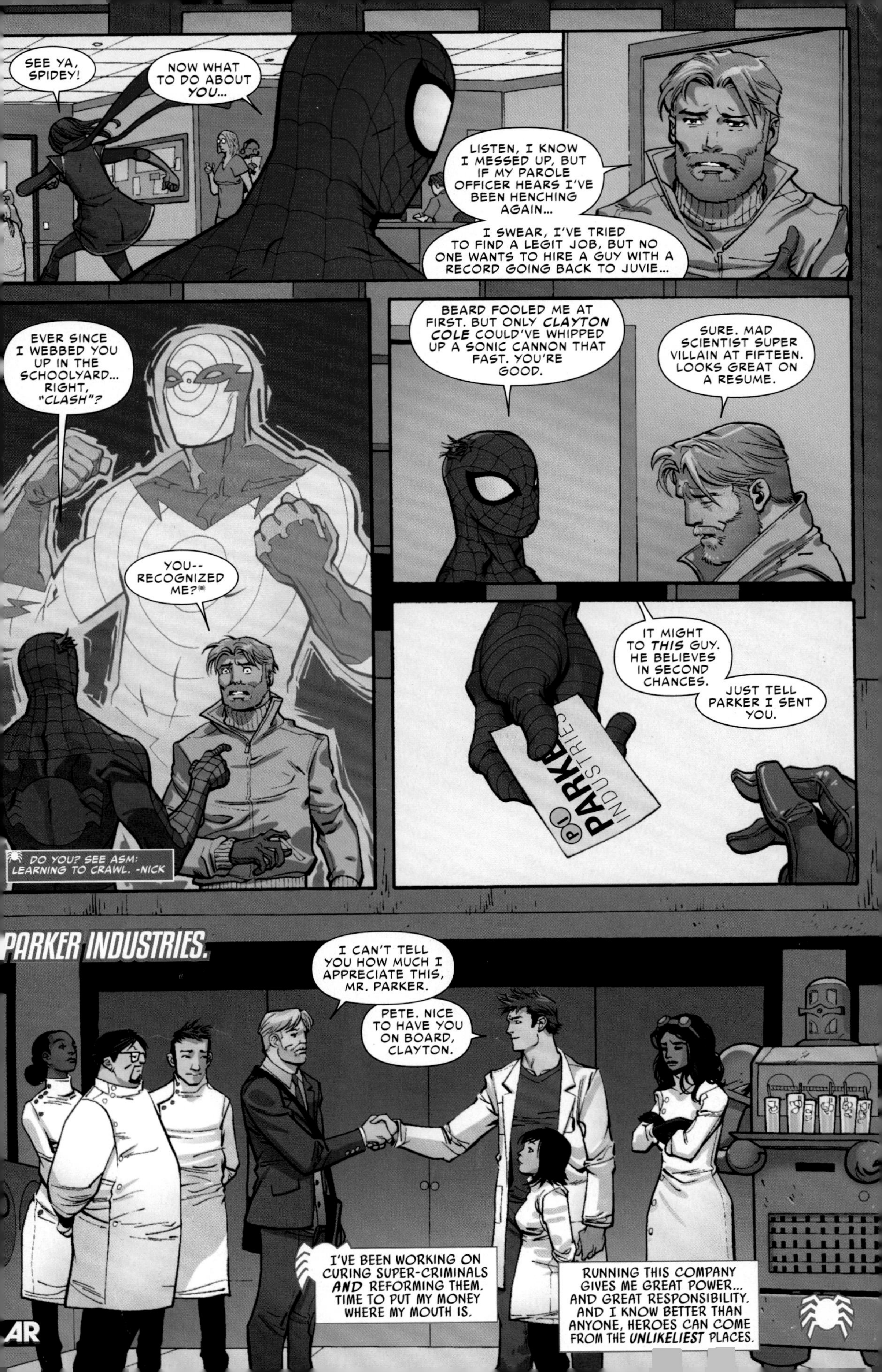
SEE YA, SPIDEY!
NOW WHAT TO DO ABOUT YOU...
LISTEN, I KNOW I MESSED UP, BUT IF MY PAROLE OFFICER HEARS I'VE BEEN HENCHING AGAIN...
I SWEAR, I'VE TRIED TO FIND A LEGIT JOB, BUT NO ONE WANTS TO HIRE A GUY WITH A RECORD GOING BACK TO JUVIE...
EVER SINCE I WEBBED YOU UP IN THE SCHOOLYARD... RIGHT, "CLASH"?
YOU-- RECOGNIZED ME?*
*DO YOU? SEE ASM: LEARNING TO CRAWL. -NICK
BEARD FOOLED ME AT FIRST. BUT ONLY CLAYTON COLE COULD'VE WHIPPED UP A SONIC CANNON THAT FAST. YOU'RE GOOD.
SURE. MAD SCIENTIST SUPER VILLAIN AT FIFTEEN. LOOKS GREAT ON A RESUME.
IT MIGHT TO THIS GUY. HE BELIEVES IN SECOND CHANCES.
JUST TELL PARKER I SENT YOU.
PI PARKER INDUSTRIES
PARKER INDUSTRIES.
I CAN'T TELL YOU HOW MUCH I APPRECIATE THIS, MR. PARKER.
PETE. NICE TO HAVE YOU ON BOARD, CLAYTON.
I'VE BEEN WORKING ON CURING SUPER-CRIMINALS AND REFORMING THEM. TIME TO PUT MY MONEY WHERE MY MOUTH IS.
RUNNING THIS COMPANY GIVES ME GREAT POWER... AND GREAT RESPONSIBILITY. AND I KNOW BETTER THAN ANYONE, HEROES CAN COME FROM THE UNLIKELIEST PLACES.

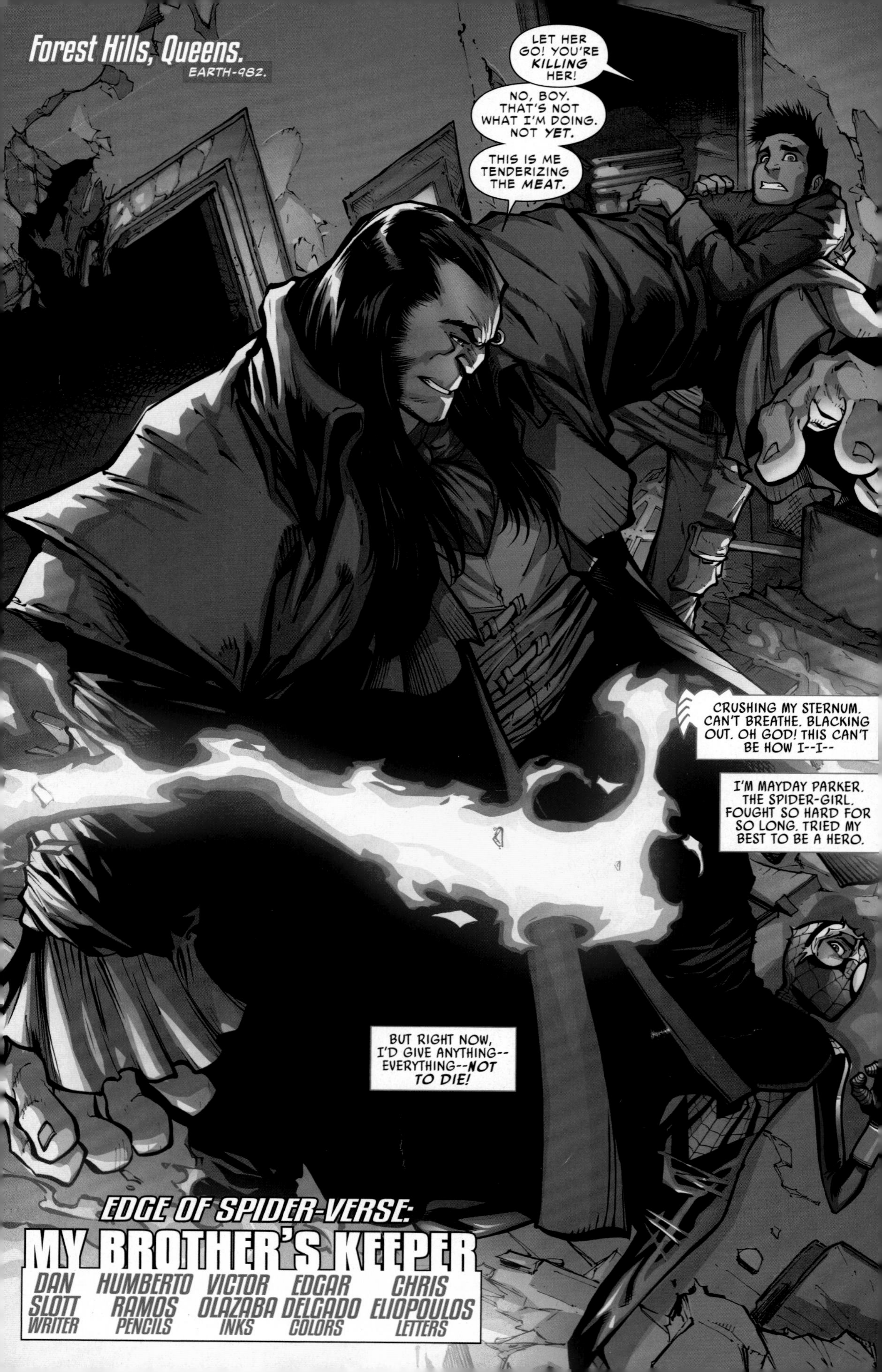

Forest Hills, Queens.
EARTH-982.
LET HER GO! YOU'RE KILLING HER!
NO, BOY. THAT'S NOT WHAT I'M DOING. NOT YET.
THIS IS ME TENDERIZING THE MEAT.
CRUSHING MY STERNUM. CAN'T BREATHE. BLACKING OUT. OH GOD! THIS CAN'T BE HOW I--I--
I'M MAYDAY PARKER. THE SPIDER-GIRL. FOUGHT SO HARD FOR SO LONG. TRIED MY BEST TO BE A HERO.
BUT RIGHT NOW, I'D GIVE ANYTHING-- EVERYTHING--NOT TO DIE!
EDGE OF SPIDER-VERSE:
MY BROTHER'S KEEPER
DAN SLOTT WRITER
HUMBERTO RAMOS PENCILS
VICTOR OLAZABA INKS
EDGAR DELGADO COLORS
CHRIS ELIOPOULOS LETTERS

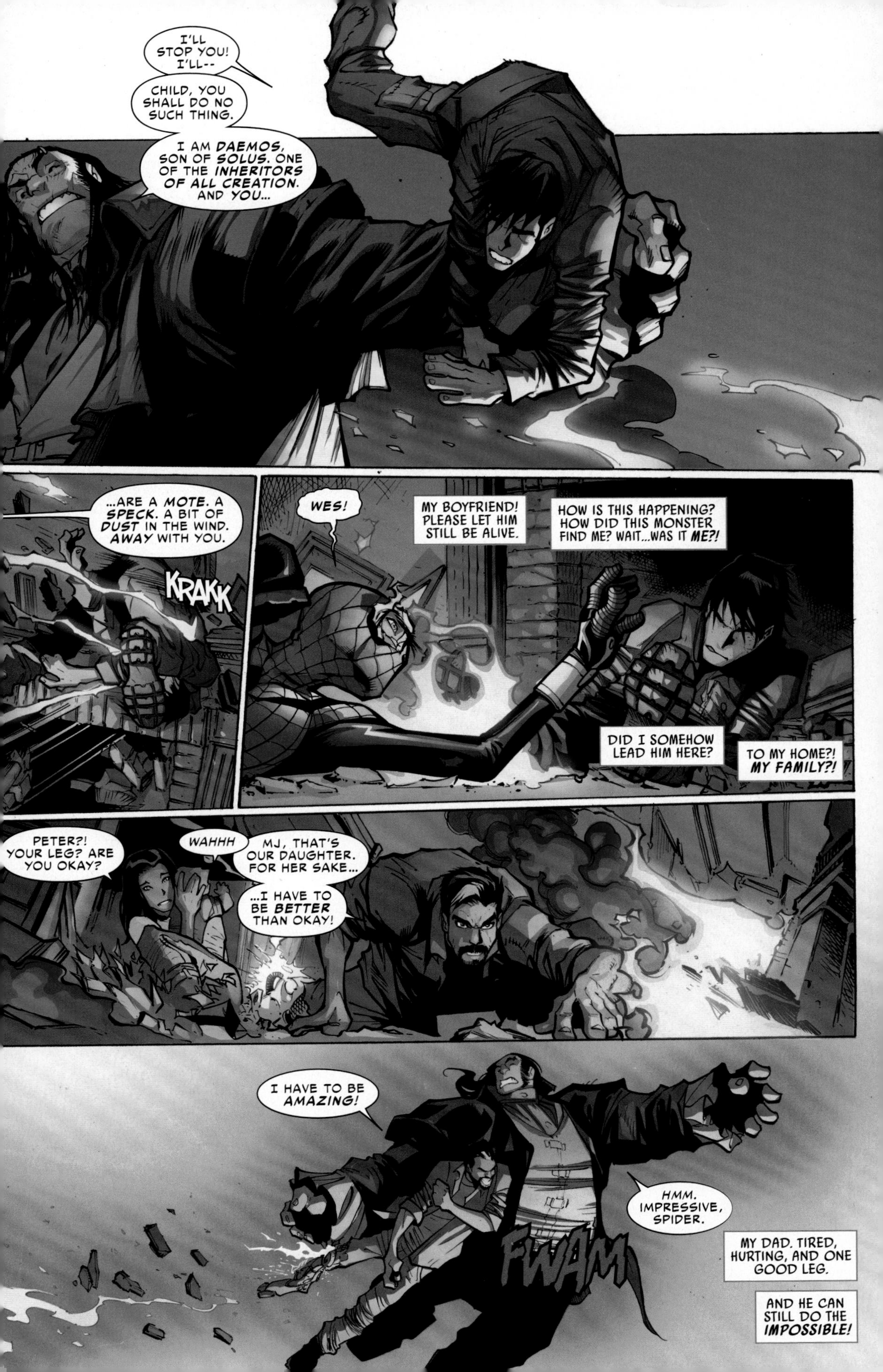
I'LL STOP YOU! I'LL--
CHILD, YOU SHALL DO NO SUCH THING.
I AM **DAEMOS**, SON OF **SOLUS**. ONE OF THE **INHERITORS OF ALL CREATION**. AND **YOU**...
...ARE A **MOTE**. A **SPECK**. A BIT OF **DUST** IN THE WIND. **AWAY** WITH YOU.
KRAKK
WES!
MY BOYFRIEND! PLEASE LET HIM STILL BE ALIVE.
HOW IS THIS HAPPENING? HOW DID THIS MONSTER FIND ME? WAIT...WAS IT **ME?!**
DID I SOMEHOW LEAD HIM HERE?
TO MY HOME?! **MY FAMILY?!**
PETER?! YOUR LEG? ARE YOU OKAY?
WAHHH
MJ, THAT'S OUR DAUGHTER. FOR HER SAKE...
...I HAVE TO BE **BETTER** THAN OKAY!
I HAVE TO BE **AMAZING!**
HMM. IMPRESSIVE, SPIDER.
FWAM
MY DAD. TIRED, HURTING, AND ONE GOOD LEG.
AND HE CAN STILL DO THE **IMPOSSIBLE!**

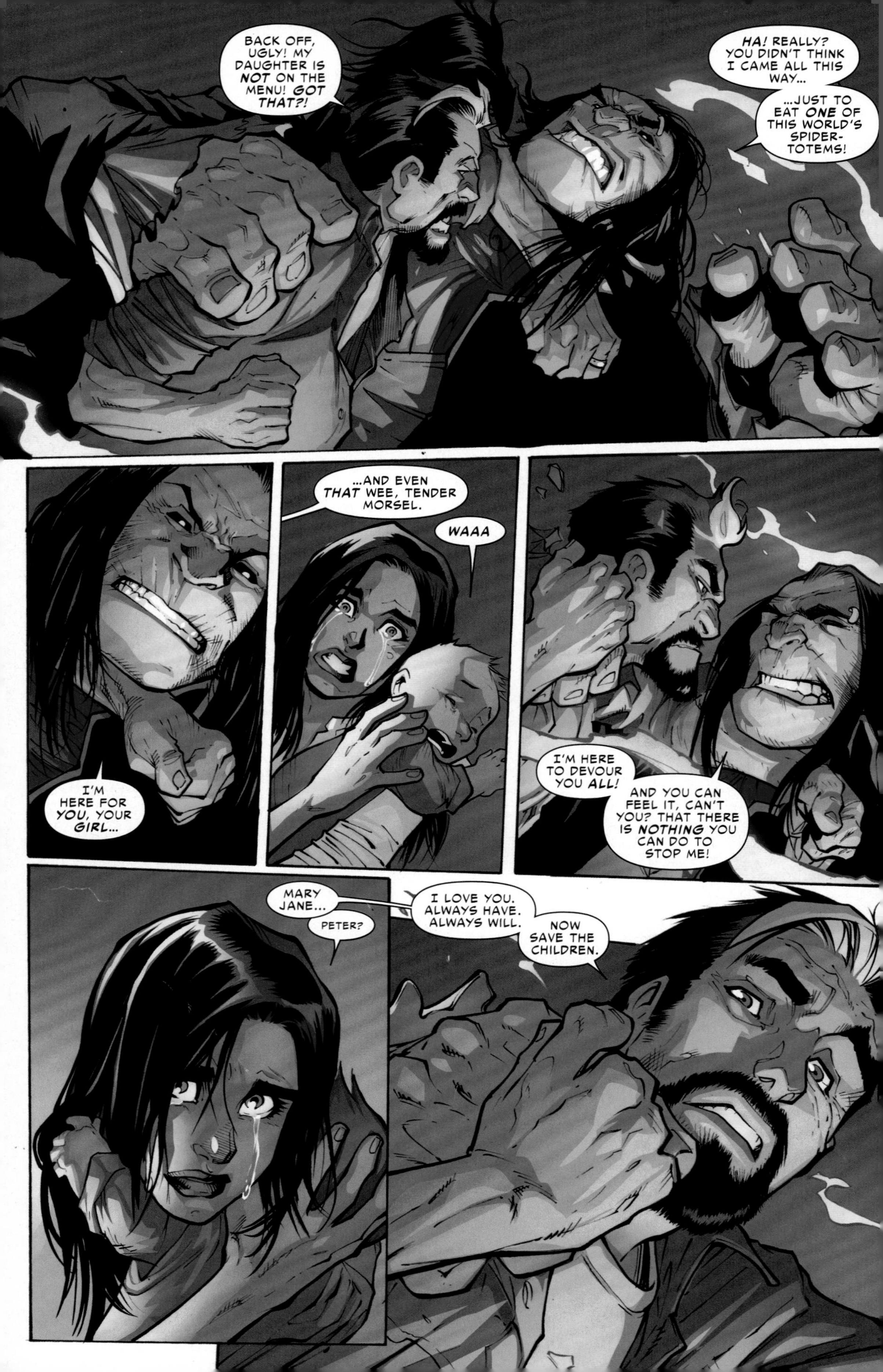
BACK OFF, UGLY! MY DAUGHTER IS NOT ON THE MENU! GOT THAT?!
HA! REALLY? YOU DIDN'T THINK I CAME ALL THIS WAY...
...JUST TO EAT ONE OF THIS WORLD'S SPIDER-TOTEMS!
I'M HERE FOR YOU, YOUR GIRL...
...AND EVEN THAT WEE, TENDER MORSEL.
WAAA
I'M HERE TO DEVOUR YOU ALL!
AND YOU CAN FEEL IT, CAN'T YOU? THAT THERE IS NOTHING YOU CAN DO TO STOP ME!
MARY JANE...
PETER?
I LOVE YOU. ALWAYS HAVE. ALWAYS WILL.
NOW SAVE THE CHILDREN.

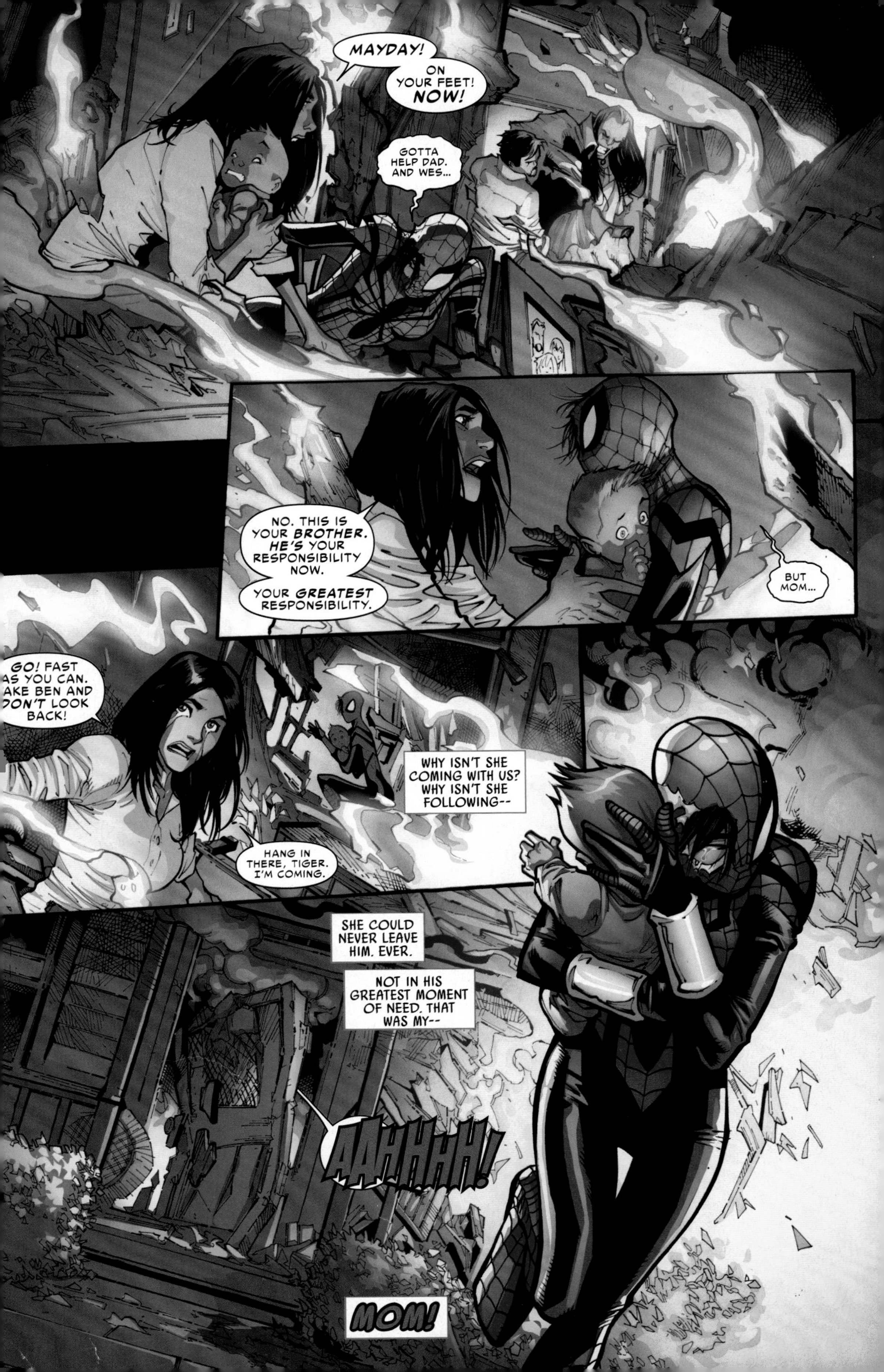
MAYDAY!
ON YOUR FEET! NOW!
GOTTA HELP DAD. AND WES...
NO. THIS IS YOUR BROTHER. HE'S YOUR RESPONSIBILITY NOW.
YOUR GREATEST RESPONSIBILITY.
BUT MOM...
GO! FAST AS YOU CAN. AKE BEN AND DON'T LOOK BACK!
WHY ISN'T SHE COMING WITH US? WHY ISN'T SHE FOLLOWING--
HANG IN THERE, TIGER. I'M COMING.
SHE COULD NEVER LEAVE HIM. EVER.
NOT IN HIS GREATEST MOMENT OF NEED. THAT WAS MY--
AAHHHHH!
MOM!

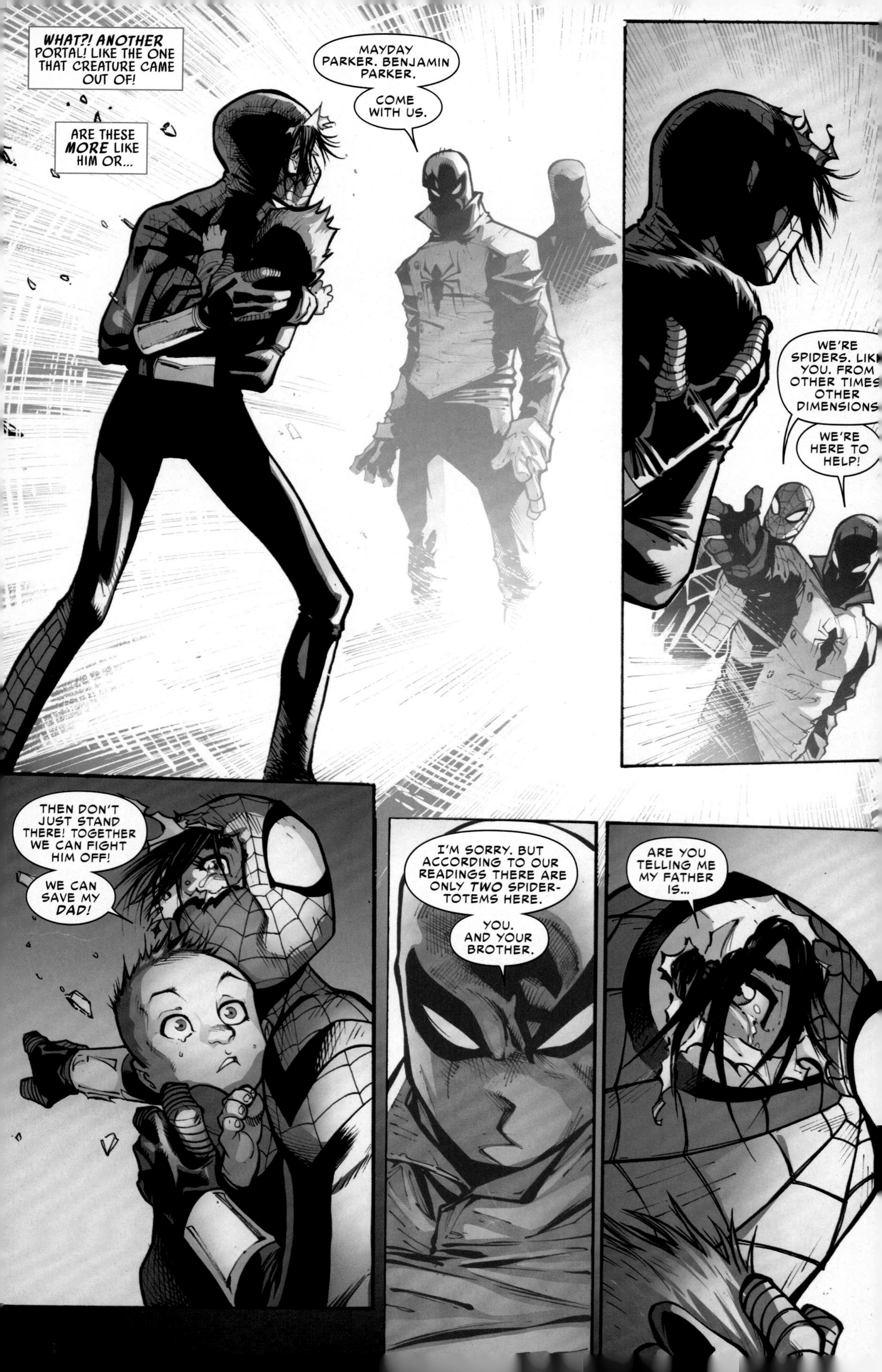
WHAT?! ANOTHER PORTAL! LIKE THE ONE THAT CREATURE CAME OUT OF!
ARE THESE MORE LIKE HIM OR...
MAYDAY PARKER. BENJAMIN PARKER.
COME WITH US.
WE'RE SPIDERS. LIK YOU. FROM OTHER TIMES OTHER DIMENSIONS
WE'RE HERE TO HELP!
THEN DON'T JUST STAND THERE! TOGETHER WE CAN FIGHT HIM OFF!
WE CAN SAVE MY DAD!
I'M SORRY. BUT ACCORDING TO OUR READINGS THERE ARE ONLY TWO SPIDER-TOTEMS HERE.
YOU. AND YOUR BROTHER.
ARE YOU TELLING ME MY FATHER IS...

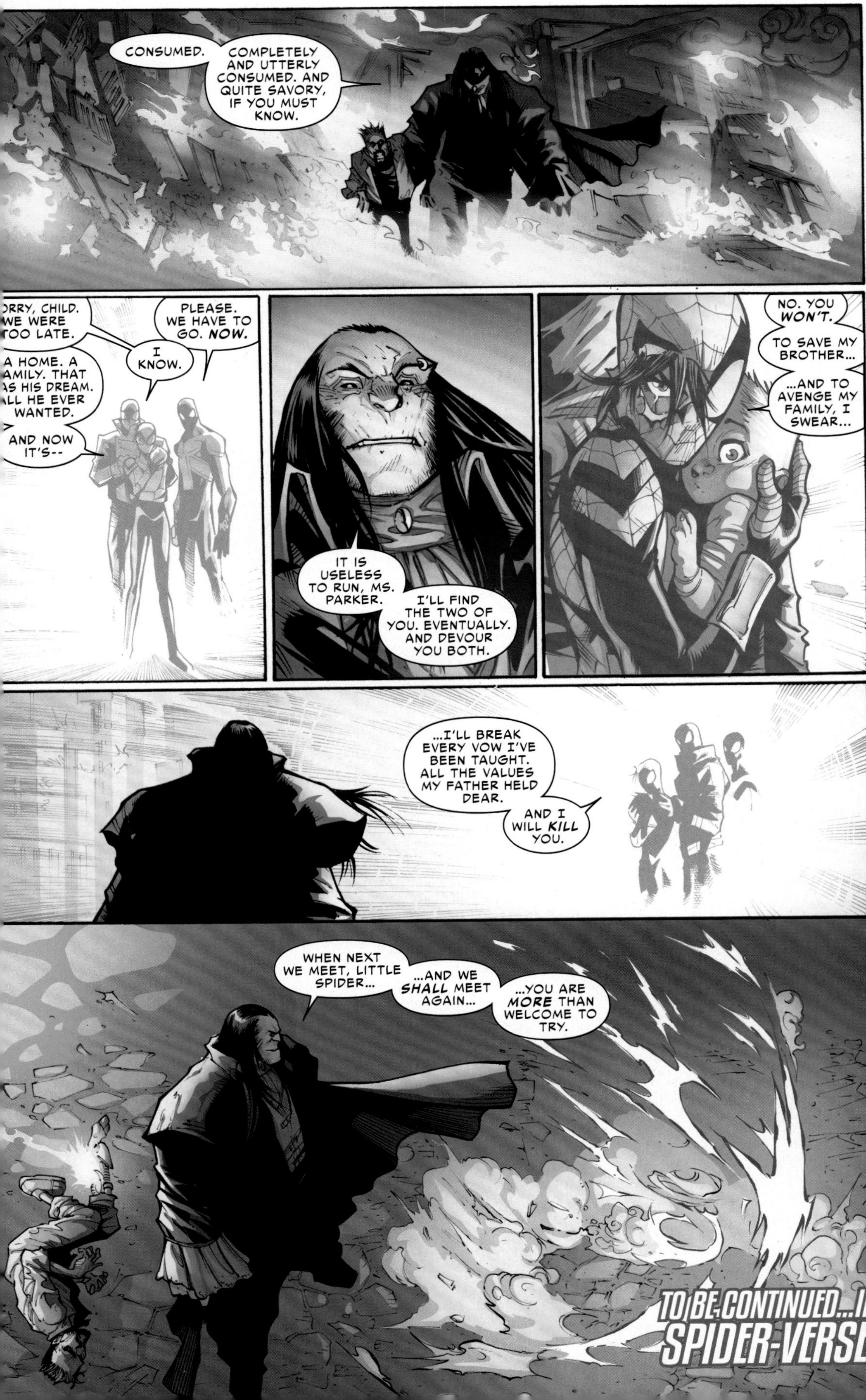
CONSUMED.
COMPLETELY AND UTTERLY CONSUMED. AND QUITE SAVORY, IF YOU MUST KNOW.
ORRY, CHILD. WE WERE TOO LATE.
PLEASE. WE HAVE TO GO. NOW.
I KNOW.
A HOME. A AMILY. THAT AS HIS DREAM. LL HE EVER WANTED.
AND NOW IT'S--
IT IS USELESS TO RUN, MS. PARKER.
I'LL FIND THE TWO OF YOU. EVENTUALLY. AND DEVOUR YOU BOTH.
NO. YOU WON'T.
TO SAVE MY BROTHER...
...AND TO AVENGE MY FAMILY, I SWEAR...
...I'LL BREAK EVERY VOW I'VE BEEN TAUGHT. ALL THE VALUES MY FATHER HELD DEAR.
AND I WILL KILL YOU.
WHEN NEXT WE MEET, LITTLE SPIDER...
...AND WE SHALL MEET AGAIN...
...YOU ARE MORE THAN WELCOME TO TRY.
TO BE CONTINUED...IN SPIDER-VERSE!

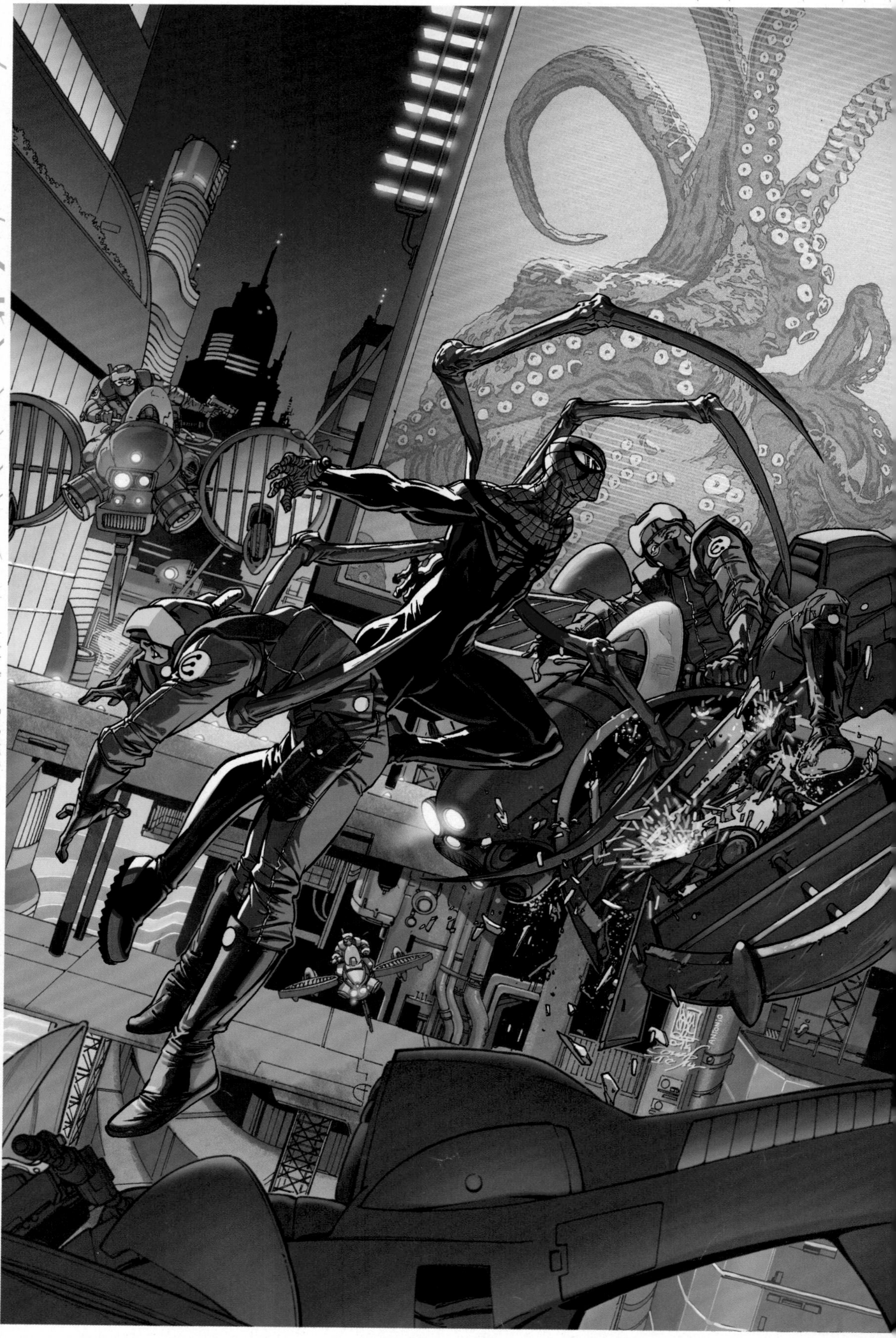

SUPERIOR SPIDER-MAN 32

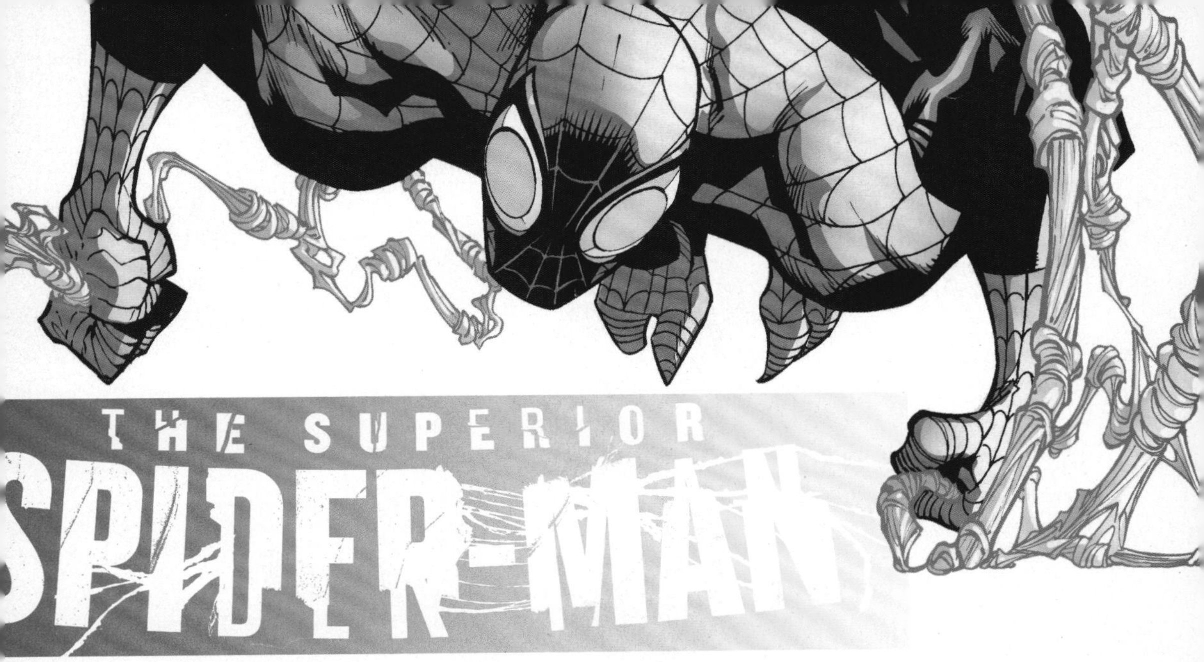
THE SUPERIOR
SPIDER-MAN

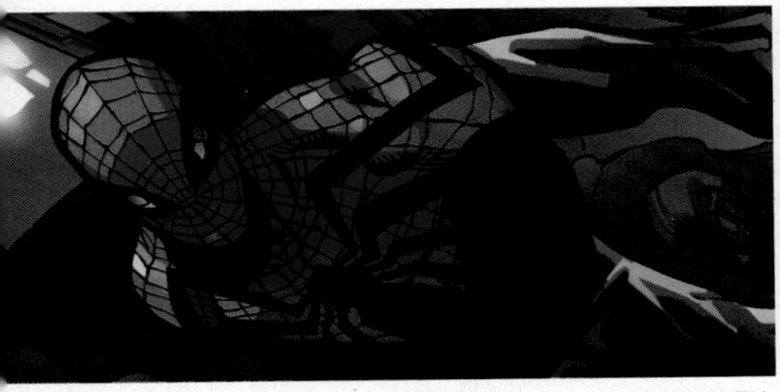

N A LAST-DITCH EFFORT TO SAVE HIMSELF FROM DEATH, **TTO OCTAVIUS** SWAPPED MINDS WITH SPIDER-MAN, EAVING **PETER PARKER** TO DIE IN HIS PLACE. TAKING ON 'ETER'S SENSE OF RESPONSIBILITY, OTTO CARRIED ON HIS MISSION AS THE SUPERIOR SPIDER-MAN.

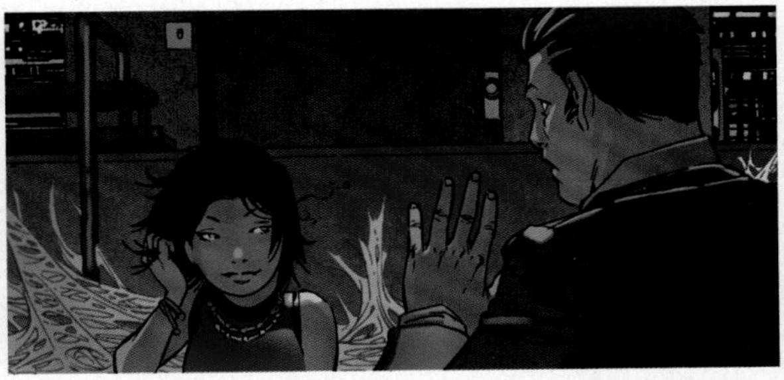

OTTO SET ABOUT IMPROVING PETER'S LIFE AND EVEN FELL IN LOVE WITH A WOMAN NAMED **ANNA MARIA MARCONI.**

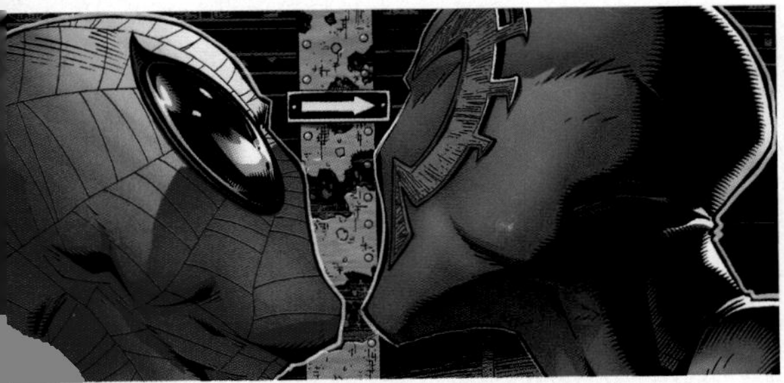

RECENTLY, WHEN A **TEMPORAL DISTORTION** THREATENED THE LIFE OF TYLER STONE, HEAD OF ALCHEMAX IN THE YEAR 2099, SPIDER-MAN 2099 TRAVELED BACK IN TIME TO HORIZON LABS BEFORE IT BECAME ALCHEMAX TO SAVE THE LIFE OF TIBERIUS STONE.

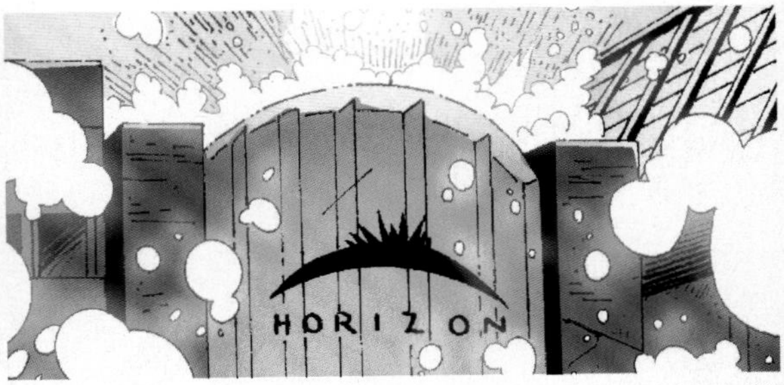
HORIZON

WHEN HORIZON LABS WAS LOST IN A TEMPORAL IMPLOSION, THE SUPERIOR SPIDER-MAN DISAPPEARED FOR 24 HOURS.* THIS IS WHERE HE WENT.

THIS STORY TAKES PLACE DURING* ***SUPERIOR SPIDER-MAN #19.*

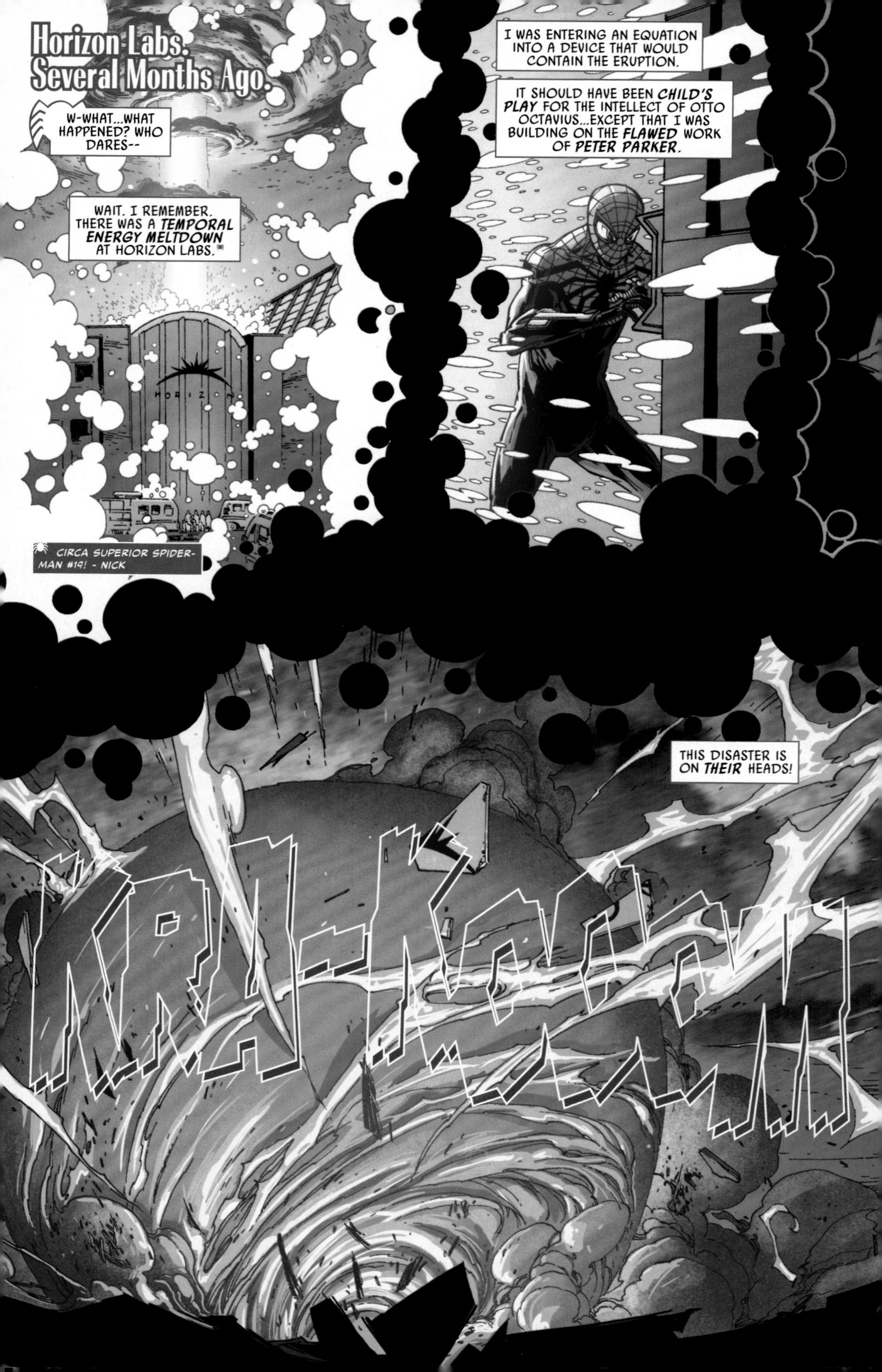
Horizon Labs. Several Months Ago.
W-WHAT...WHAT HAPPENED? WHO DARES--
WAIT. I REMEMBER. THERE WAS A TEMPORAL ENERGY MELTDOWN AT HORIZON LABS.*
CIRCA SUPERIOR SPIDER-MAN #19! - NICK
I WAS ENTERING AN EQUATION INTO A DEVICE THAT WOULD CONTAIN THE ERUPTION.
IT SHOULD HAVE BEEN CHILD'S PLAY FOR THE INTELLECT OF OTTO OCTAVIUS...EXCEPT THAT I WAS BUILDING ON THE FLAWED WORK OF PETER PARKER.
THIS DISASTER IS ON THEIR HEADS!
KRA-KOOOM

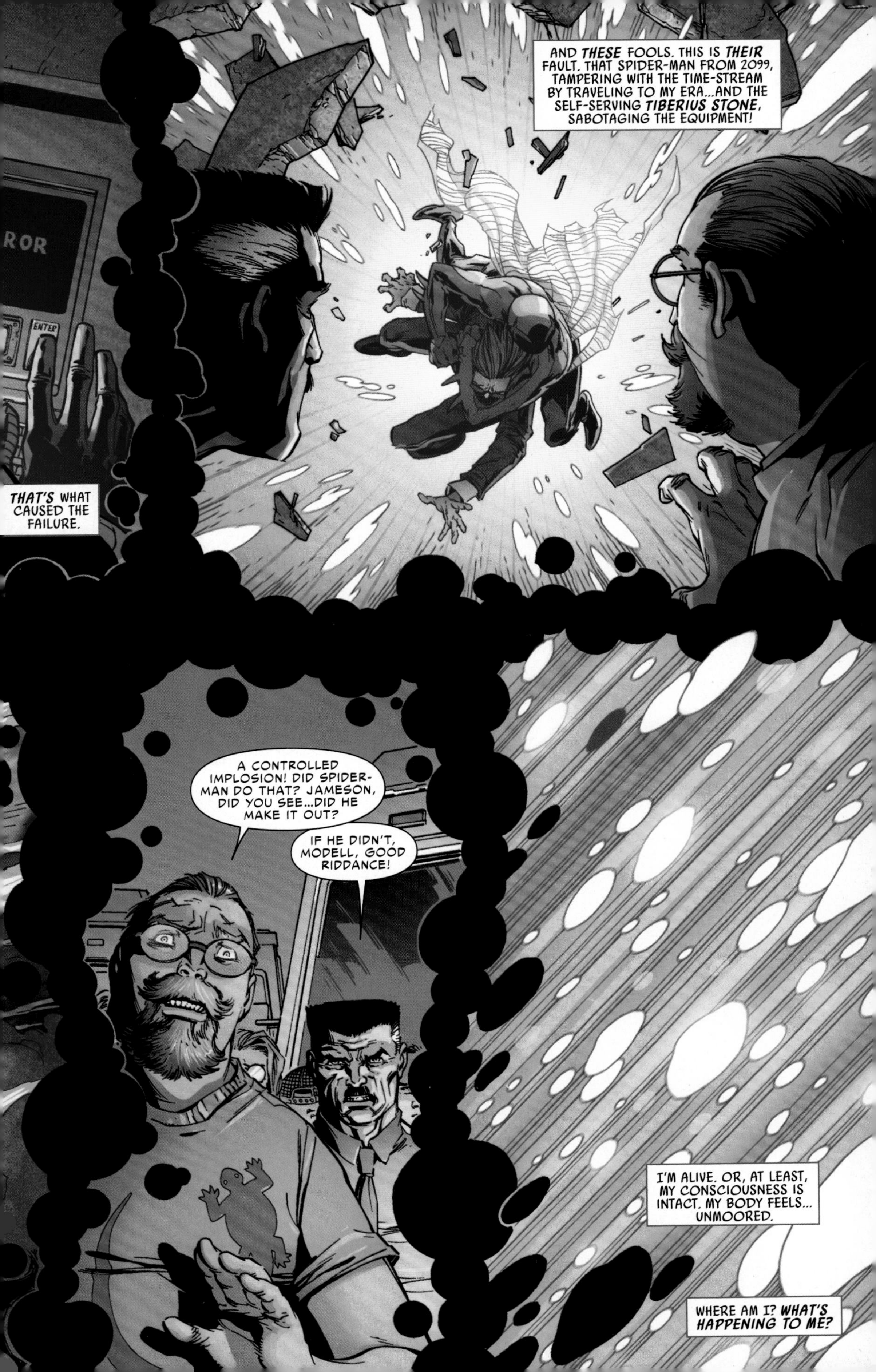
AND THESE FOOLS. THIS IS THEIR FAULT. THAT SPIDER-MAN FROM 2099, TAMPERING WITH THE TIME-STREAM BY TRAVELING TO MY ERA...AND THE SELF-SERVING TIBERIUS STONE, SABOTAGING THE EQUIPMENT!
ROR
ENTER
THAT'S WHAT CAUSED THE FAILURE.
A CONTROLLED IMPLOSION! DID SPIDER-MAN DO THAT? JAMESON, DID YOU SEE...DID HE MAKE IT OUT?
IF HE DIDN'T, MODELL, GOOD RIDDANCE!
I'M ALIVE. OR, AT LEAST, MY CONSCIOUSNESS IS INTACT. MY BODY FEELS... UNMOORED.
WHERE AM I? WHAT'S HAPPENING TO ME?

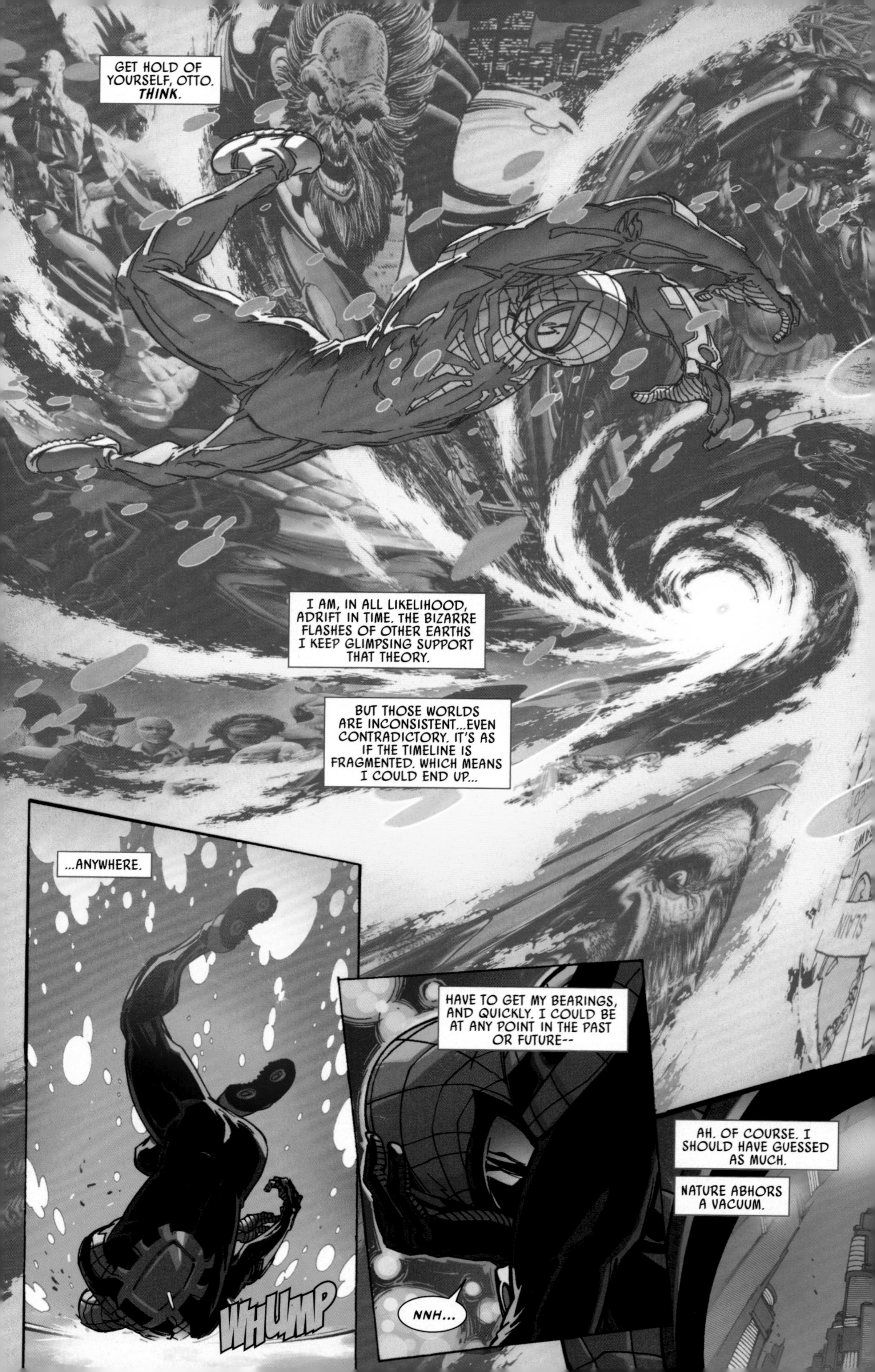
GET HOLD OF YOURSELF, OTTO. *THINK.*
I AM, IN ALL LIKELIHOOD, ADRIFT IN TIME. THE BIZARRE FLASHES OF OTHER EARTHS I KEEP GLIMPSING SUPPORT THAT THEORY.
BUT THOSE WORLDS ARE INCONSISTENT...EVEN CONTRADICTORY. IT'S AS IF THE TIMELINE IS FRAGMENTED. WHICH MEANS I COULD END UP...
...ANYWHERE.
WHUMP
HAVE TO GET MY BEARINGS, AND QUICKLY. I COULD BE AT ANY POINT IN THE PAST OR FUTURE--
NNH...
AH. OF COURSE. I SHOULD HAVE GUESSED AS MUCH.
NATURE ABHORS A VACUUM.

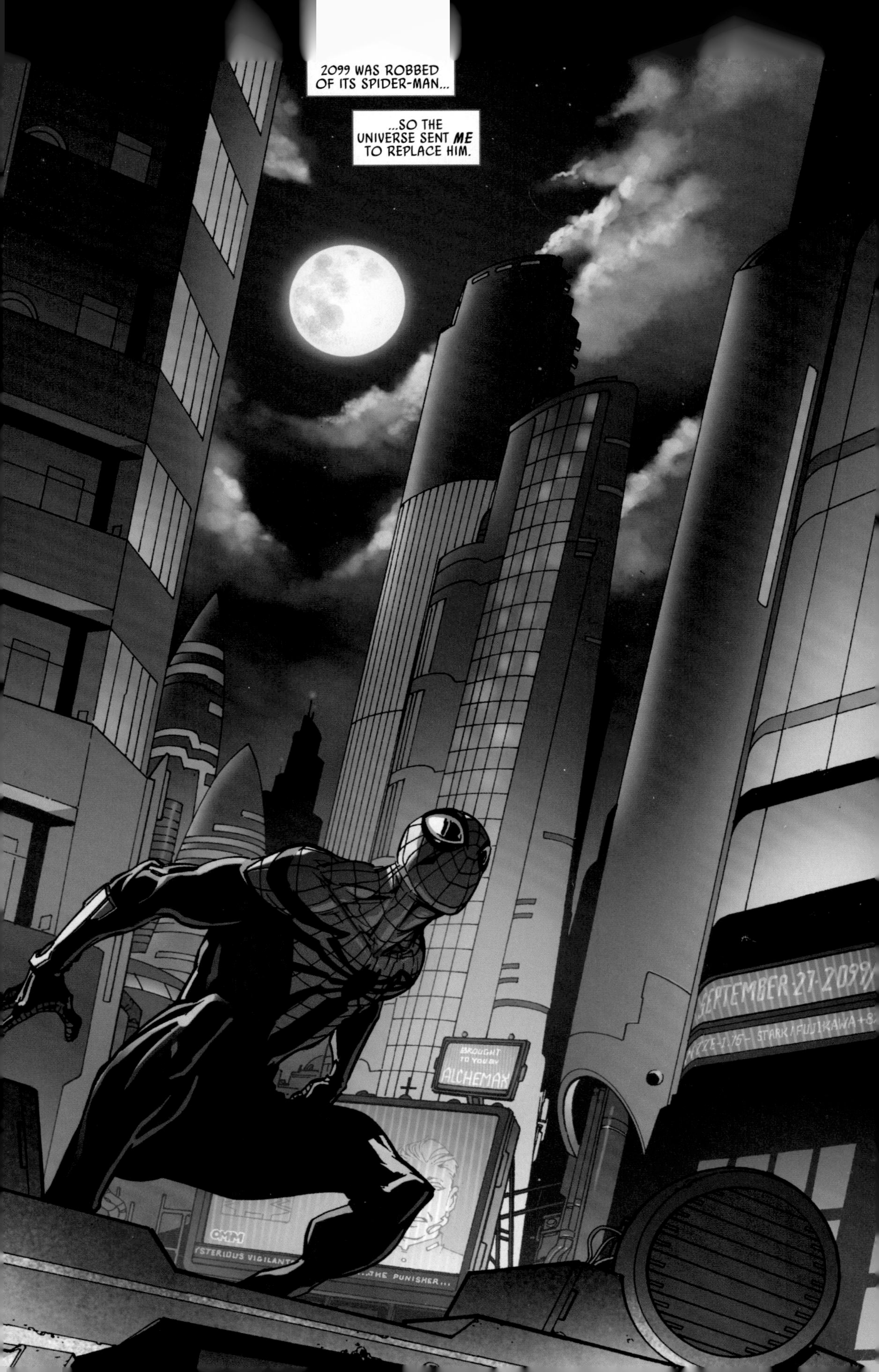
2099 WAS ROBBED OF ITS SPIDER-MAN...
...SO THE UNIVERSE SENT *ME* TO REPLACE HIM.
BROUGHT TO YOU BY ALCHEMAX
SEPTEMBER 27 2099
STARK FUJIKAWA
OMM
...THE PUNISHER...

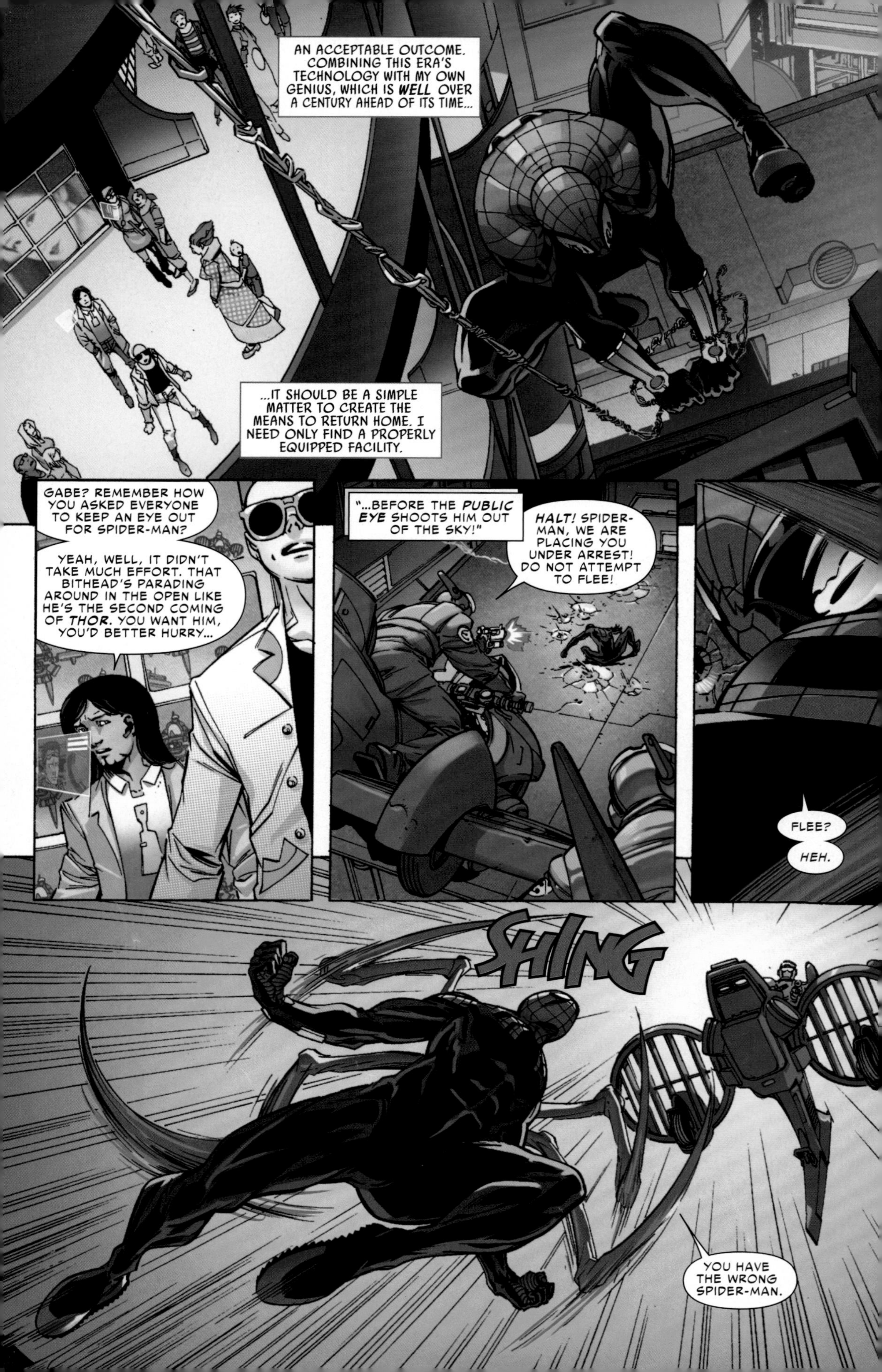
AN ACCEPTABLE OUTCOME. COMBINING THIS ERA'S TECHNOLOGY WITH MY OWN GENIUS, WHICH IS WELL OVER A CENTURY AHEAD OF ITS TIME...
...IT SHOULD BE A SIMPLE MATTER TO CREATE THE MEANS TO RETURN HOME. I NEED ONLY FIND A PROPERLY EQUIPPED FACILITY.
GABE? REMEMBER HOW YOU ASKED EVERYONE TO KEEP AN EYE OUT FOR SPIDER-MAN?
YEAH, WELL, IT DIDN'T TAKE MUCH EFFORT. THAT BITHEAD'S PARADING AROUND IN THE OPEN LIKE HE'S THE SECOND COMING OF THOR. YOU WANT HIM, YOU'D BETTER HURRY...
"...BEFORE THE PUBLIC EYE SHOOTS HIM OUT OF THE SKY!"
HALT! SPIDER-MAN, WE ARE PLACING YOU UNDER ARREST! DO NOT ATTEMPT TO FLEE!
FLEE?
HEH.
SHING
YOU HAVE THE WRONG SPIDER-MAN.

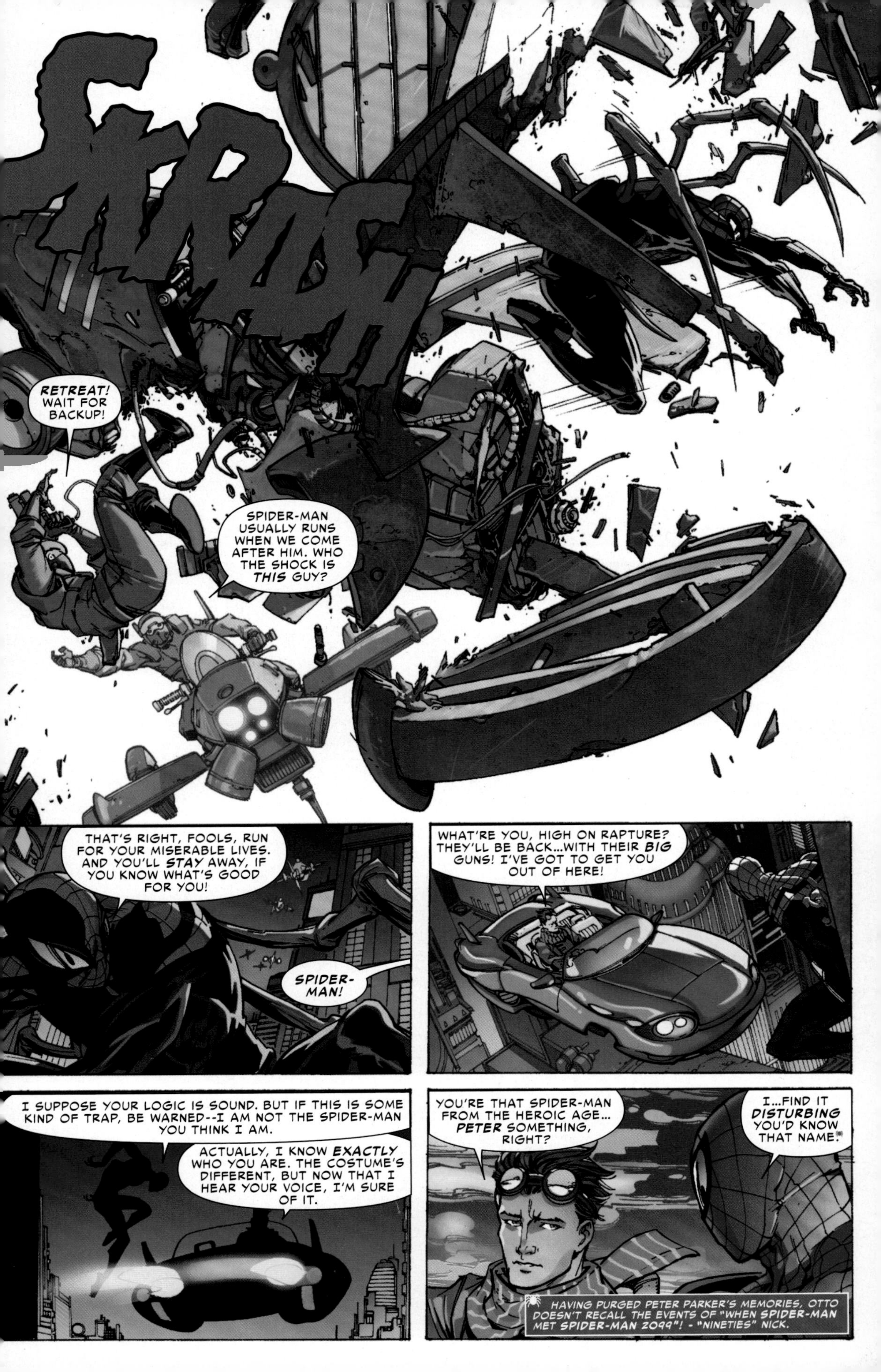
SKRASH
RETREAT! WAIT FOR BACKUP!
SPIDER-MAN USUALLY RUNS WHEN WE COME AFTER HIM. WHO THE SHOCK IS THIS GUY?
THAT'S RIGHT, FOOLS, RUN FOR YOUR MISERABLE LIVES. AND YOU'LL STAY AWAY, IF YOU KNOW WHAT'S GOOD FOR YOU!
SPIDER-MAN!
WHAT'RE YOU, HIGH ON RAPTURE? THEY'LL BE BACK...WITH THEIR BIG GUNS! I'VE GOT TO GET YOU OUT OF HERE!
I SUPPOSE YOUR LOGIC IS SOUND. BUT IF THIS IS SOME KIND OF TRAP, BE WARNED--I AM NOT THE SPIDER-MAN YOU THINK I AM.
ACTUALLY, I KNOW EXACTLY WHO YOU ARE. THE COSTUME'S DIFFERENT, BUT NOW THAT I HEAR YOUR VOICE, I'M SURE OF IT.
YOU'RE THAT SPIDER-MAN FROM THE HEROIC AGE... PETER SOMETHING, RIGHT?
I...FIND IT DISTURBING YOU'D KNOW THAT NAME.
HAVING PURGED PETER PARKER'S MEMORIES, OTTO DOESN'T RECALL THE EVENTS OF "WHEN SPIDER-MAN MET SPIDER-MAN 2099"! - "NINETIES" NICK.

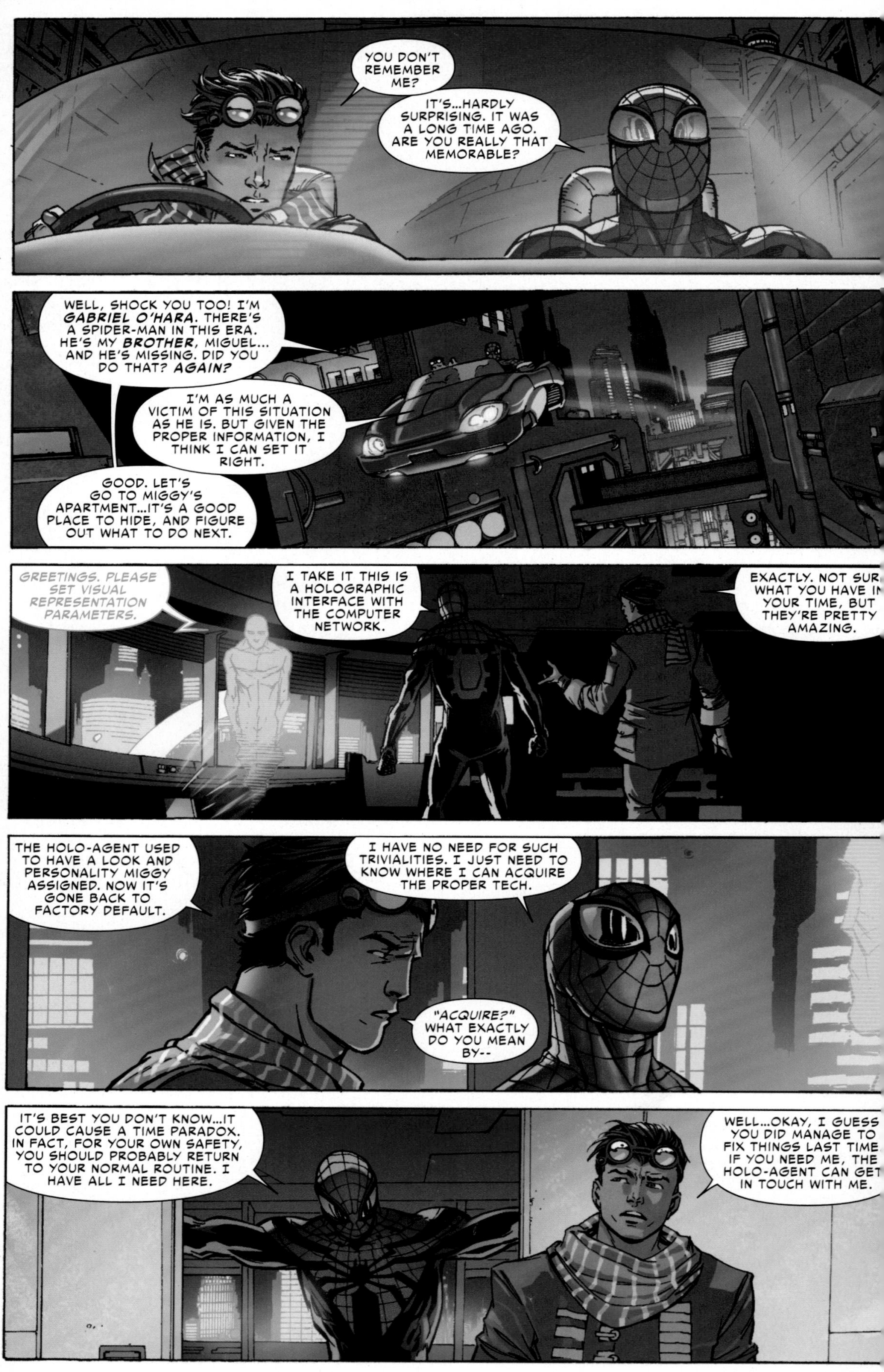

YOU DON'T REMEMBER ME?
IT'S...HARDLY SURPRISING. IT WAS A LONG TIME AGO. ARE YOU REALLY THAT MEMORABLE?
WELL, SHOCK YOU TOO! I'M GABRIEL O'HARA. THERE'S A SPIDER-MAN IN THIS ERA. HE'S MY BROTHER, MIGUEL... AND HE'S MISSING. DID YOU DO THAT? AGAIN?
I'M AS MUCH A VICTIM OF THIS SITUATION AS HE IS. BUT GIVEN THE PROPER INFORMATION, I THINK I CAN SET IT RIGHT.
GOOD. LET'S GO TO MIGGY'S APARTMENT...IT'S A GOOD PLACE TO HIDE, AND FIGURE OUT WHAT TO DO NEXT.
GREETINGS. PLEASE SET VISUAL REPRESENTATION PARAMETERS.
I TAKE IT THIS IS A HOLOGRAPHIC INTERFACE WITH THE COMPUTER NETWORK.
EXACTLY. NOT SUR WHAT YOU HAVE IN YOUR TIME, BUT THEY'RE PRETTY AMAZING.
THE HOLO-AGENT USED TO HAVE A LOOK AND PERSONALITY MIGGY ASSIGNED. NOW IT'S GONE BACK TO FACTORY DEFAULT.
I HAVE NO NEED FOR SUCH TRIVIALITIES. I JUST NEED TO KNOW WHERE I CAN ACQUIRE THE PROPER TECH.
"ACQUIRE?" WHAT EXACTLY DO YOU MEAN BY--
IT'S BEST YOU DON'T KNOW...IT COULD CAUSE A TIME PARADOX. IN FACT, FOR YOUR OWN SAFETY, YOU SHOULD PROBABLY RETURN TO YOUR NORMAL ROUTINE. I HAVE ALL I NEED HERE.
WELL...OKAY, I GUESS YOU DID MANAGE TO FIX THINGS LAST TIME. IF YOU NEED ME, THE HOLO-AGENT CAN GET IN TOUCH WITH ME.

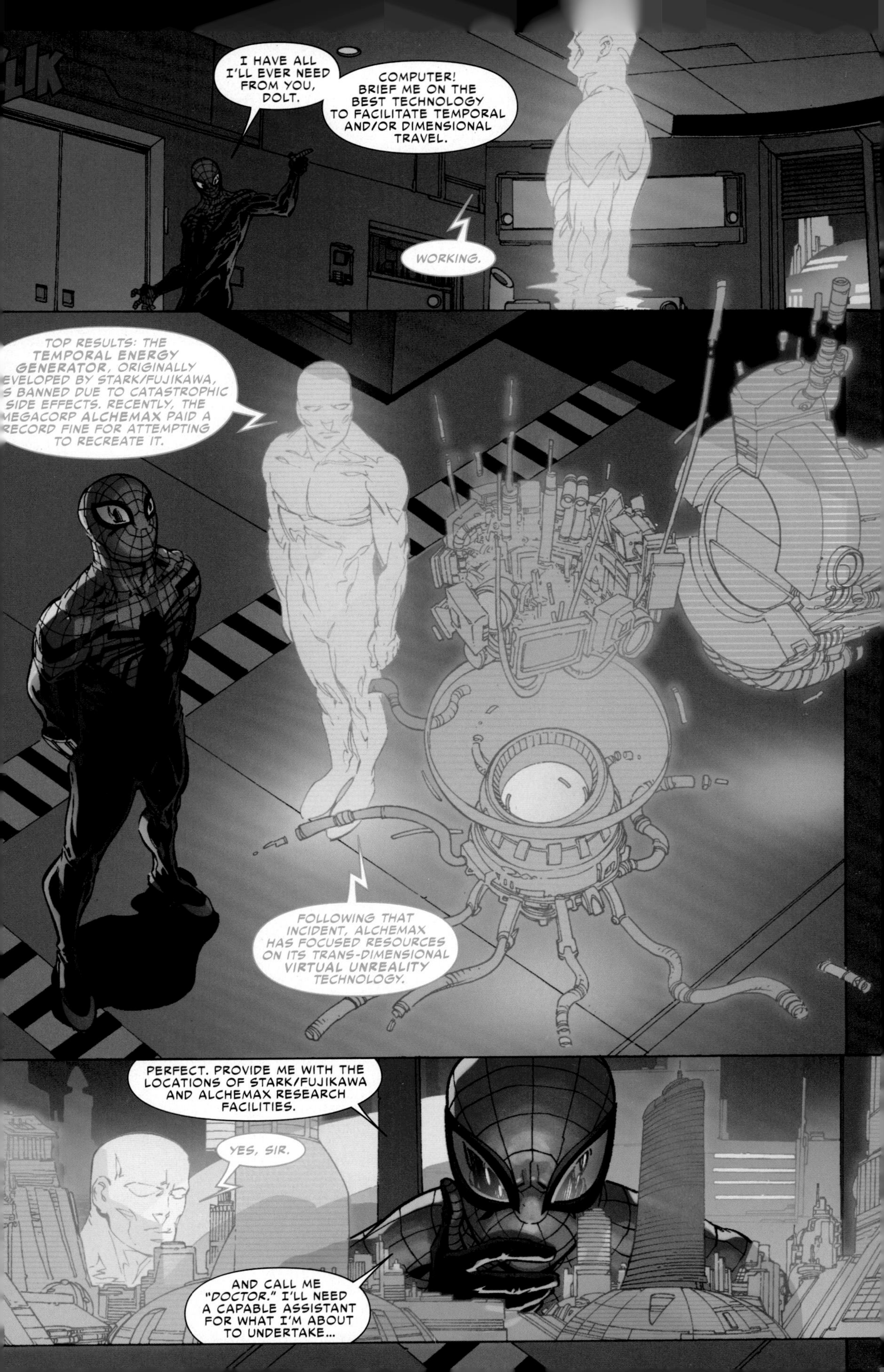
I HAVE ALL I'LL EVER NEED FROM YOU, DOLT.
COMPUTER! BRIEF ME ON THE BEST TECHNOLOGY TO FACILITATE TEMPORAL AND/OR DIMENSIONAL TRAVEL.
WORKING.
TOP RESULTS: THE TEMPORAL ENERGY GENERATOR, ORIGINALLY EVELOPED BY STARK/FUJIKAWA, S BANNED DUE TO CATASTROPHIC SIDE EFFECTS. RECENTLY, THE MEGACORP ALCHEMAX PAID A RECORD FINE FOR ATTEMPTING TO RECREATE IT.
FOLLOWING THAT INCIDENT, ALCHEMAX HAS FOCUSED RESOURCES ON ITS TRANS-DIMENSIONAL VIRTUAL UNREALITY TECHNOLOGY.
PERFECT. PROVIDE ME WITH THE LOCATIONS OF STARK/FUJIKAWA AND ALCHEMAX RESEARCH FACILITIES.
YES, SIR.
AND CALL ME "DOCTOR." I'LL NEED A CAPABLE ASSISTANT FOR WHAT I'M ABOUT TO UNDERTAKE...

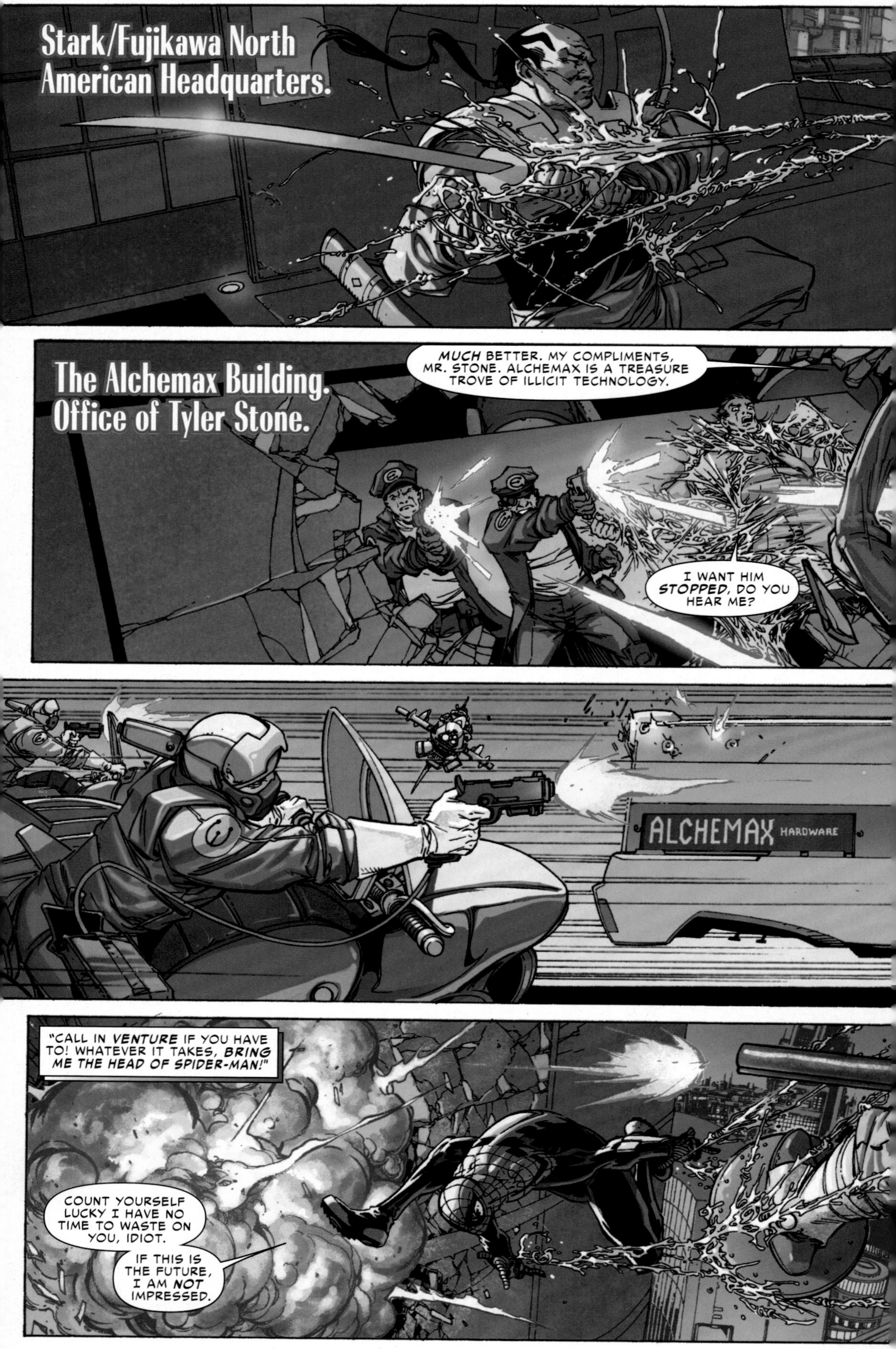
Stark/Fujikawa North American Headquarters.
The Alchemax Building. Office of Tyler Stone.
MUCH BETTER. MY COMPLIMENTS, MR. STONE. ALCHEMAX IS A TREASURE TROVE OF ILLICIT TECHNOLOGY.
I WANT HIM STOPPED, DO YOU HEAR ME?
ALCHEMAX HARDWARE
"CALL IN VENTURE IF YOU HAVE TO! WHATEVER IT TAKES, BRING ME THE HEAD OF SPIDER-MAN!"
COUNT YOURSELF LUCKY I HAVE NO TIME TO WASTE ON YOU, IDIOT.
IF THIS IS THE FUTURE, I AM NOT IMPRESSED.

DISAPPOINTING. YOUR COMPANY IS ACTUALLY ABIDING BY THE LAW, SPECIALIST. SLIM PICKINGS INDEED.

"BRING ALL THE RESOURCES OF THE PUBLIC EYE DOWN ON HIM!

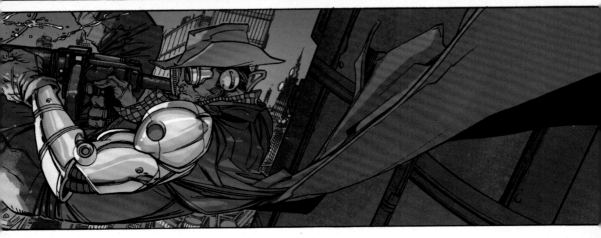

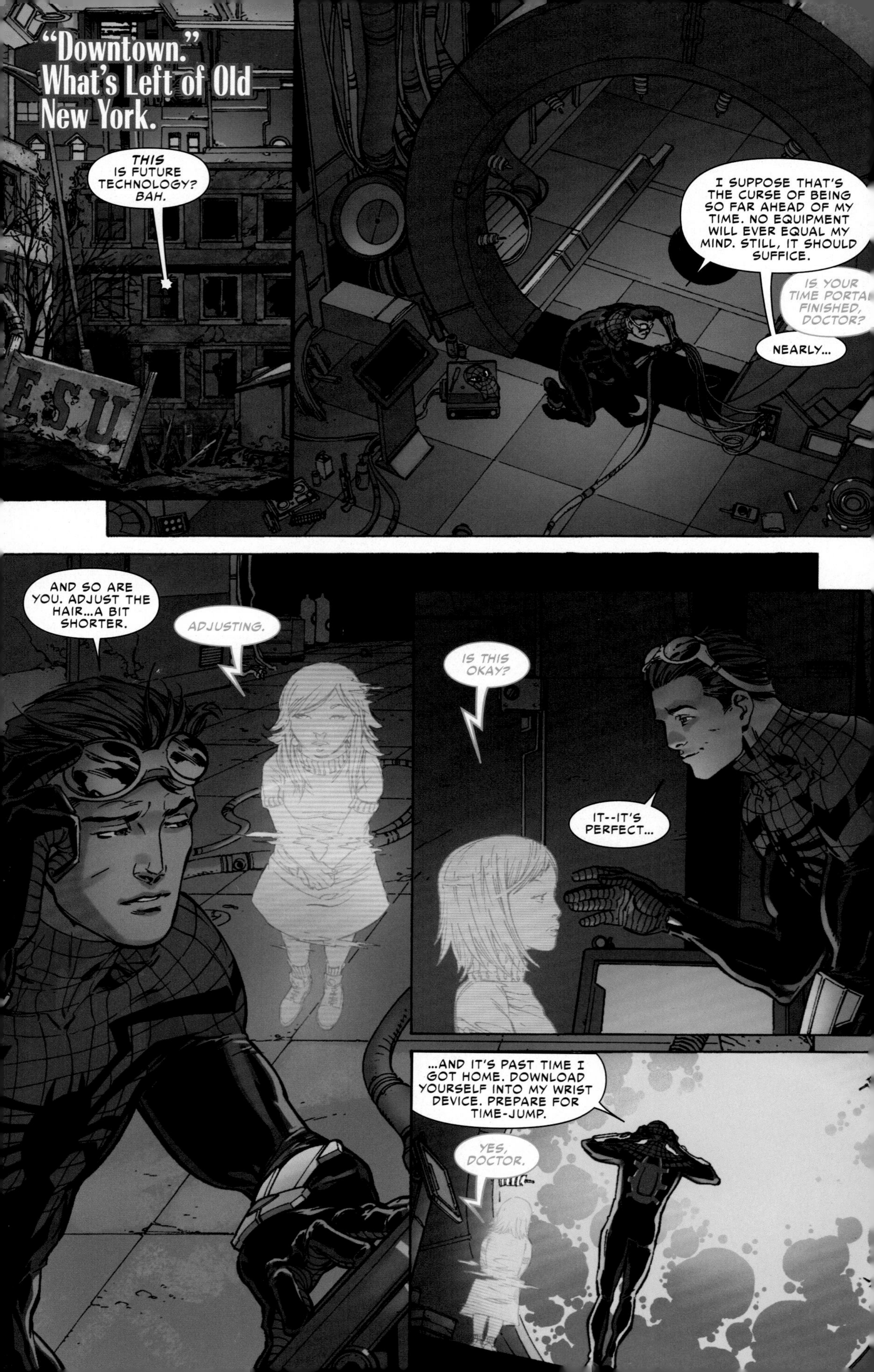
"Downtown." What's Left of Old New York.
THIS IS FUTURE TECHNOLOGY? BAH.
ESU
I SUPPOSE THAT'S THE CURSE OF BEING SO FAR AHEAD OF MY TIME. NO EQUIPMENT WILL EVER EQUAL MY MIND. STILL, IT SHOULD SUFFICE.
IS YOUR TIME PORTAL FINISHED, DOCTOR?
NEARLY...
AND SO ARE YOU. ADJUST THE HAIR...A BIT SHORTER.
ADJUSTING.
IS THIS OKAY?
IT--IT'S PERFECT...
...AND IT'S PAST TIME I GOT HOME. DOWNLOAD YOURSELF INTO MY WRIST DEVICE. PREPARE FOR TIME-JUMP.
YES, DOCTOR.

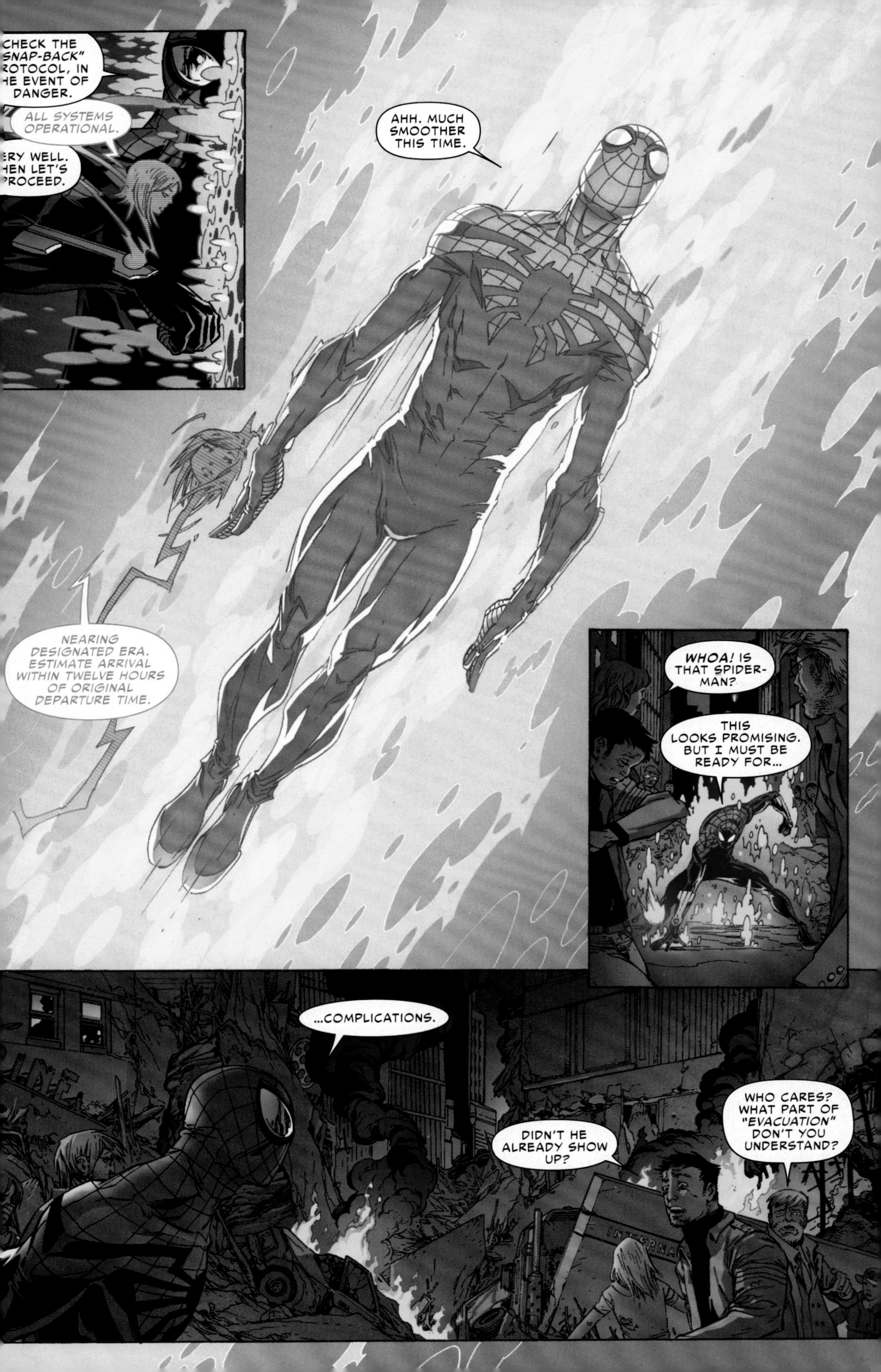
CHECK THE "SNAP-BACK" ROTOCOL, IN HE EVENT OF DANGER.
ALL SYSTEMS OPERATIONAL.
ERY WELL. HEN LET'S PROCEED.
AHH. MUCH SMOOTHER THIS TIME.
NEARING DESIGNATED ERA. ESTIMATE ARRIVAL WITHIN TWELVE HOURS OF ORIGINAL DEPARTURE TIME.
WHOA! IS THAT SPIDER-MAN?
THIS LOOKS PROMISING. BUT I MUST BE READY FOR...
...COMPLICATIONS.
DIDN'T HE ALREADY SHOW UP?
WHO CARES? WHAT PART OF "EVACUATION" DON'T YOU UNDERSTAND?

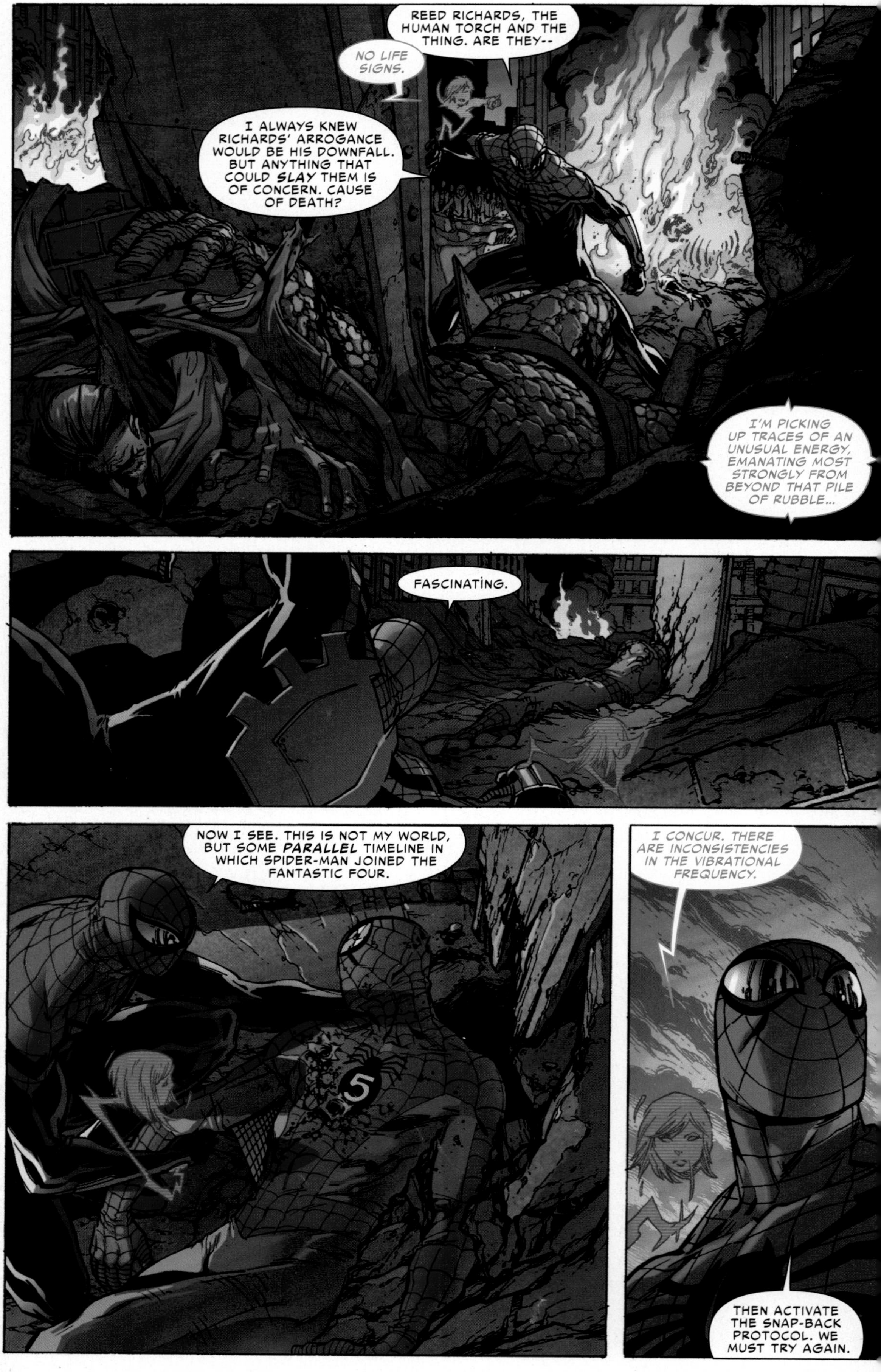
REED RICHARDS, THE HUMAN TORCH AND THE THING. ARE THEY--
NO LIFE SIGNS.
I ALWAYS KNEW RICHARDS' ARROGANCE WOULD BE HIS DOWNFALL. BUT ANYTHING THAT COULD SLAY THEM IS OF CONCERN. CAUSE OF DEATH?
I'M PICKING UP TRACES OF AN UNUSUAL ENERGY, EMANATING MOST STRONGLY FROM BEYOND THAT PILE OF RUBBLE...
FASCINATING.
NOW I SEE. THIS IS NOT MY WORLD, BUT SOME PARALLEL TIMELINE IN WHICH SPIDER-MAN JOINED THE FANTASTIC FOUR.
I CONCUR. THERE ARE INCONSISTENCIES IN THE VIBRATIONAL FREQUENCY.
THEN ACTIVATE THE SNAP-BACK PROTOCOL. WE MUST TRY AGAIN.

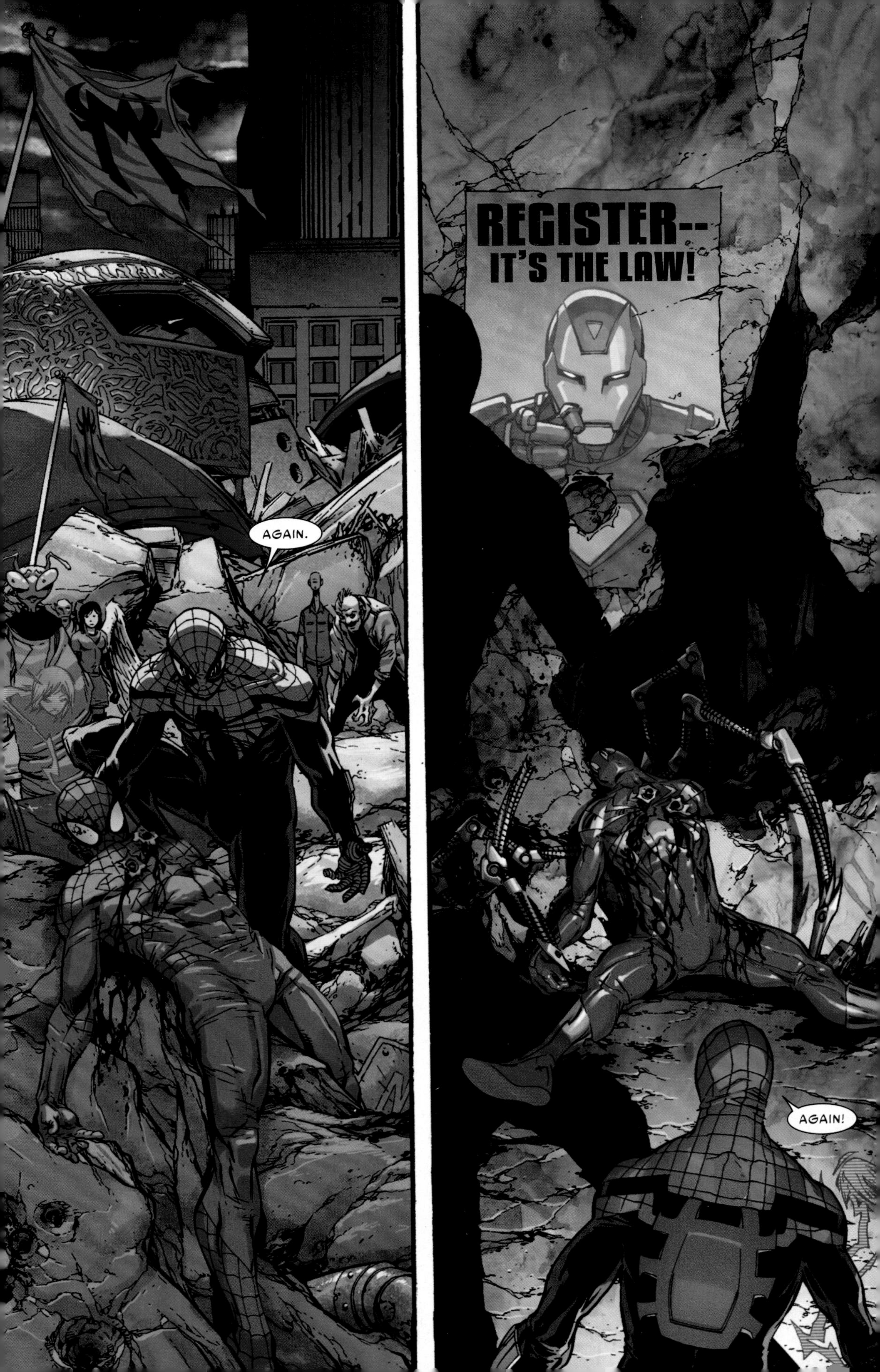
AGAIN.
REGISTER--
IT'S THE LAW!
AGAIN!

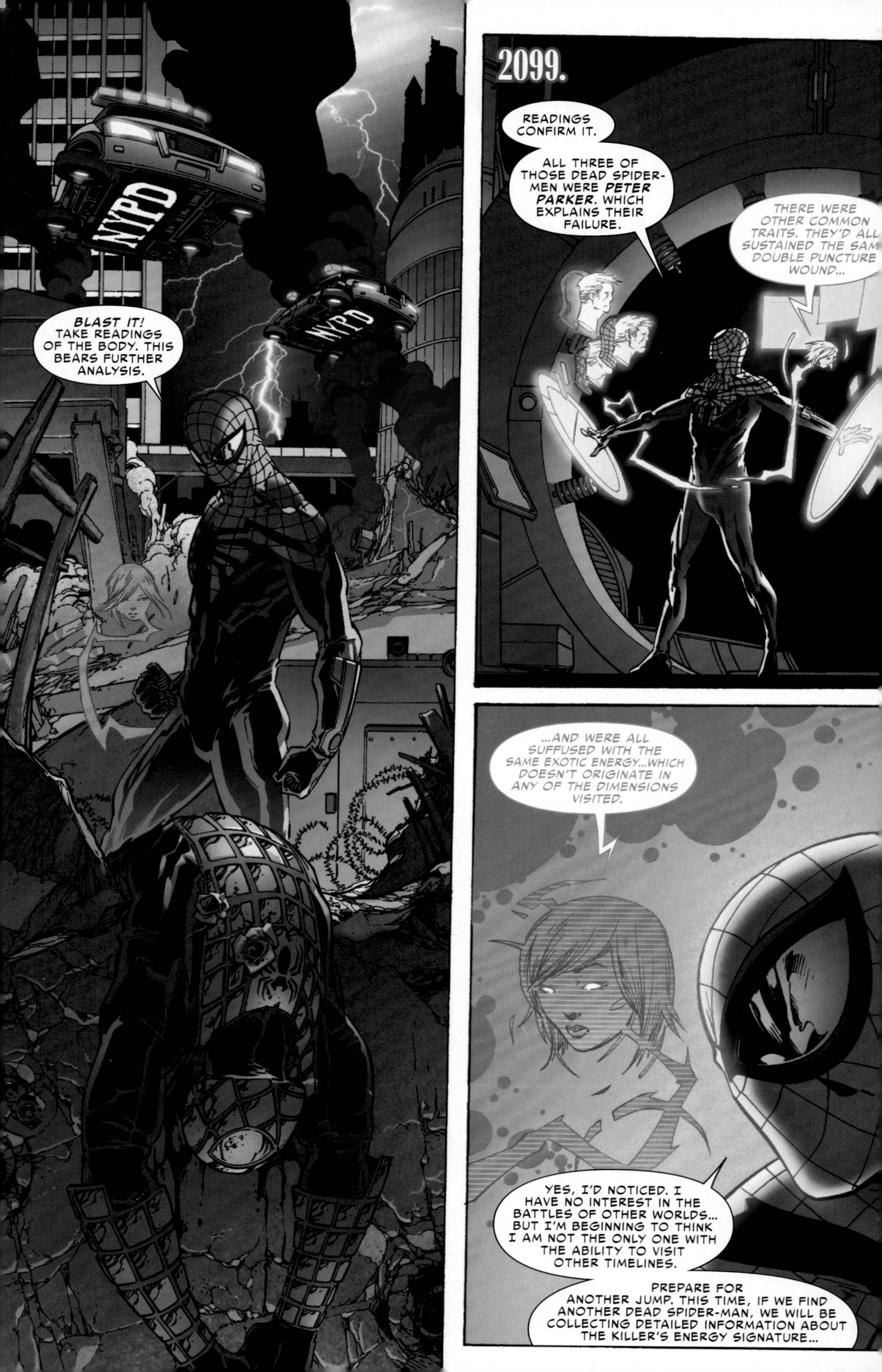
NYPD
NYPD
BLAST IT! TAKE READINGS OF THE BODY. THIS BEARS FURTHER ANALYSIS.
2099.
READINGS CONFIRM IT.
ALL THREE OF THOSE DEAD SPIDER-MEN WERE PETER PARKER. WHICH EXPLAINS THEIR FAILURE.
THERE WERE OTHER COMMON TRAITS. THEY'D ALL SUSTAINED THE SAM DOUBLE PUNCTURE WOUND...
...AND WERE ALL SUFFUSED WITH THE SAME EXOTIC ENERGY...WHICH DOESN'T ORIGINATE IN ANY OF THE DIMENSIONS VISITED.
YES, I'D NOTICED. I HAVE NO INTEREST IN THE BATTLES OF OTHER WORLDS... BUT I'M BEGINNING TO THINK I AM NOT THE ONLY ONE WITH THE ABILITY TO VISIT OTHER TIMELINES.
PREPARE FOR ANOTHER JUMP. THIS TIME, IF WE FIND ANOTHER DEAD SPIDER-MAN, WE WILL BE COLLECTING DETAILED INFORMATION ABOUT THE KILLER'S ENERGY SIGNATURE...

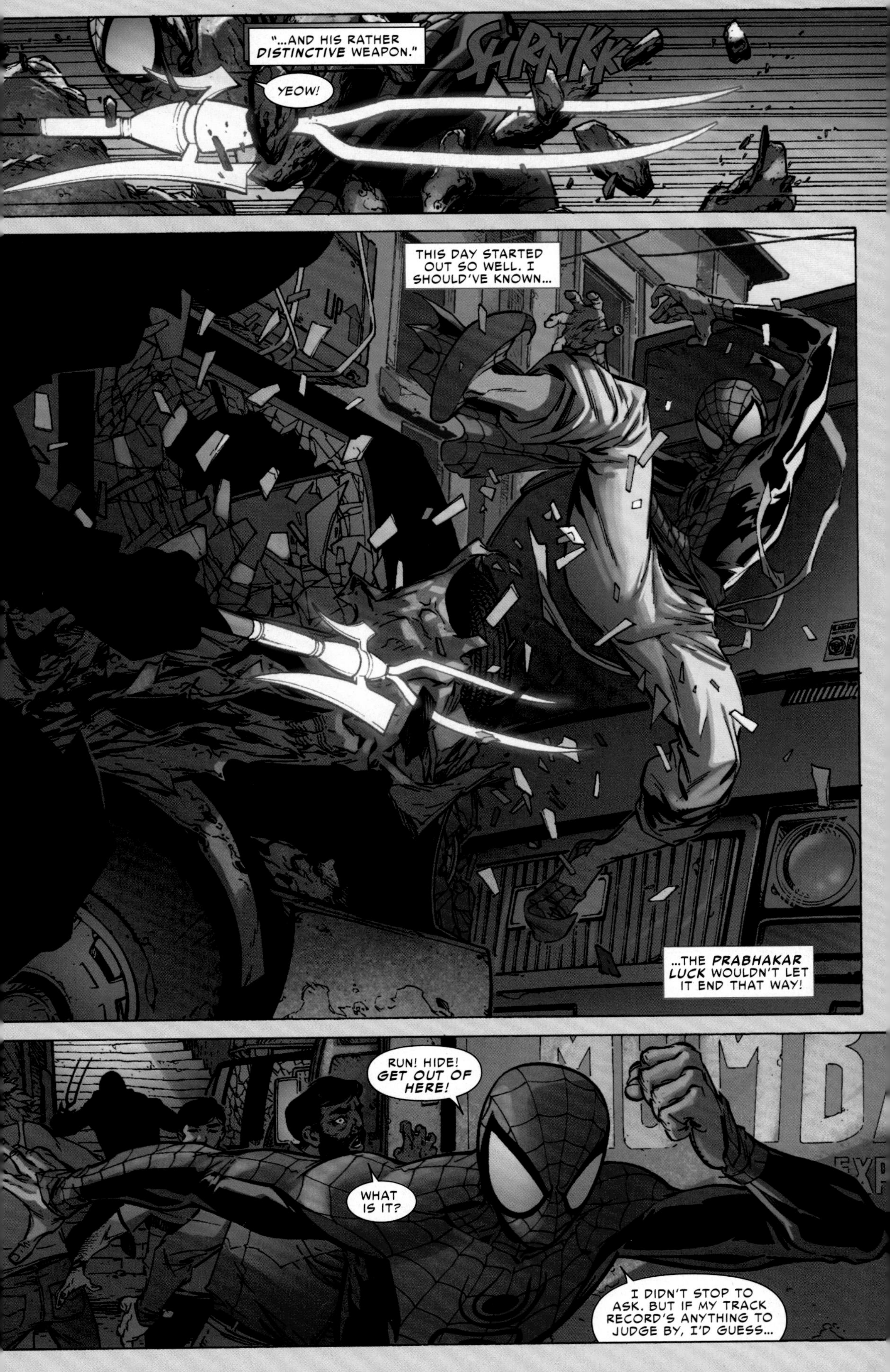
"...AND HIS RATHER DISTINCTIVE WEAPON."
YEOW!
SHRNKK
THIS DAY STARTED OUT SO WELL. I SHOULD'VE KNOWN...
...THE PRABHAKAR LUCK WOULDN'T LET IT END THAT WAY!
RUN! HIDE! GET OUT OF HERE!
WHAT IS IT?
I DIDN'T STOP TO ASK. BUT IF MY TRACK RECORD'S ANYTHING TO JUDGE BY, I'D GUESS...

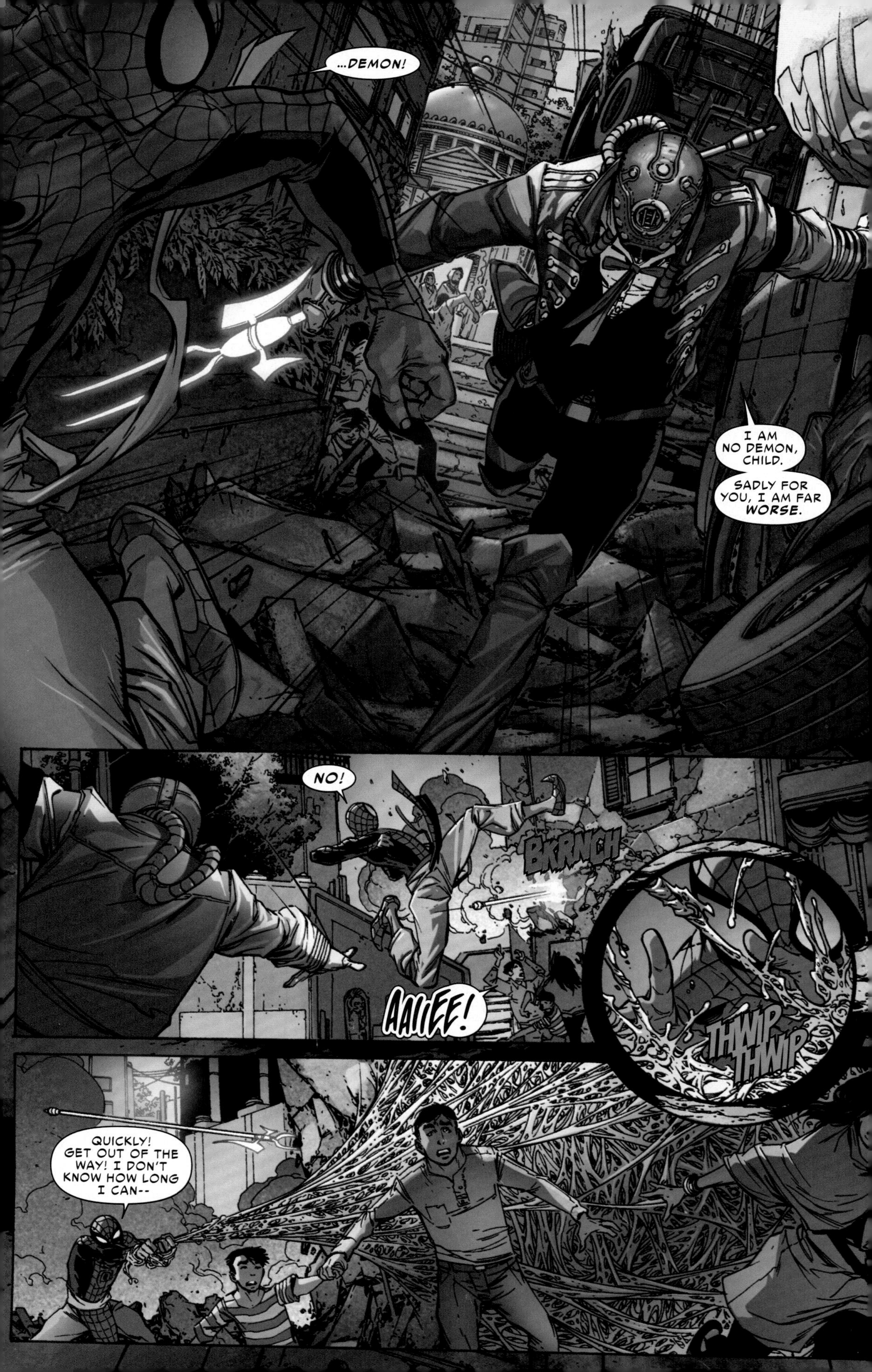
...DEMON!
I AM NO DEMON, CHILD.
SADLY FOR YOU, I AM FAR WORSE.
NO!
BKRNCH
AAIIEE!
THWIP THWIP
QUICKLY! GET OUT OF THE WAY! I DON'T KNOW HOW LONG I CAN--

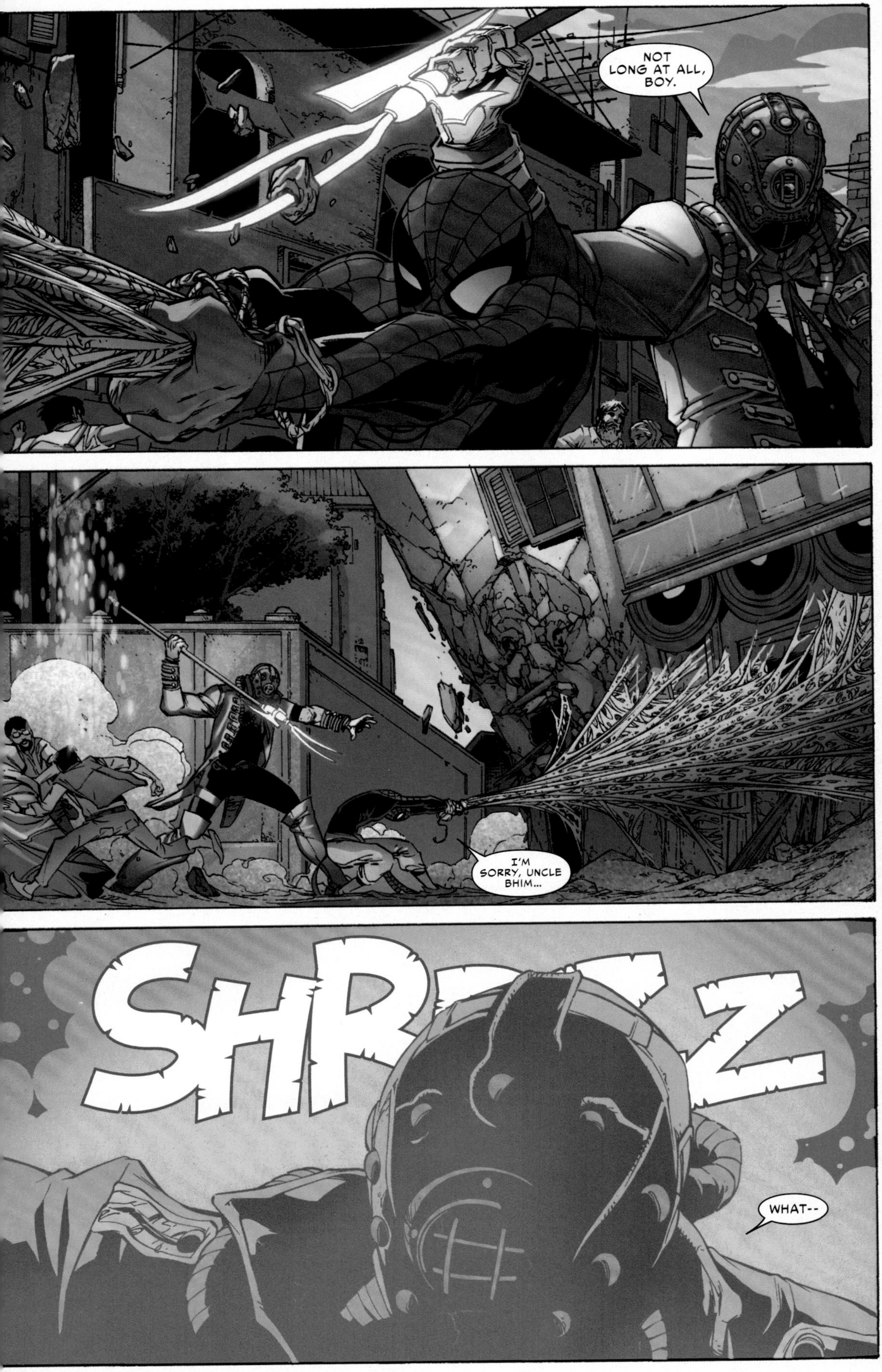
NOT LONG AT ALL, BOY.
I'M SORRY, UNCLE BHIM...
WHAT--

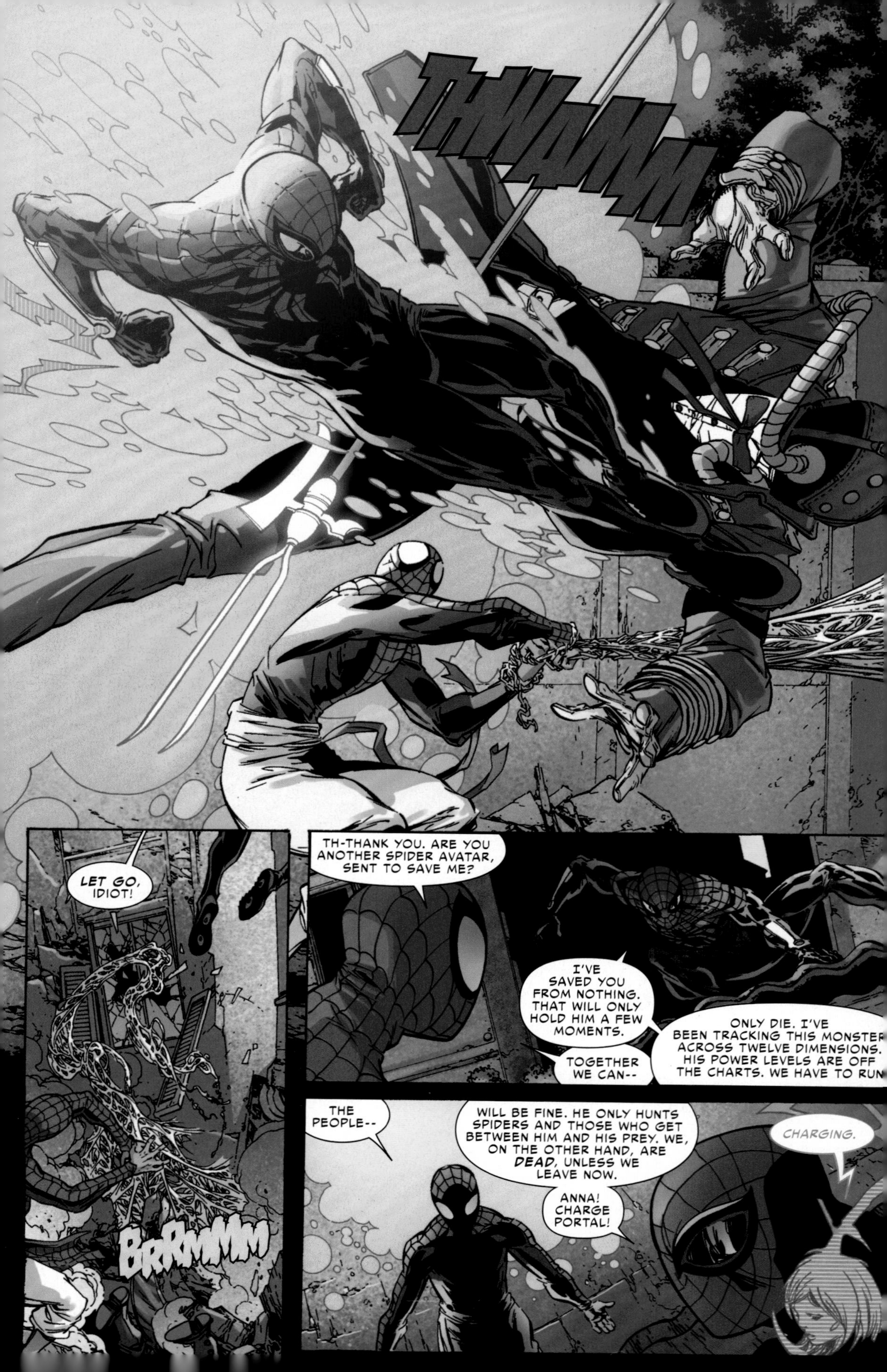
THWUMM
LET GO, IDIOT!
BRRMMM
TH-THANK YOU. ARE YOU ANOTHER SPIDER AVATAR, SENT TO SAVE ME?
I'VE SAVED YOU FROM NOTHING. THAT WILL ONLY HOLD HIM A FEW MOMENTS.
TOGETHER WE CAN--
ONLY DIE. I'VE BEEN TRACKING THIS MONSTER ACROSS TWELVE DIMENSIONS. HIS POWER LEVELS ARE OFF THE CHARTS. WE HAVE TO RUN
THE PEOPLE--
WILL BE FINE. HE ONLY HUNTS SPIDERS AND THOSE WHO GET BETWEEN HIM AND HIS PREY. WE, ON THE OTHER HAND, ARE DEAD, UNLESS WE LEAVE NOW.
ANNA! CHARGE PORTAL!
CHARGING.

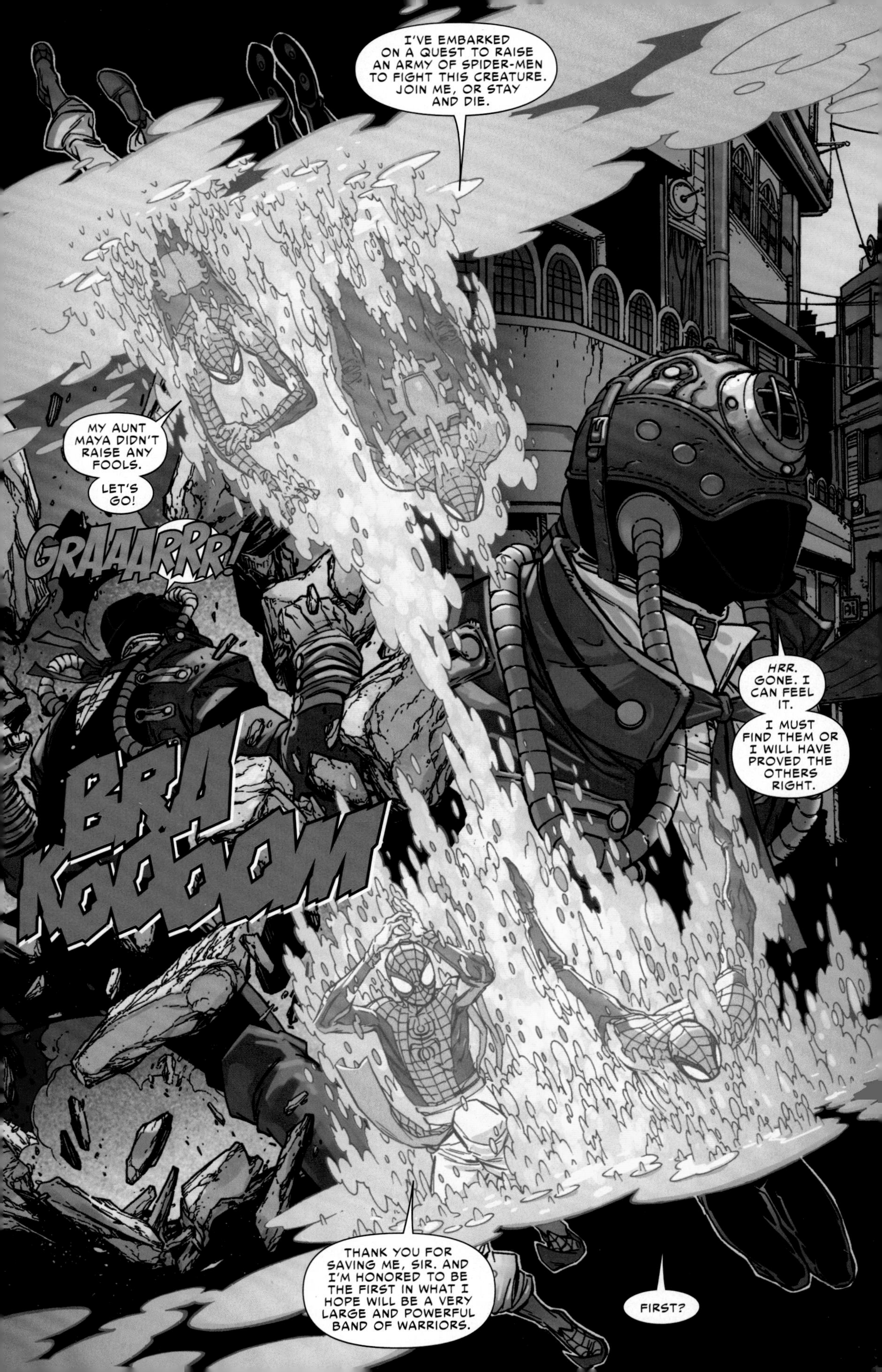
I'VE EMBARKED ON A QUEST TO RAISE AN ARMY OF SPIDER-MEN TO FIGHT THIS CREATURE. JOIN ME, OR STAY AND DIE.
MY AUNT MAYA DIDN'T RAISE ANY FOOLS.
LET'S GO!
GRAAARRR!
BRU KOOOOM
HRR. GONE. I CAN FEEL IT.
I MUST FIND THEM OR I WILL HAVE PROVED THE OTHERS RIGHT.
THANK YOU FOR SAVING ME, SIR. AND I'M HONORED TO BE THE FIRST IN WHAT I HOPE WILL BE A VERY LARGE AND POWERFUL BAND OF WARRIORS.
FIRST?

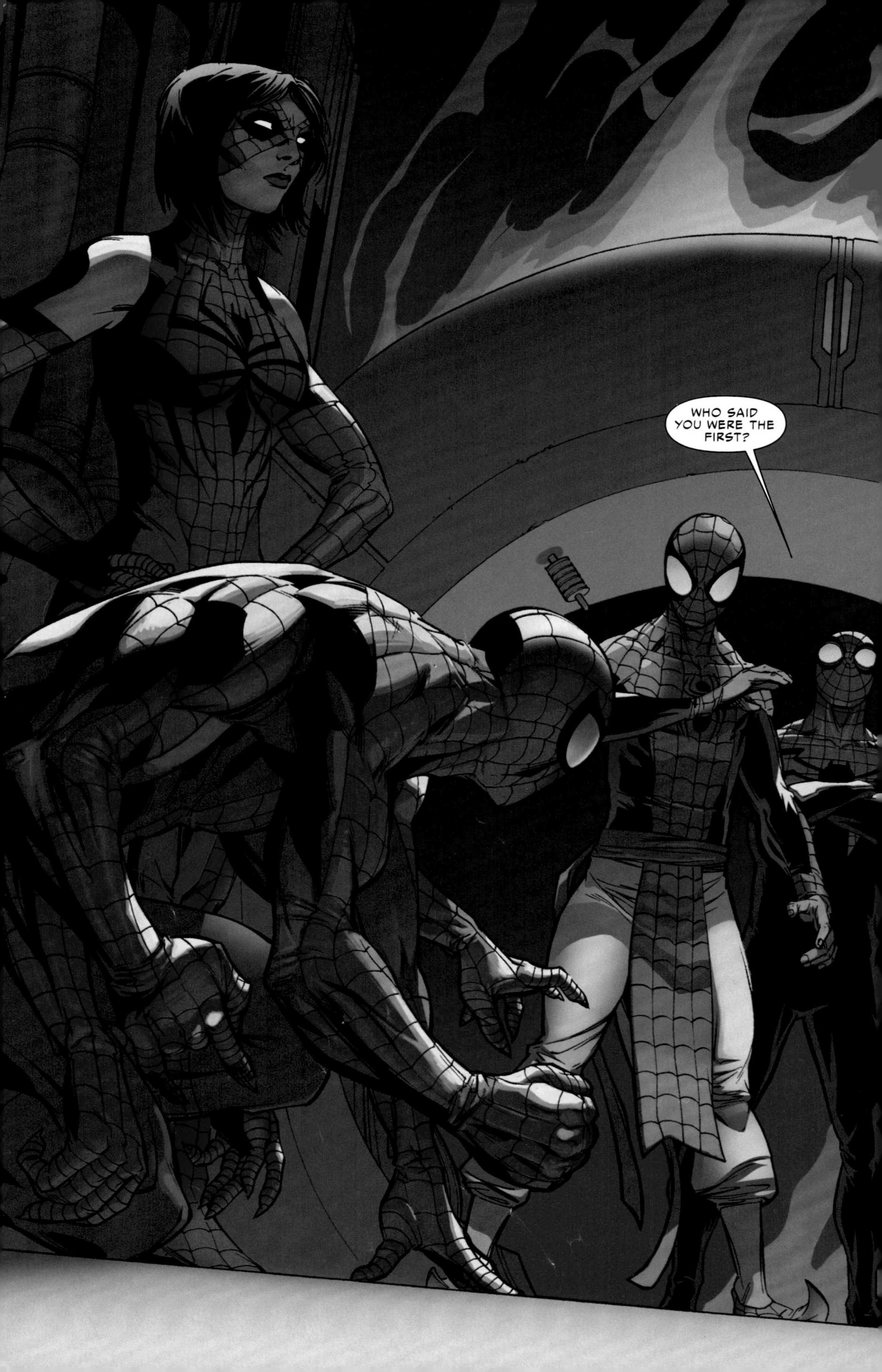
WHO SAID YOU WERE THE FIRST?

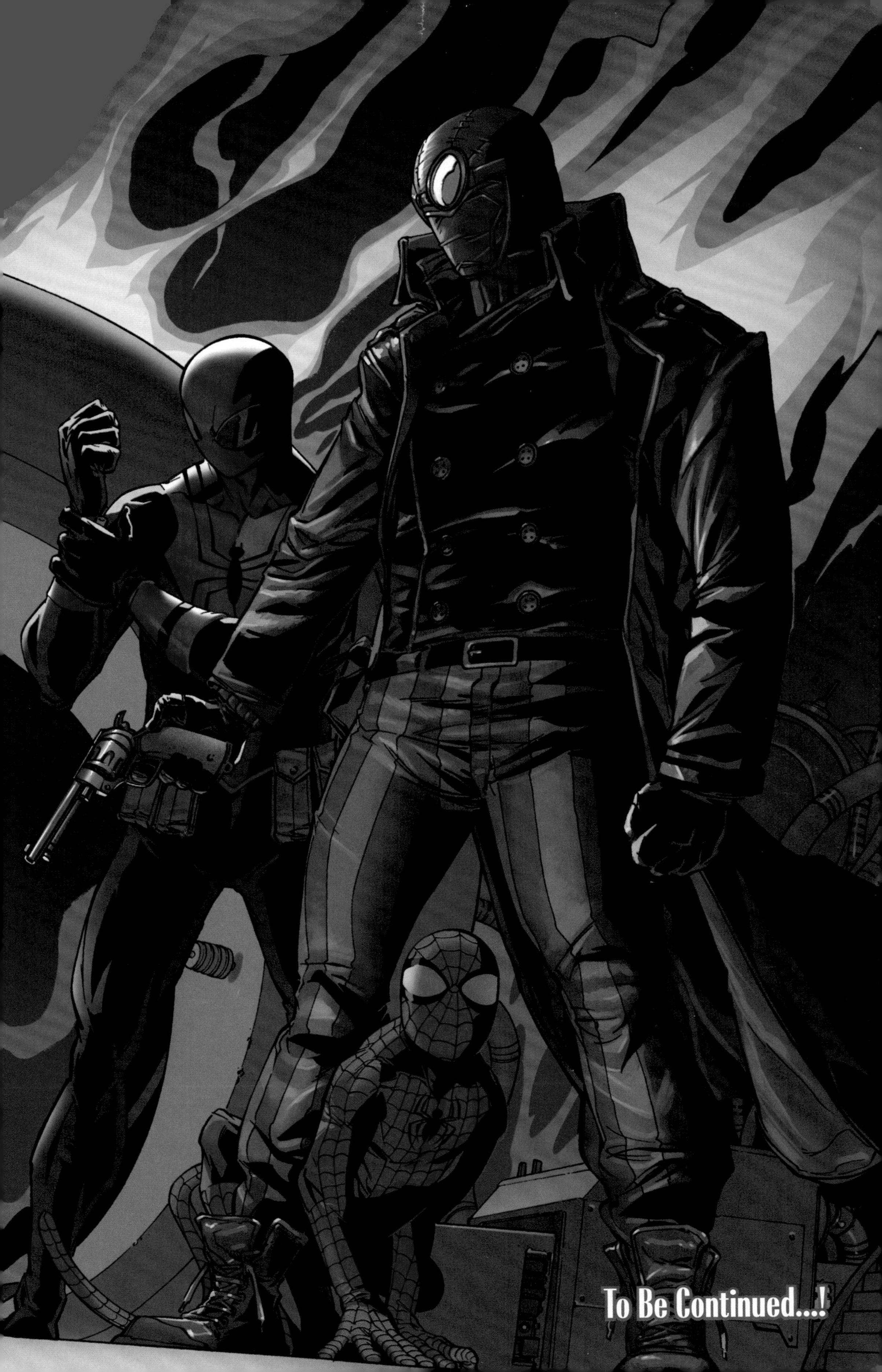
To Be Continued...!

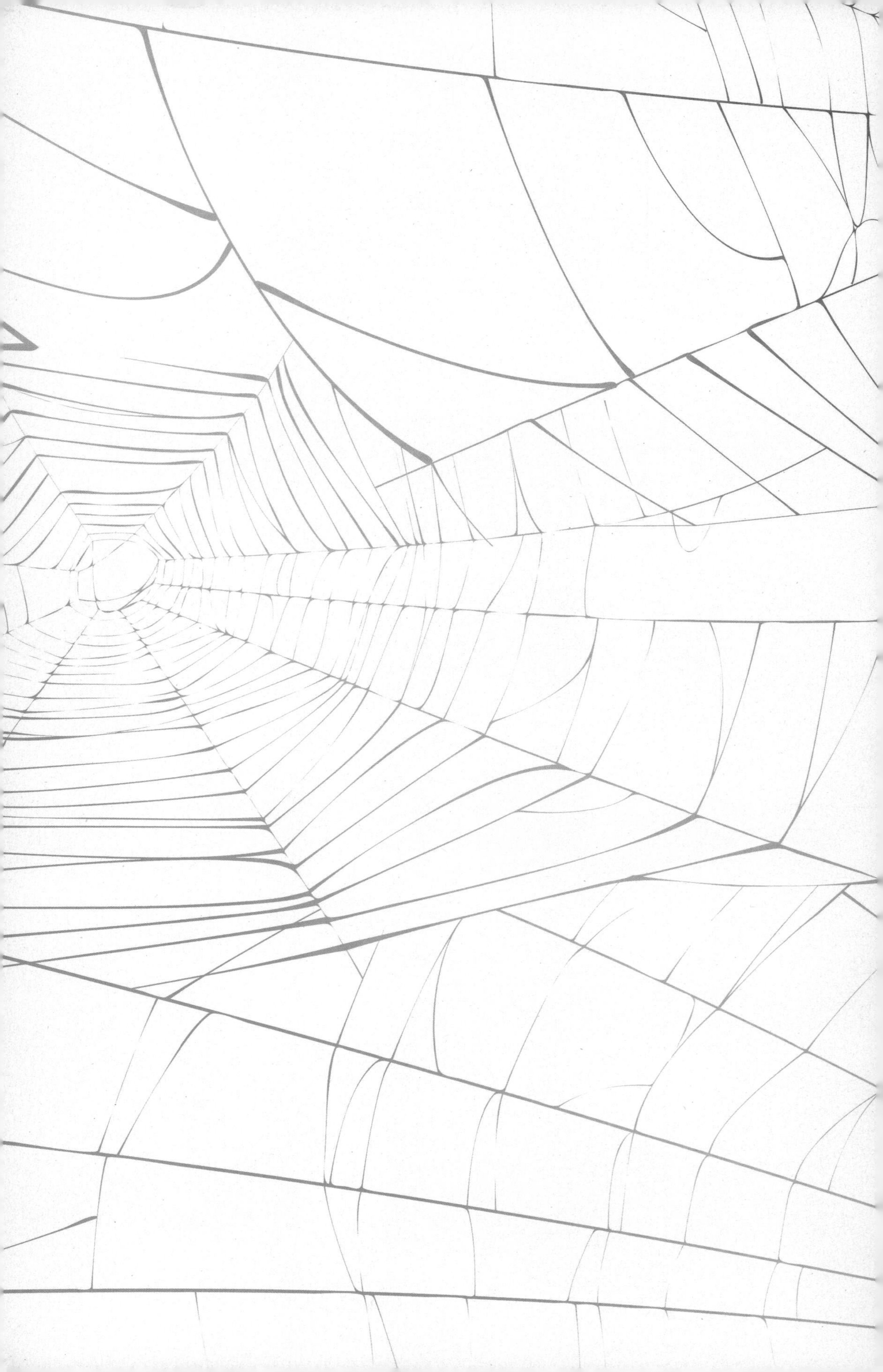

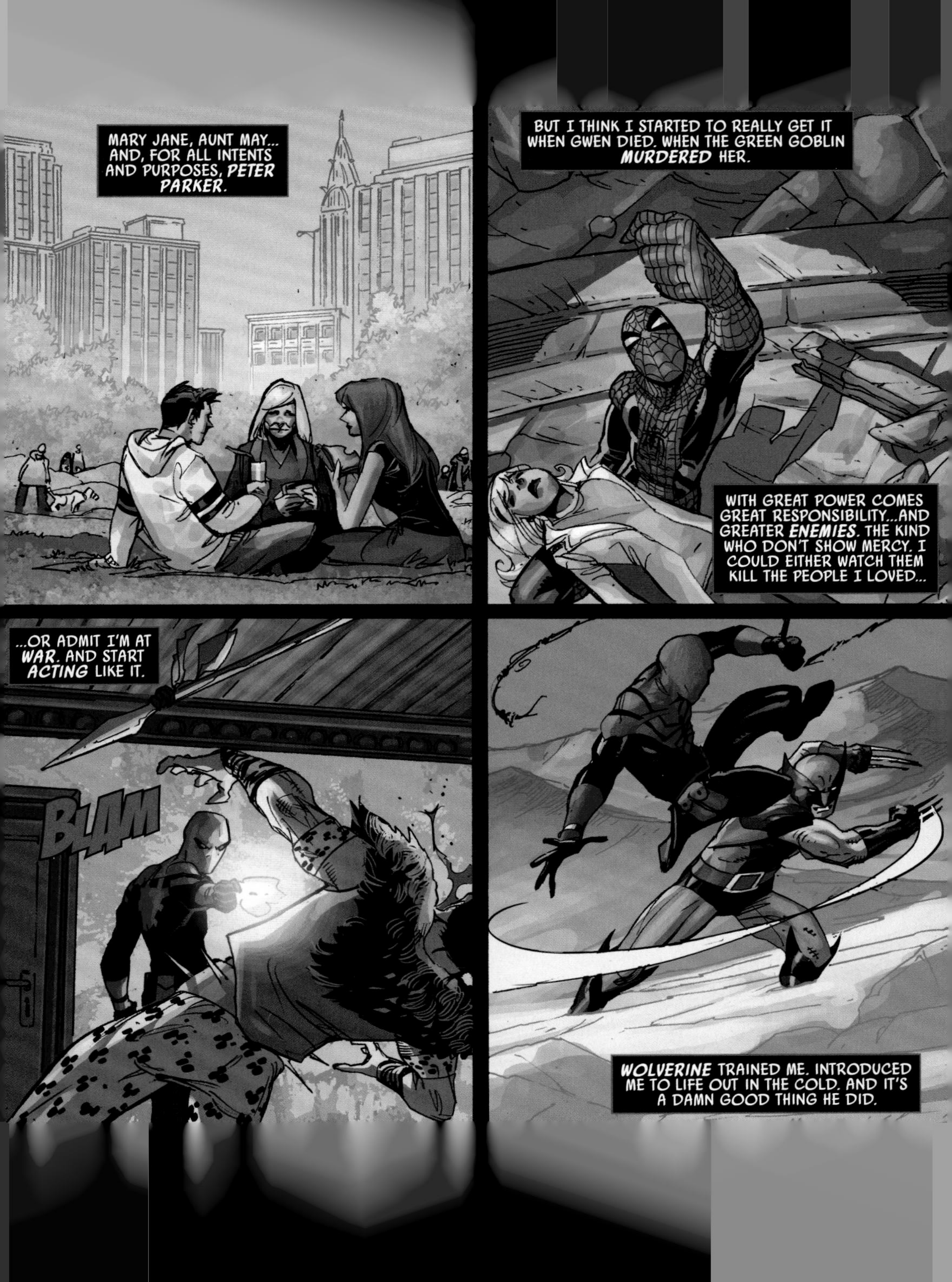
MARY JANE, AUNT MAY... AND, FOR ALL INTENTS AND PURPOSES, PETER PARKER.
BUT I THINK I STARTED TO REALLY GET IT WHEN GWEN DIED. WHEN THE GREEN GOBLIN MURDERED HER.
WITH GREAT POWER COMES GREAT RESPONSIBILITY...AND GREATER ENEMIES. THE KIND WHO DON'T SHOW MERCY. I COULD EITHER WATCH THEM KILL THE PEOPLE I LOVED...
...OR ADMIT I'M AT WAR. AND START ACTING LIKE IT.
BLAM
WOLVERINE TRAINED ME. INTRODUCED ME TO LIFE OUT IN THE COLD. AND IT'S A DAMN GOOD THING HE DID.

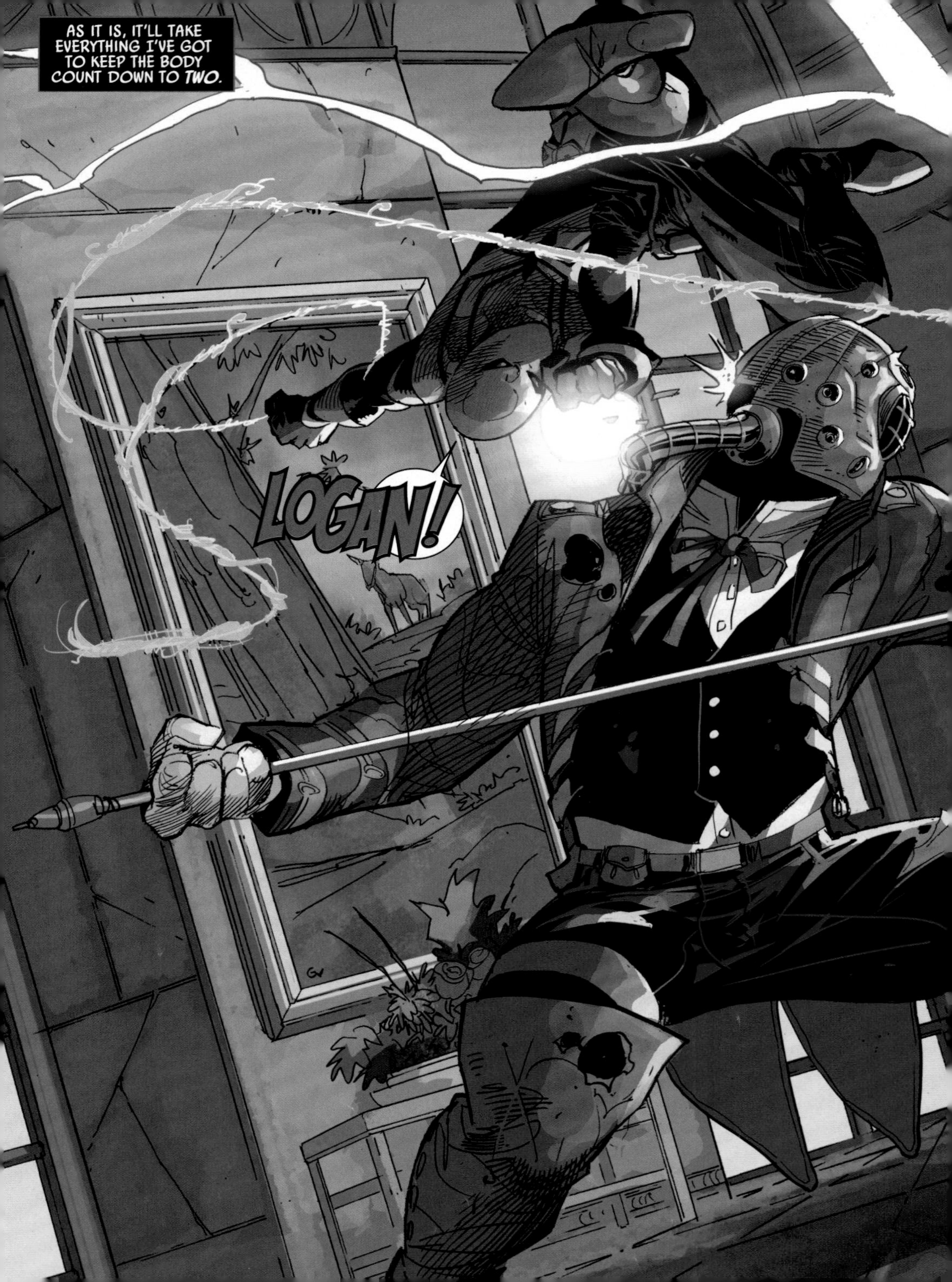
AS IT IS, IT'LL TAKE EVERYTHING I'VE GOT TO KEEP THE BODY COUNT DOWN TO *TWO*.
LOGAN!

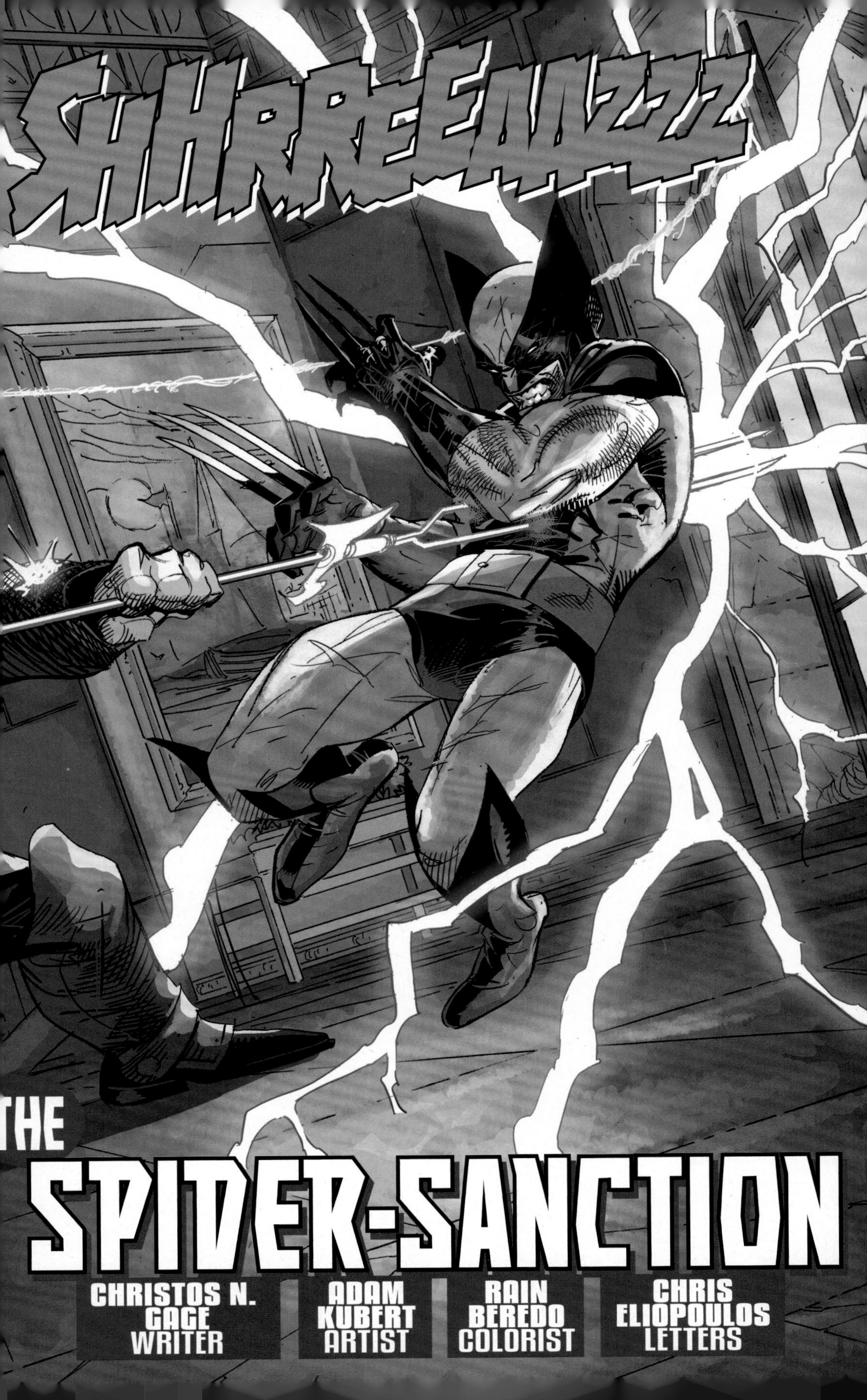
SHHREEAAZZZ
THE SPIDER-SANCTION
CHRISTOS N. GAGE WRITER
ADAM KUBERT ARTIST
RAIN BEREDO COLORIST
CHRIS ELIOPOULOS LETTERS

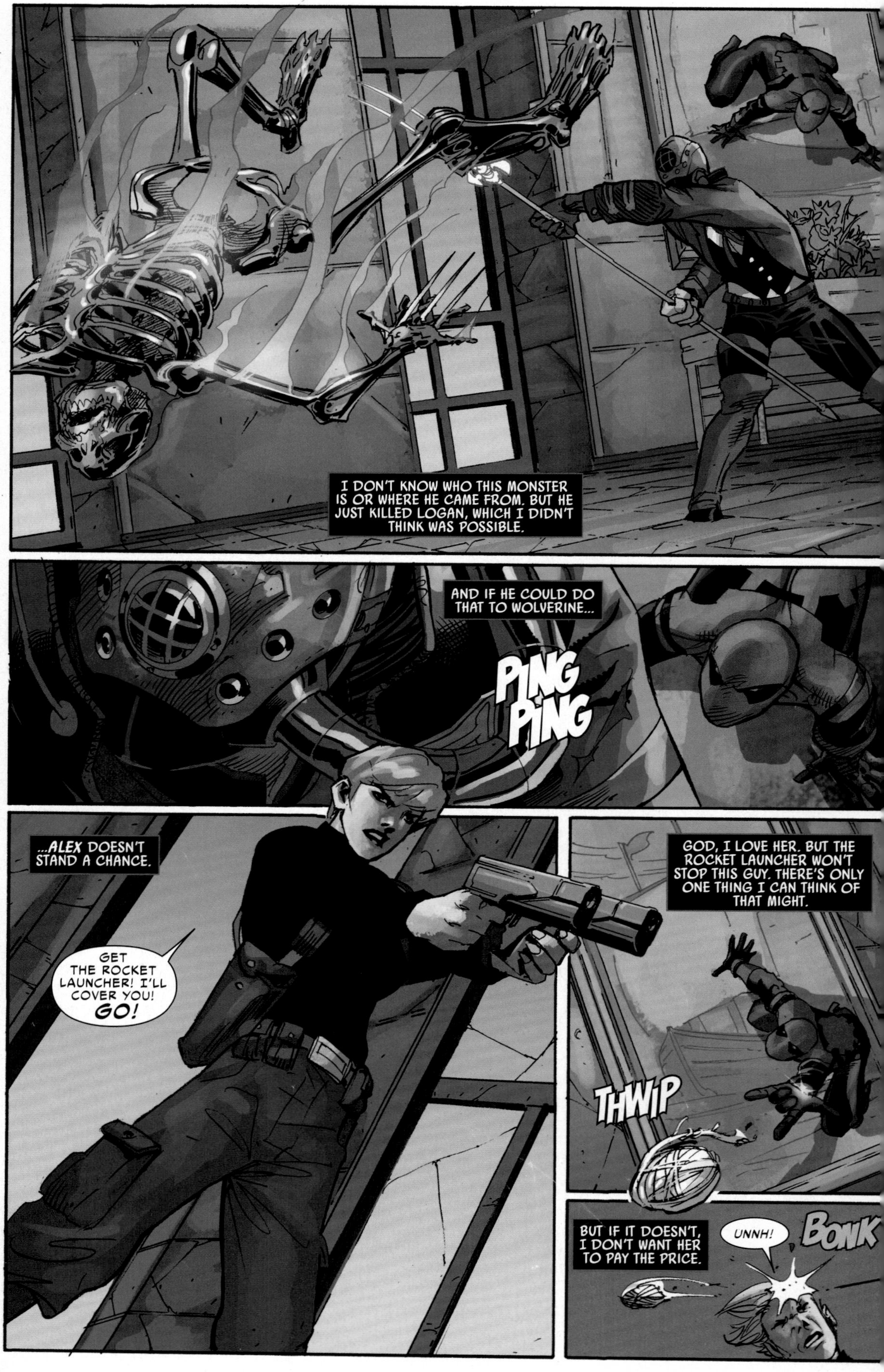

I DON'T KNOW WHO THIS MONSTER IS OR WHERE HE CAME FROM. BUT HE JUST KILLED LOGAN, WHICH I DIDN'T THINK WAS POSSIBLE.
AND IF HE COULD DO THAT TO WOLVERINE...
PING PING
...ALEX DOESN'T STAND A CHANCE.
GET THE ROCKET LAUNCHER! I'LL COVER YOU! GO!
GOD, I LOVE HER. BUT THE ROCKET LAUNCHER WON'T STOP THIS GUY. THERE'S ONLY ONE THING I CAN THINK OF THAT MIGHT.
THWIP
BUT IF IT DOESN'T, I DON'T WANT HER TO PAY THE PRICE.
UNNH!
BONK

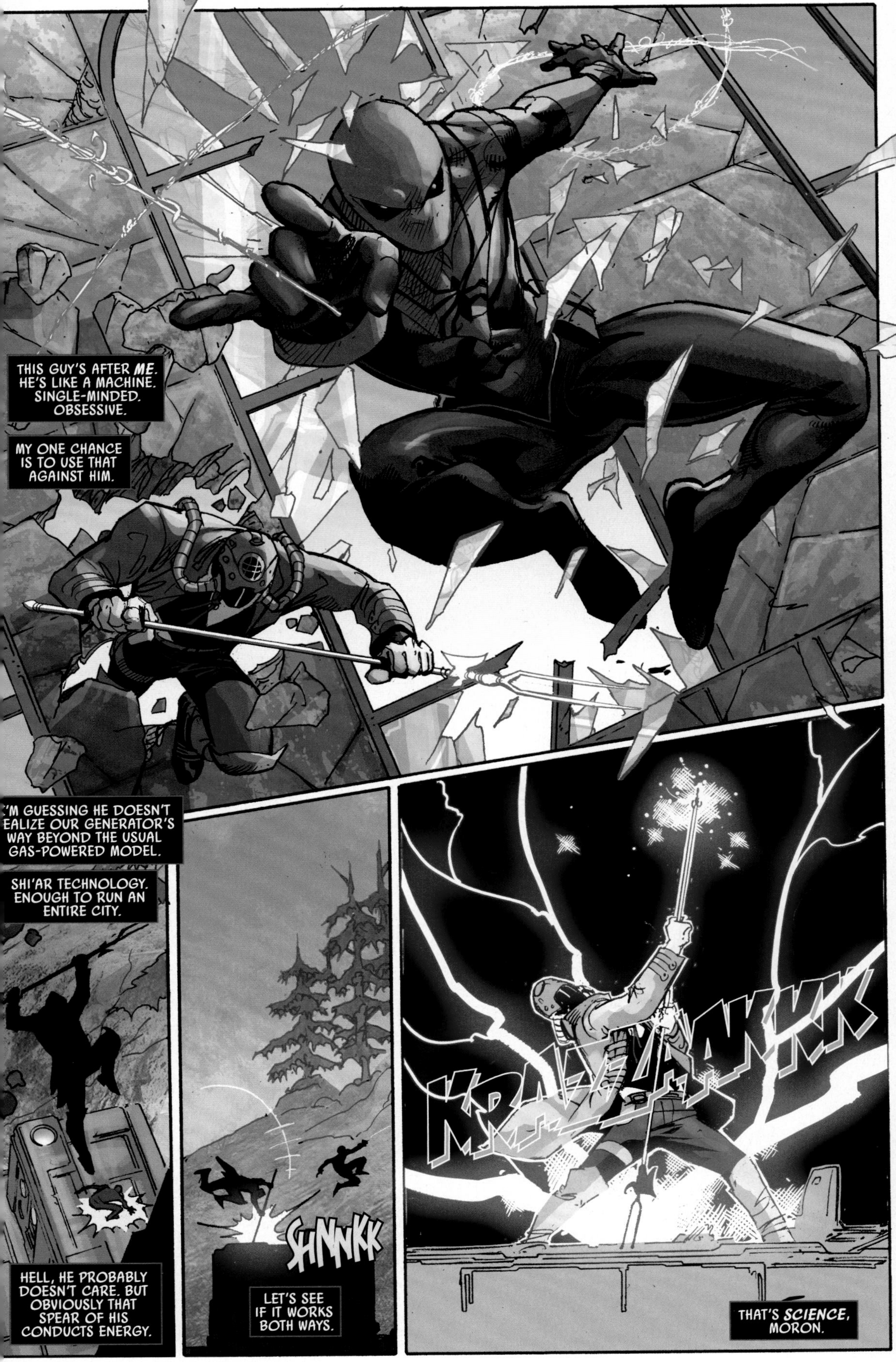
THIS GUY'S AFTER ME. HE'S LIKE A MACHINE. SINGLE-MINDED. OBSESSIVE.
MY ONE CHANCE IS TO USE THAT AGAINST HIM.
I'M GUESSING HE DOESN'T REALIZE OUR GENERATOR'S WAY BEYOND THE USUAL GAS-POWERED MODEL.
SHI'AR TECHNOLOGY. ENOUGH TO RUN AN ENTIRE CITY.
HELL, HE PROBABLY DOESN'T CARE. BUT OBVIOUSLY THAT SPEAR OF HIS CONDUCTS ENERGY.
SHNNKK
LET'S SEE IF IT WORKS BOTH WAYS.
KRAKAKOOM
THAT'S SCIENCE, MORON.

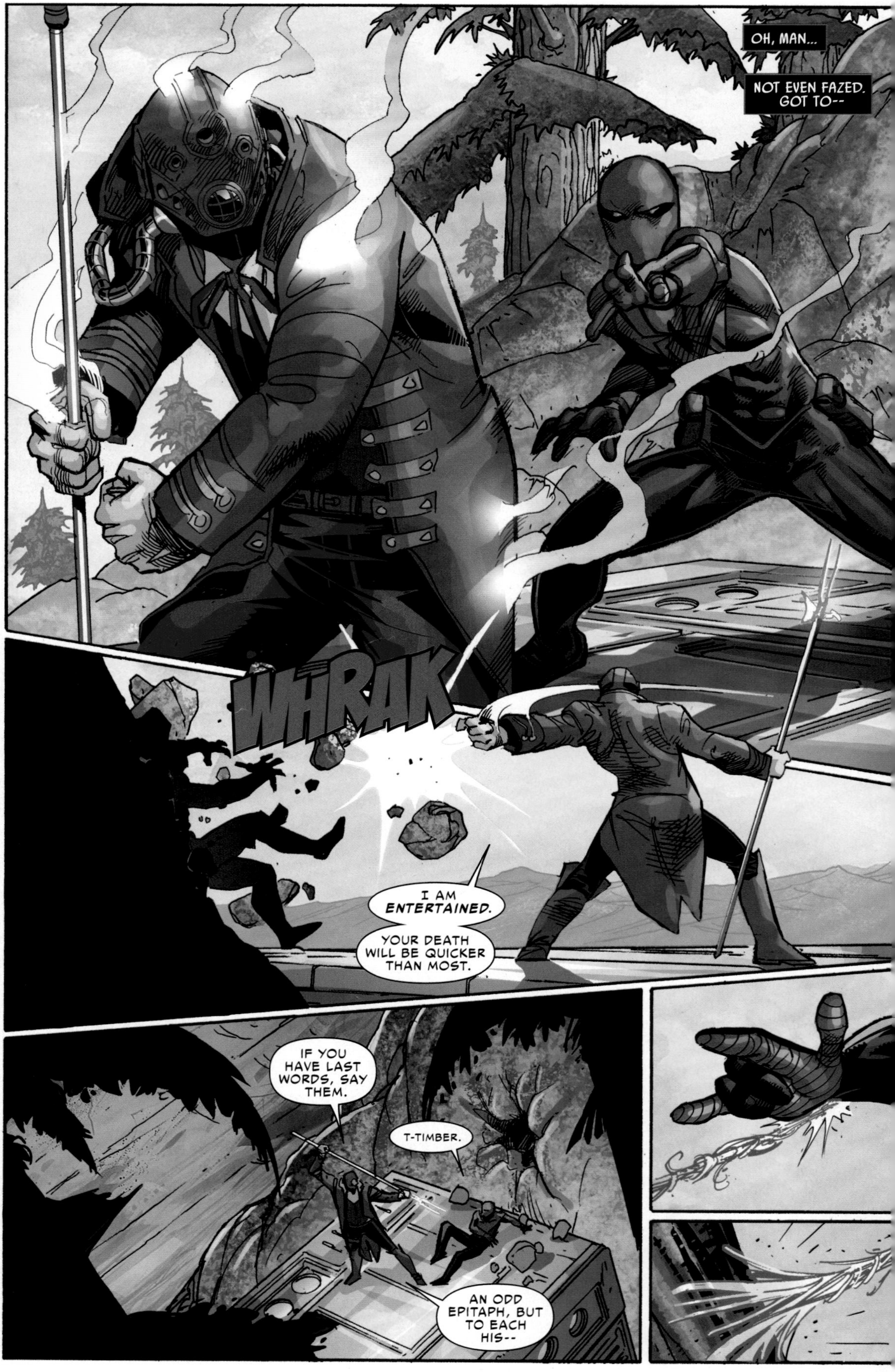
OH, MAN...
NOT EVEN FAZED. GOT TO--
WHRAK
I AM ENTERTAINED.
YOUR DEATH WILL BE QUICKER THAN MOST.
IF YOU HAVE LAST WORDS, SAY THEM.
T-TIMBER.
AN ODD EPITAPH, BUT TO EACH HIS--

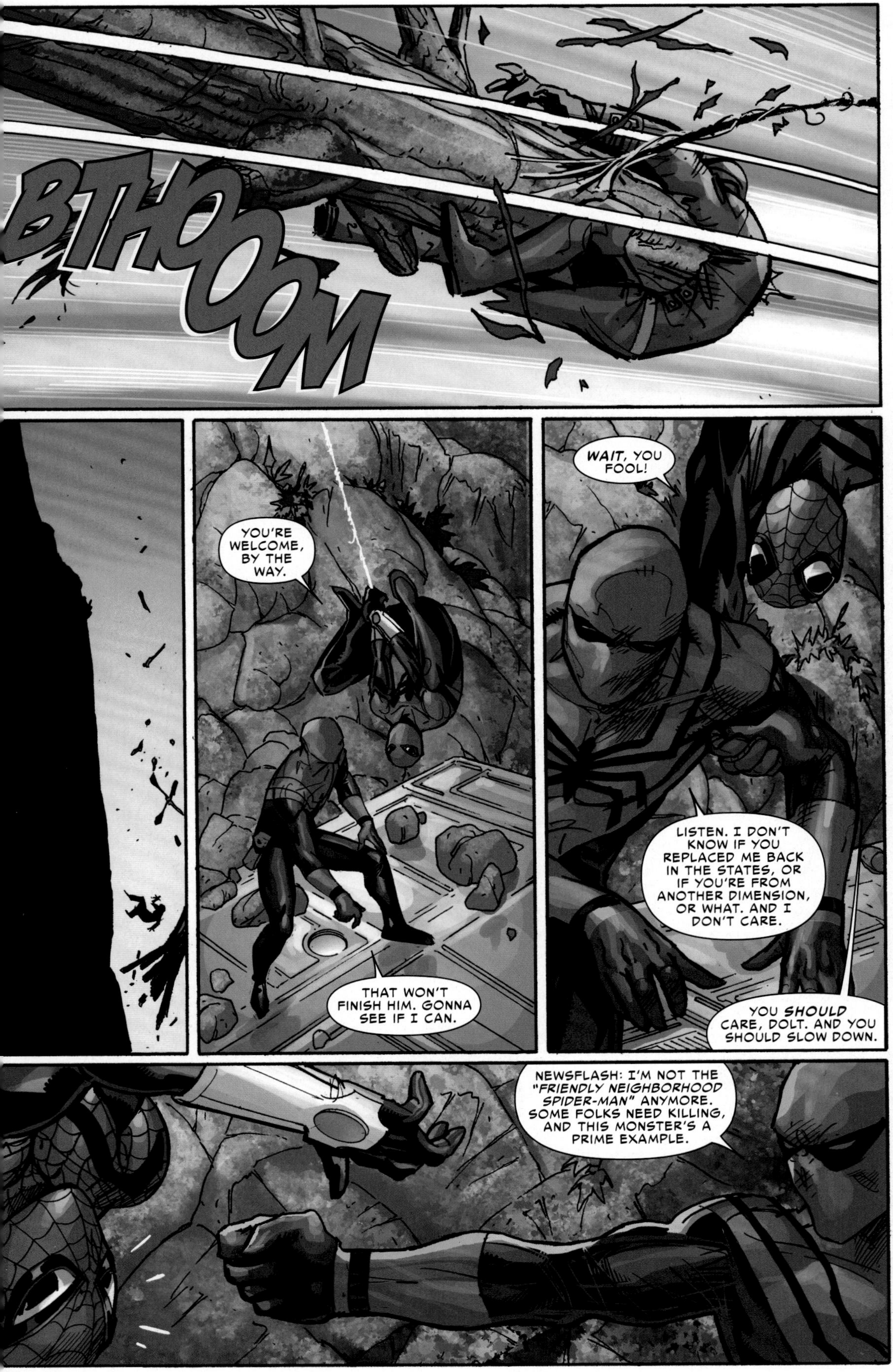
BTHOOOOM
YOU'RE WELCOME, BY THE WAY.
THAT WON'T FINISH HIM. GONNA SEE IF I CAN.
WAIT, YOU FOOL!
LISTEN. I DON'T KNOW IF YOU REPLACED ME BACK IN THE STATES, OR IF YOU'RE FROM ANOTHER DIMENSION, OR WHAT. AND I DON'T CARE.
YOU ***SHOULD*** CARE, DOLT. AND YOU SHOULD SLOW DOWN.
NEWSFLASH: I'M NOT THE "*FRIENDLY NEIGHBORHOOD SPIDER-MAN*" ANYMORE. SOME FOLKS NEED KILLING, AND THIS MONSTER'S A PRIME EXAMPLE.

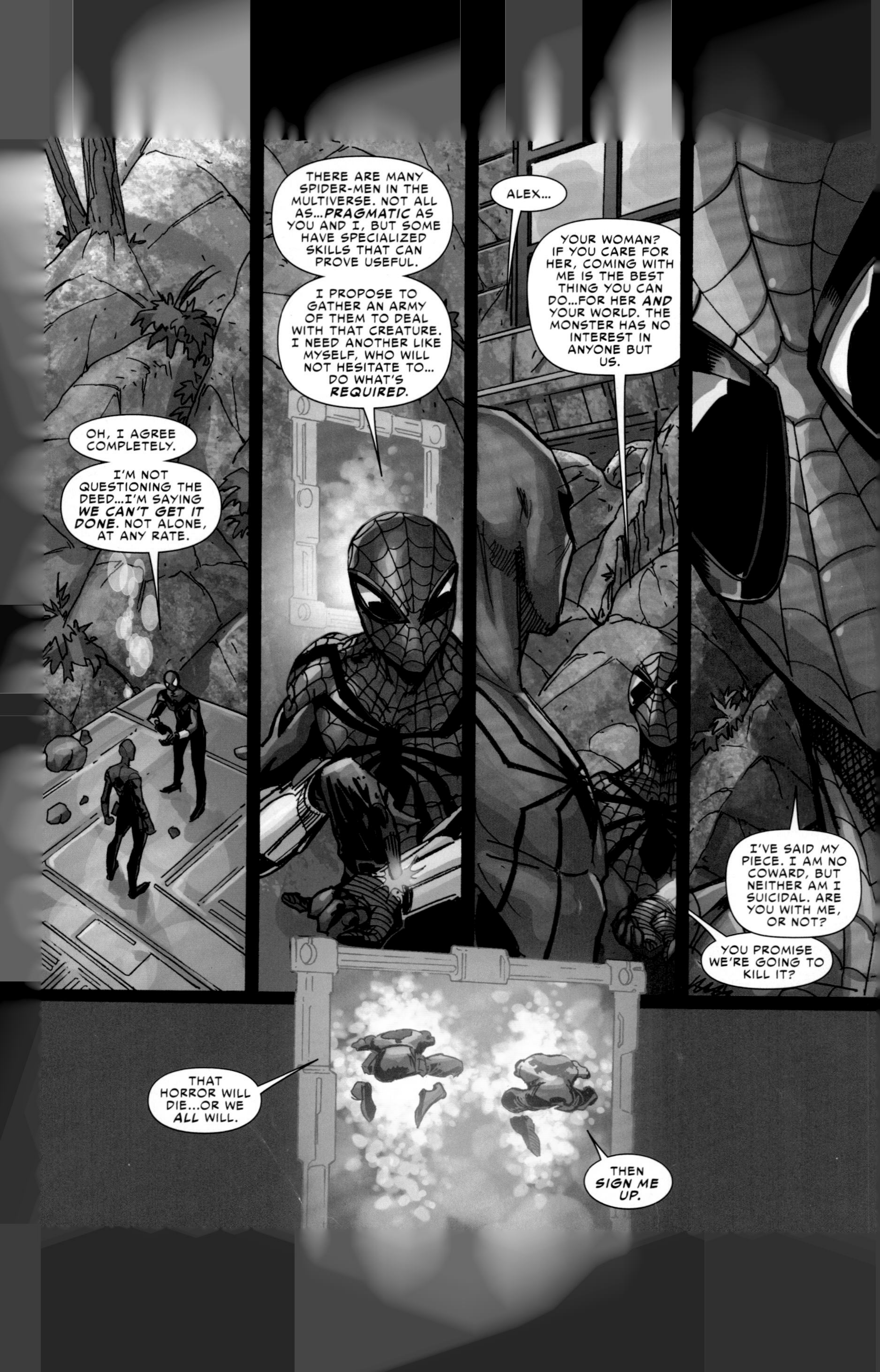
OH, I AGREE COMPLETELY.
I'M NOT QUESTIONING THE DEED...I'M SAYING WE CAN'T GET IT DONE. NOT ALONE, AT ANY RATE.
THERE ARE MANY SPIDER-MEN IN THE MULTIVERSE. NOT ALL AS...PRAGMATIC AS YOU AND I, BUT SOME HAVE SPECIALIZED SKILLS THAT CAN PROVE USEFUL.
I PROPOSE TO GATHER AN ARMY OF THEM TO DEAL WITH THAT CREATURE. I NEED ANOTHER LIKE MYSELF, WHO WILL NOT HESITATE TO... DO WHAT'S REQUIRED.
ALEX...
YOUR WOMAN? IF YOU CARE FOR HER, COMING WITH ME IS THE BEST THING YOU CAN DO...FOR HER AND YOUR WORLD. THE MONSTER HAS NO INTEREST IN ANYONE BUT US.
I'VE SAID MY PIECE. I AM NO COWARD, BUT NEITHER AM I SUICIDAL. ARE YOU WITH ME, OR NOT?
YOU PROMISE WE'RE GOING TO KILL IT?
THAT HORROR WILL DIE...OR WE ALL WILL.
THEN SIGN ME UP.

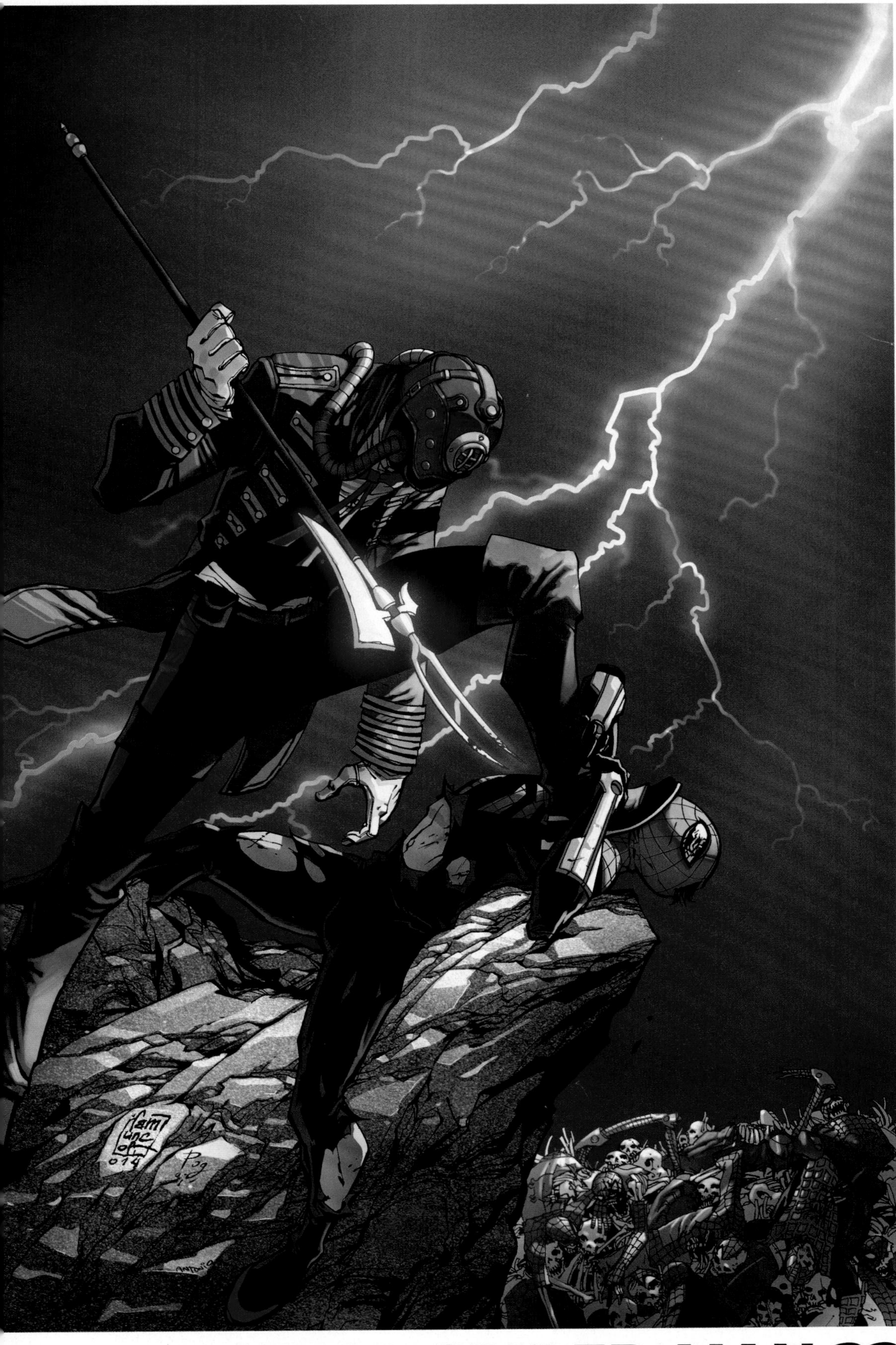

SUPERIOR SPIDER-MAN 33

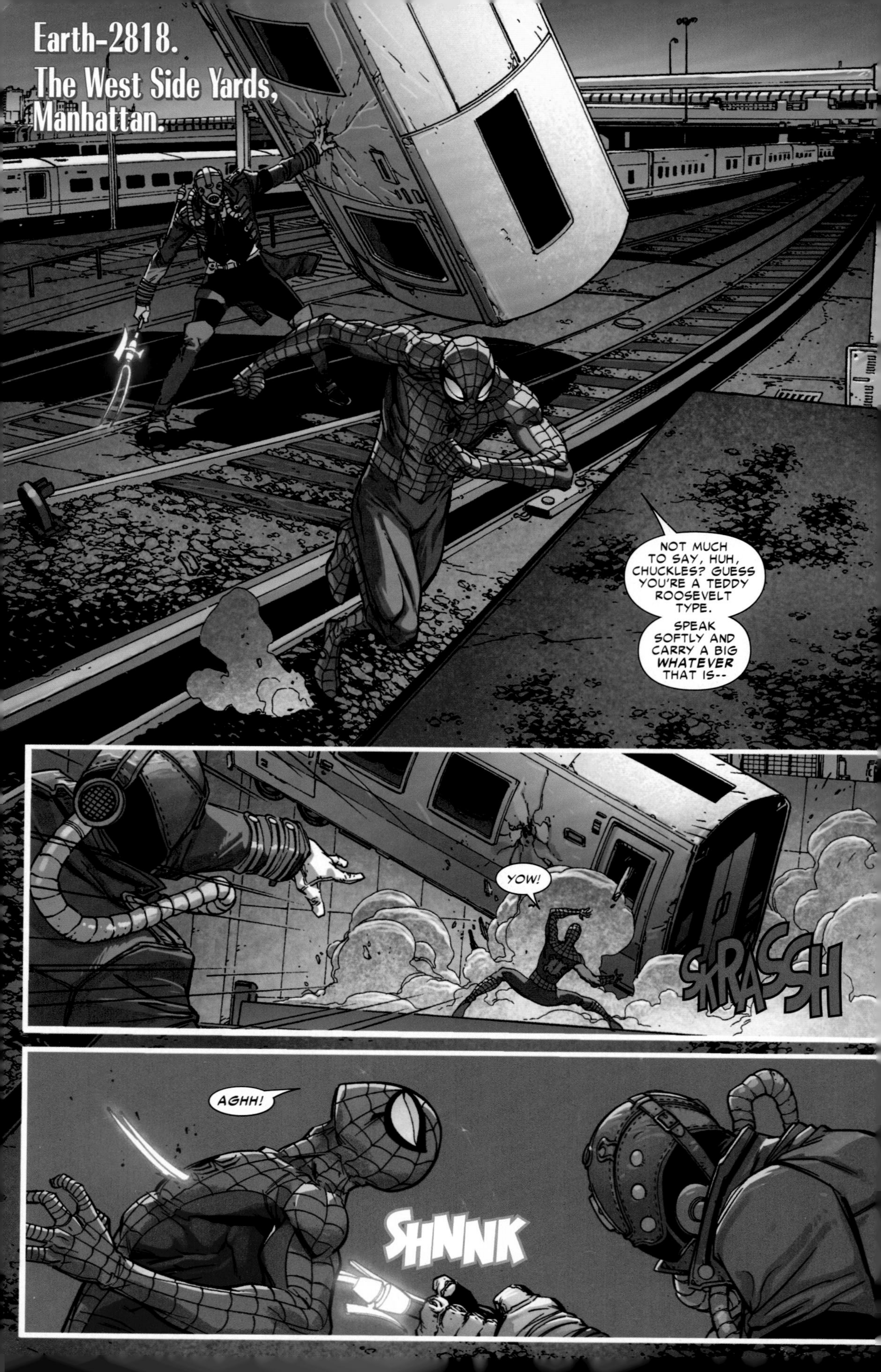
Earth-2818.
The West Side Yards, Manhattan.
NOT MUCH TO SAY, HUH, CHUCKLES? GUESS YOU'RE A TEDDY ROOSEVELT TYPE.
SPEAK SOFTLY AND CARRY A BIG *WHATEVER* THAT IS--
YOW!
SKRASSH
AGHH!
SHNNK

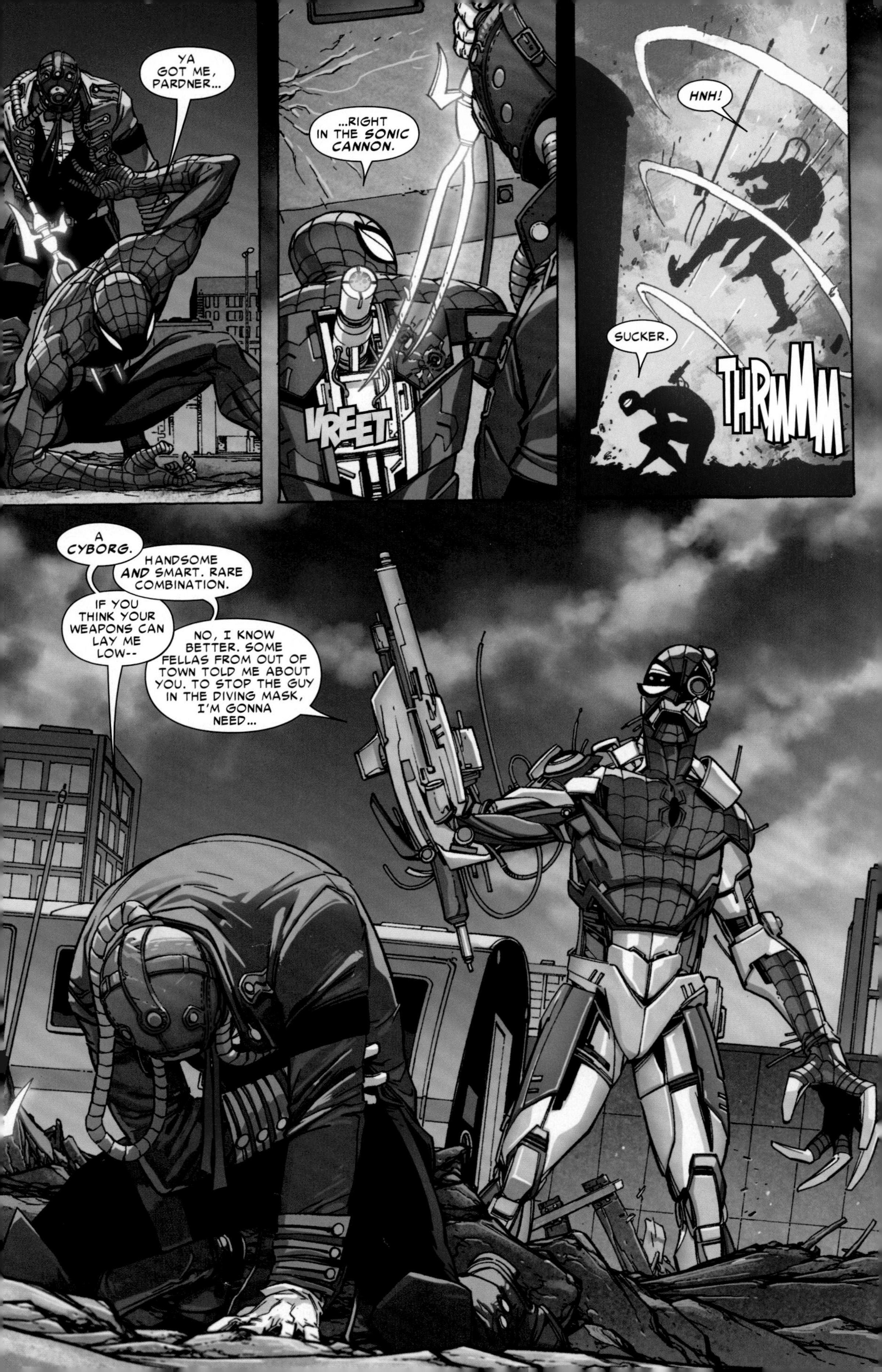
YA GOT ME, PARDNER...
...RIGHT IN THE SONIC CANNON.
VREEET
HNH!
SUCKER.
THRMMM
A CYBORG.
HANDSOME AND SMART. RARE COMBINATION.
IF YOU THINK YOUR WEAPONS CAN LAY ME LOW--
NO, I KNOW BETTER. SOME FELLAS FROM OUT OF TOWN TOLD ME ABOUT YOU. TO STOP THE GUY IN THE DIVING MASK, I'M GONNA NEED...

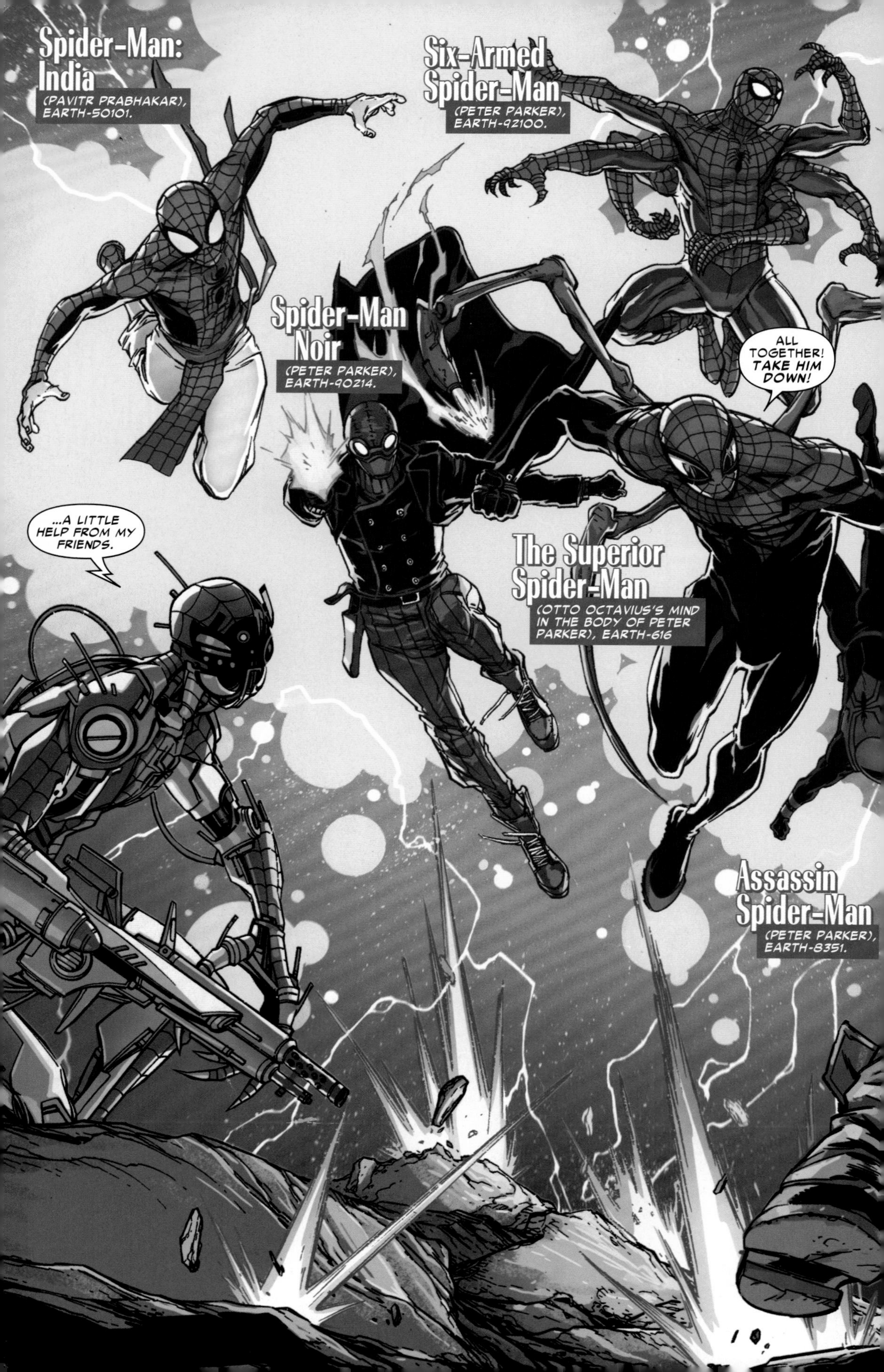

Spider-Man: India
(PAVITR PRABHAKAR), EARTH-50101.
Six-Armed Spider-Man
(PETER PARKER), EARTH-92100.
Spider-Man Noir
(PETER PARKER), EARTH-90214.
ALL TOGETHER! TAKE HIM DOWN!
...A LITTLE HELP FROM MY FRIENDS.
The Superior Spider-Man
(OTTO OCTAVIUS'S MIND IN THE BODY OF PETER PARKER), EARTH-616
Assassin Spider-Man
(PETER PARKER), EARTH-8351.

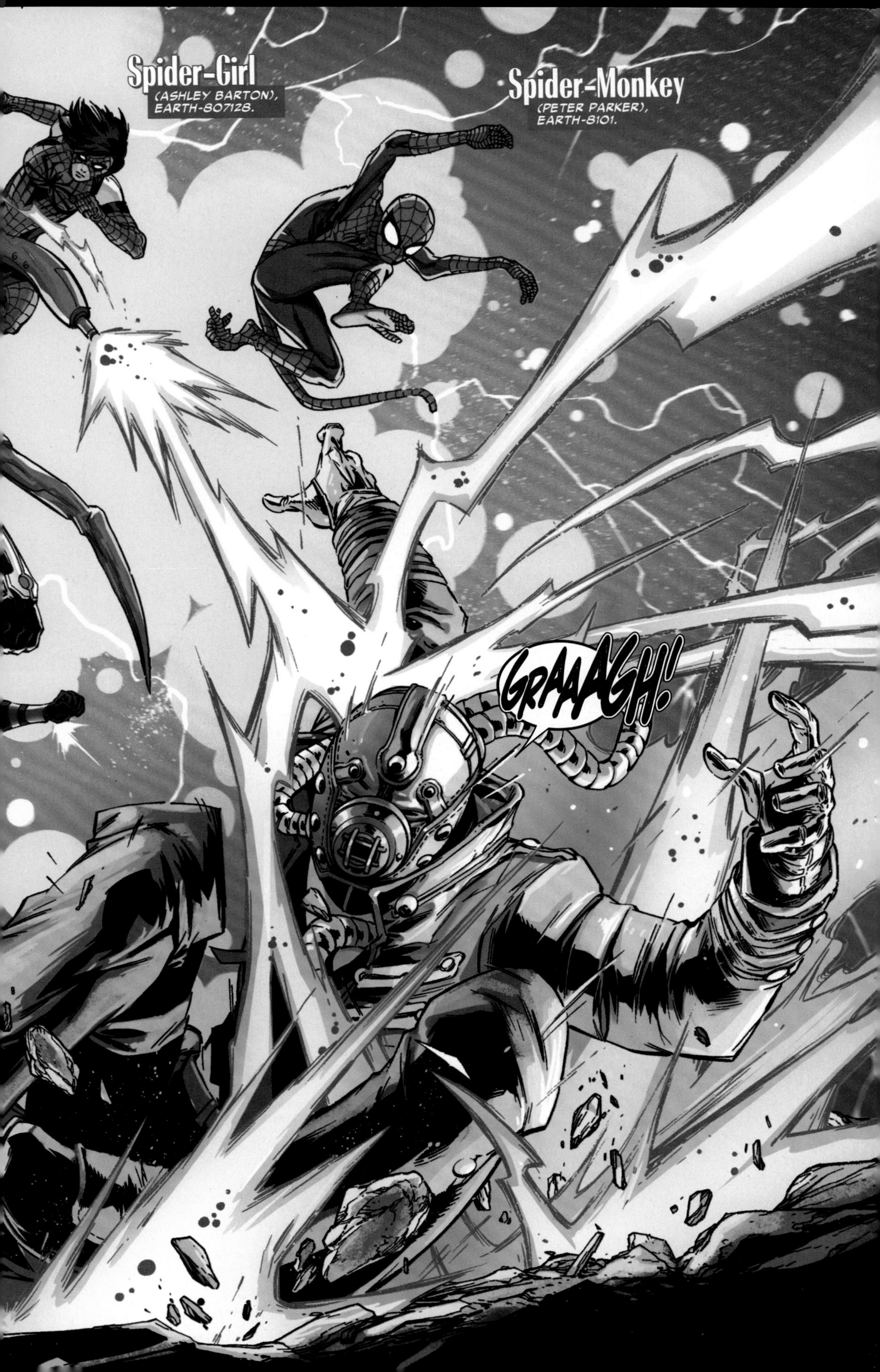
Spider-Girl
(ASHLEY BARTON), EARTH-807128.
Spider-Monkey
(PETER PARKER), EARTH-8101.
GRAAAGH!

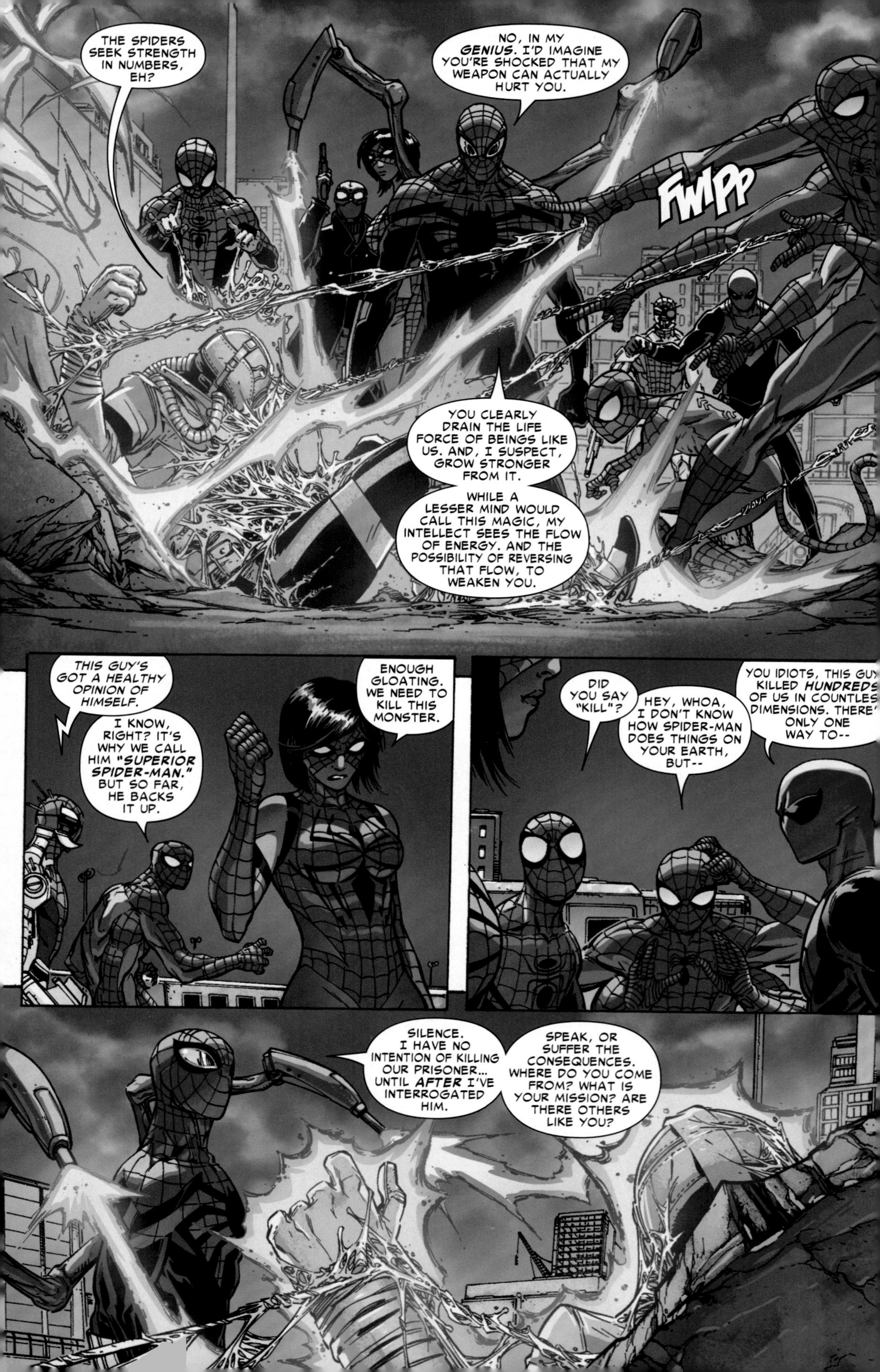
THE SPIDERS SEEK STRENGTH IN NUMBERS, EH?
NO, IN MY GENIUS. I'D IMAGINE YOU'RE SHOCKED THAT MY WEAPON CAN ACTUALLY HURT YOU.
FWIPP
YOU CLEARLY DRAIN THE LIFE FORCE OF BEINGS LIKE US. AND, I SUSPECT, GROW STRONGER FROM IT.
WHILE A LESSER MIND WOULD CALL THIS MAGIC, MY INTELLECT SEES THE FLOW OF ENERGY. AND THE POSSIBILITY OF REVERSING THAT FLOW, TO WEAKEN YOU.
THIS GUY'S GOT A HEALTHY OPINION OF HIMSELF.
I KNOW, RIGHT? IT'S WHY WE CALL HIM "SUPERIOR SPIDER-MAN." BUT SO FAR, HE BACKS IT UP.
ENOUGH GLOATING. WE NEED TO KILL THIS MONSTER.
DID YOU SAY "KILL"?
HEY, WHOA, I DON'T KNOW HOW SPIDER-MAN DOES THINGS ON YOUR EARTH, BUT--
YOU IDIOTS, THIS GUY KILLED HUNDREDS OF US IN COUNTLESS DIMENSIONS. THERE'S ONLY ONE WAY TO--
SILENCE. I HAVE NO INTENTION OF KILLING OUR PRISONER... UNTIL AFTER I'VE INTERROGATED HIM.
SPEAK, OR SUFFER THE CONSEQUENCES. WHERE DO YOU COME FROM? WHAT IS YOUR MISSION? ARE THERE OTHERS LIKE YOU?

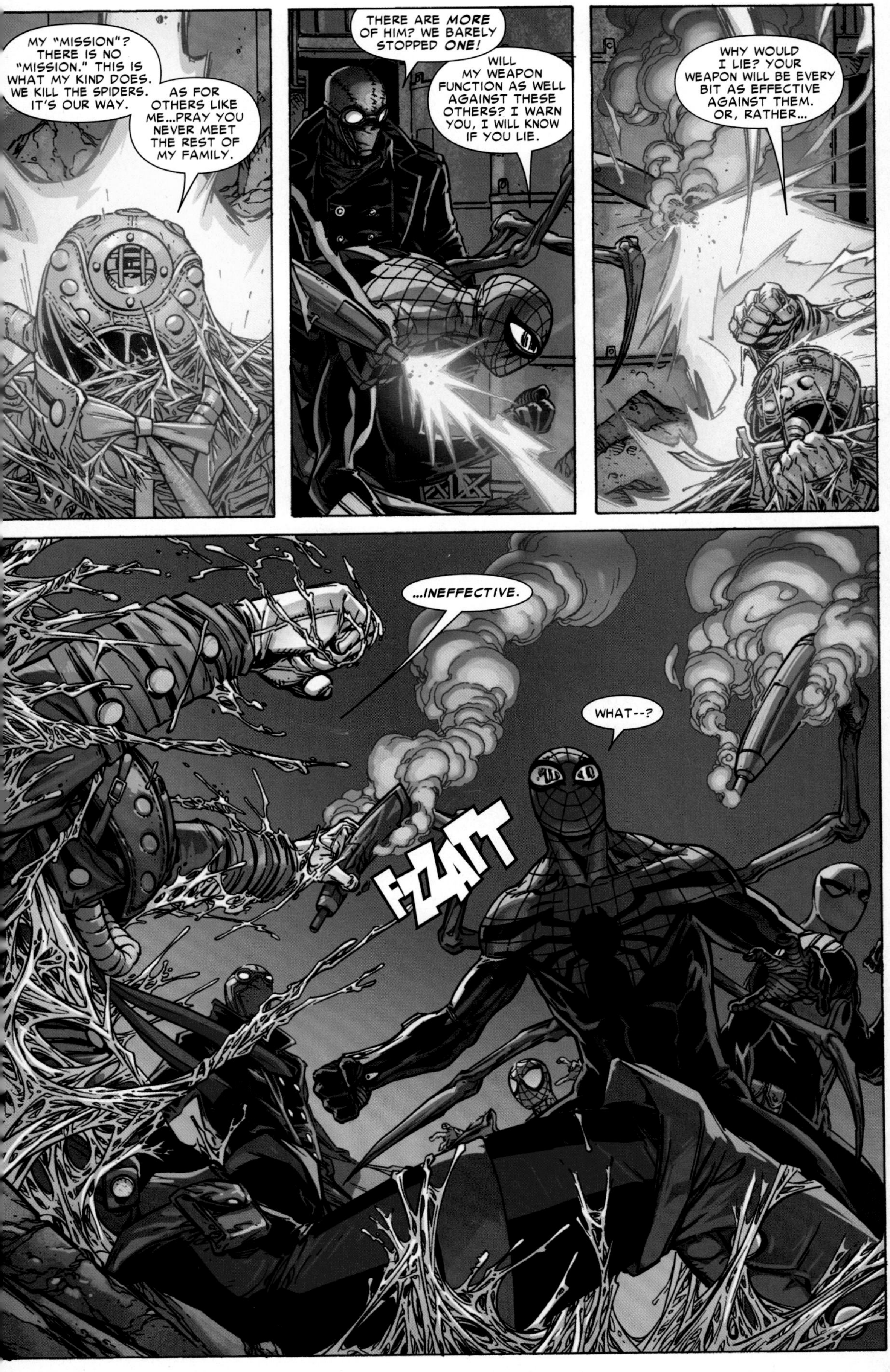
MY "MISSION"? THERE IS NO "MISSION." THIS IS WHAT MY KIND DOES. WE KILL THE SPIDERS. IT'S OUR WAY.
AS FOR OTHERS LIKE ME...PRAY YOU NEVER MEET THE REST OF MY FAMILY.
THERE ARE MORE OF HIM? WE BARELY STOPPED ONE!
WILL MY WEAPON FUNCTION AS WELL AGAINST THESE OTHERS? I WARN YOU, I WILL KNOW IF YOU LIE.
WHY WOULD I LIE? YOUR WEAPON WILL BE EVERY BIT AS EFFECTIVE AGAINST THEM. OR, RATHER...
...INEFFECTIVE.
WHAT--?
FZZATT

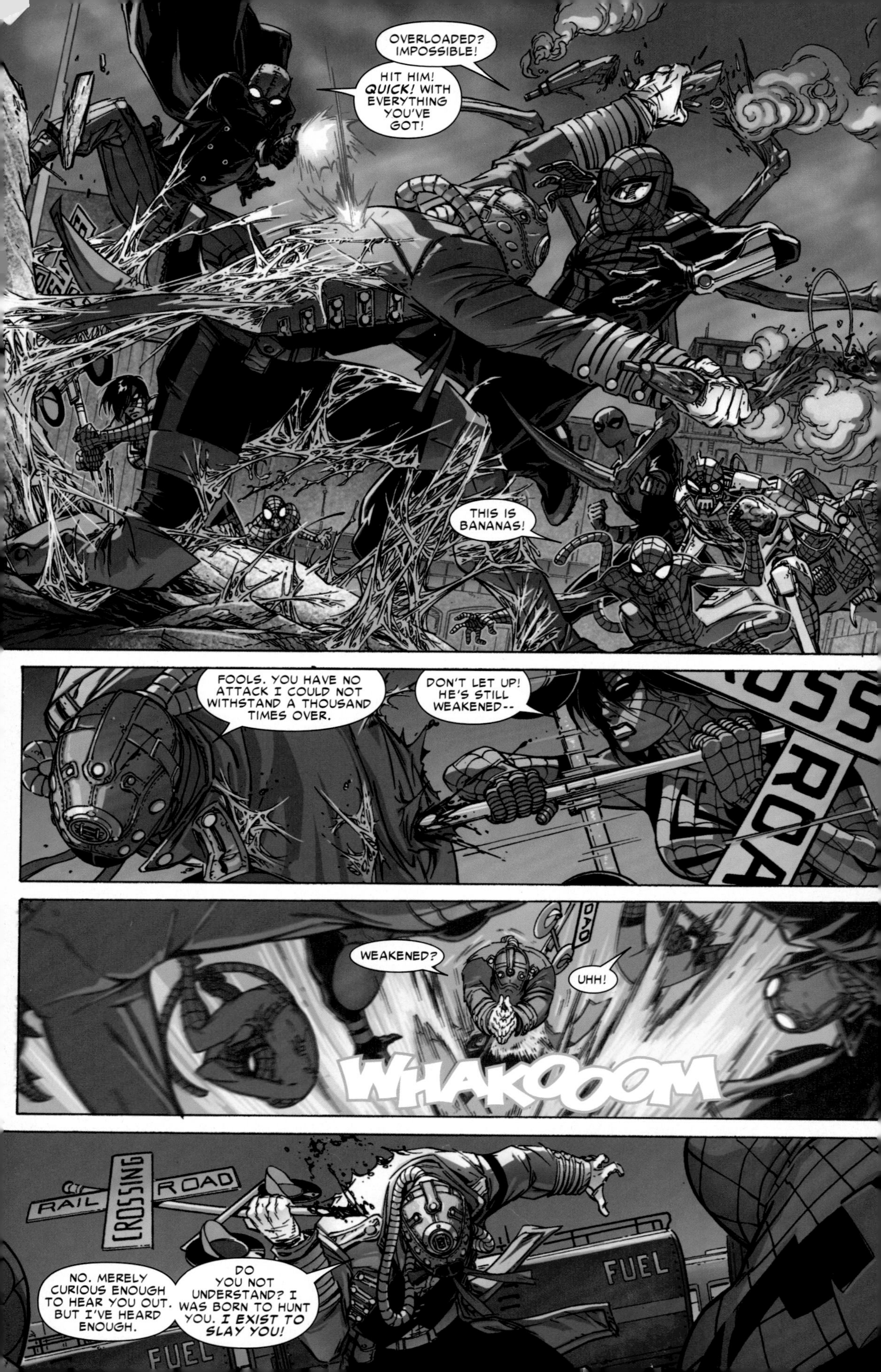
OVERLOADED? IMPOSSIBLE!
HIT HIM! QUICK! WITH EVERYTHING YOU'VE GOT!
THIS IS BANANAS!
FOOLS. YOU HAVE NO ATTACK I COULD NOT WITHSTAND A THOUSAND TIMES OVER.
DON'T LET UP! HE'S STILL WEAKENED--
WEAKENED?
UHH!
WHAKOOOM
RAIL
CROSSING
ROAD
FUEL
NO. MERELY CURIOUS ENOUGH TO HEAR YOU OUT. BUT I'VE HEARD ENOUGH.
DO YOU NOT UNDERSTAND? I WAS BORN TO HUNT YOU. I EXIST TO SLAY YOU!

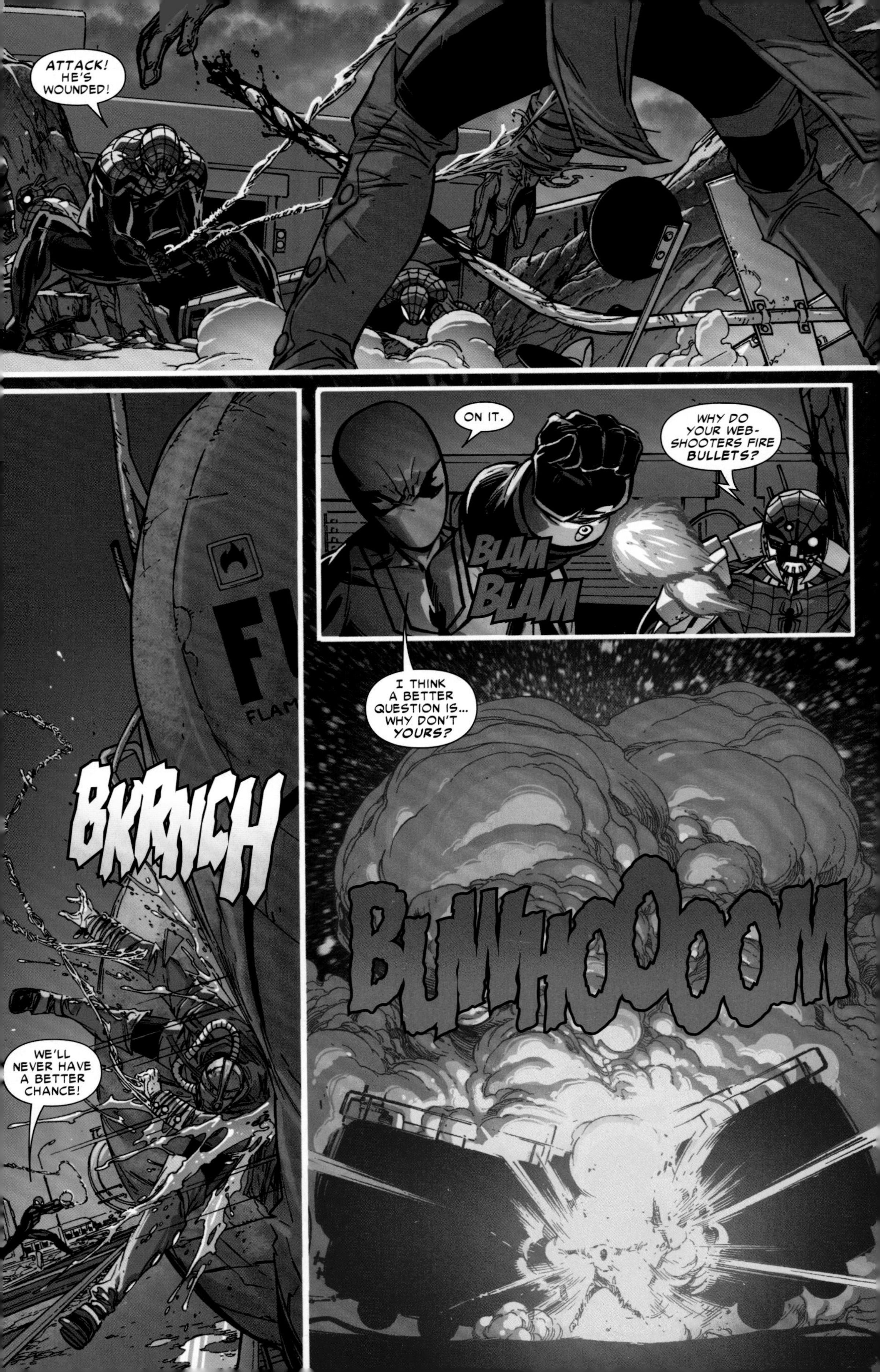
ATTACK! HE'S WOUNDED!
ON IT.
WHY DO YOUR WEB-SHOOTERS FIRE BULLETS?
BLAM
BLAM
I THINK A BETTER QUESTION IS... WHY DON'T YOURS?
FLAM
BKRNCH
BUMHOOOOM
WE'LL NEVER HAVE A BETTER CHANCE!

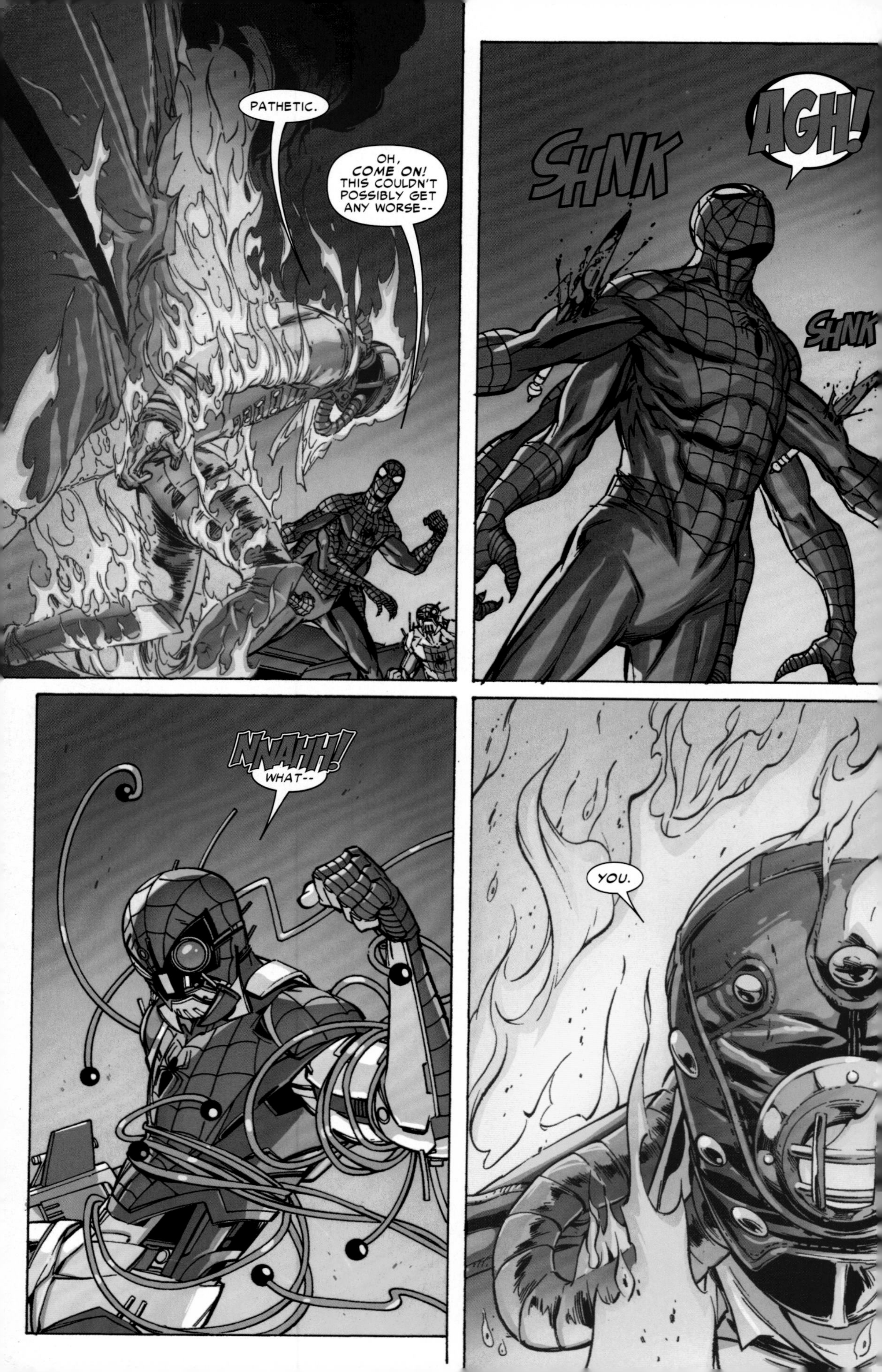
PATHETIC.
OH, COME ON! THIS COULDN'T POSSIBLY GET ANY WORSE--
SHNK
AGH!
SHNK
NNAHH!
WHAT--
YOU.

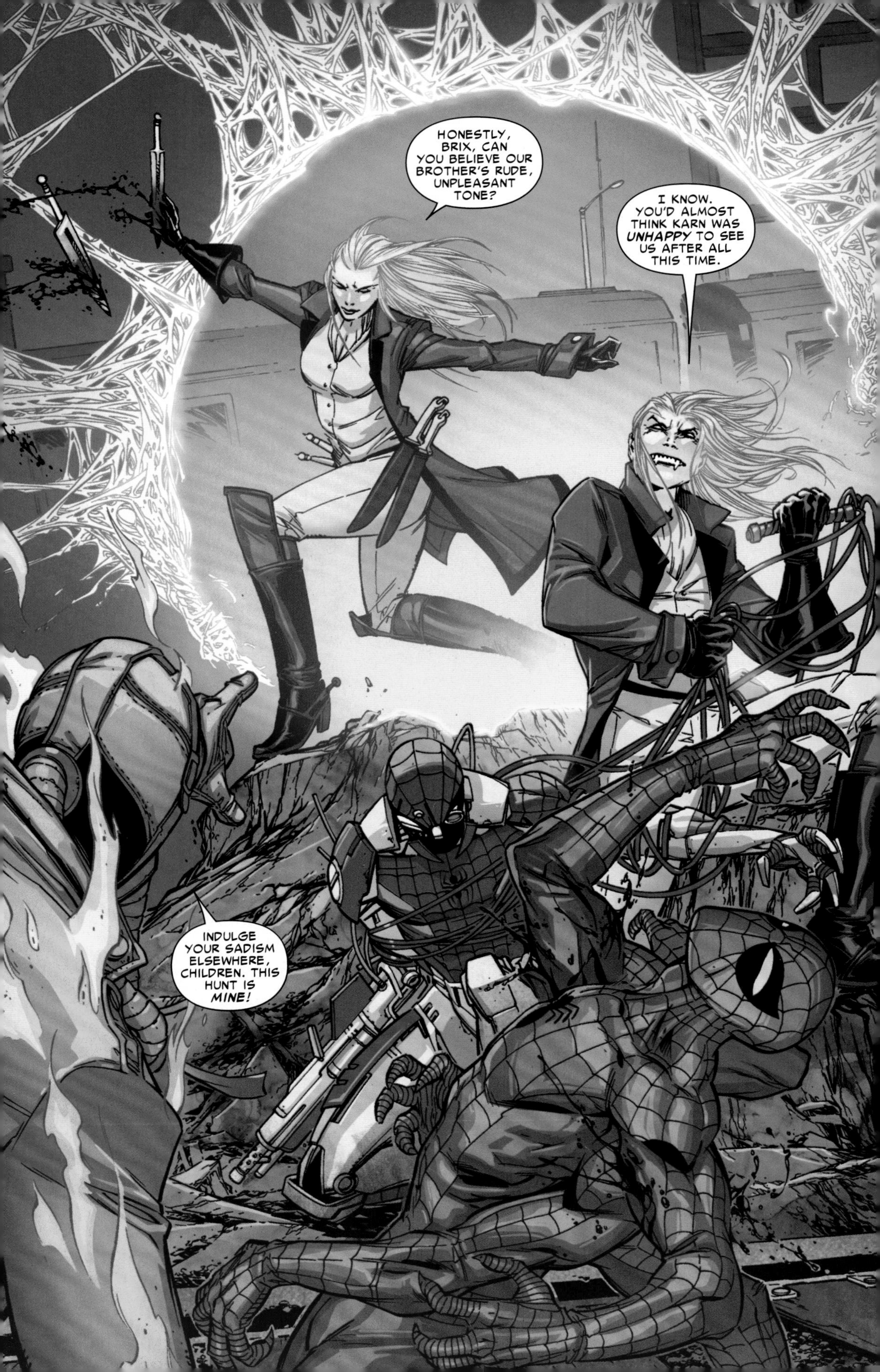
HONESTLY, BRIX, CAN YOU BELIEVE OUR BROTHER'S RUDE, UNPLEASANT TONE?
I KNOW. YOU'D ALMOST THINK KARN WAS *UNHAPPY* TO SEE US AFTER ALL THIS TIME.
INDULGE YOUR SADISM ELSEWHERE, CHILDREN. THIS HUNT IS *MINE!*

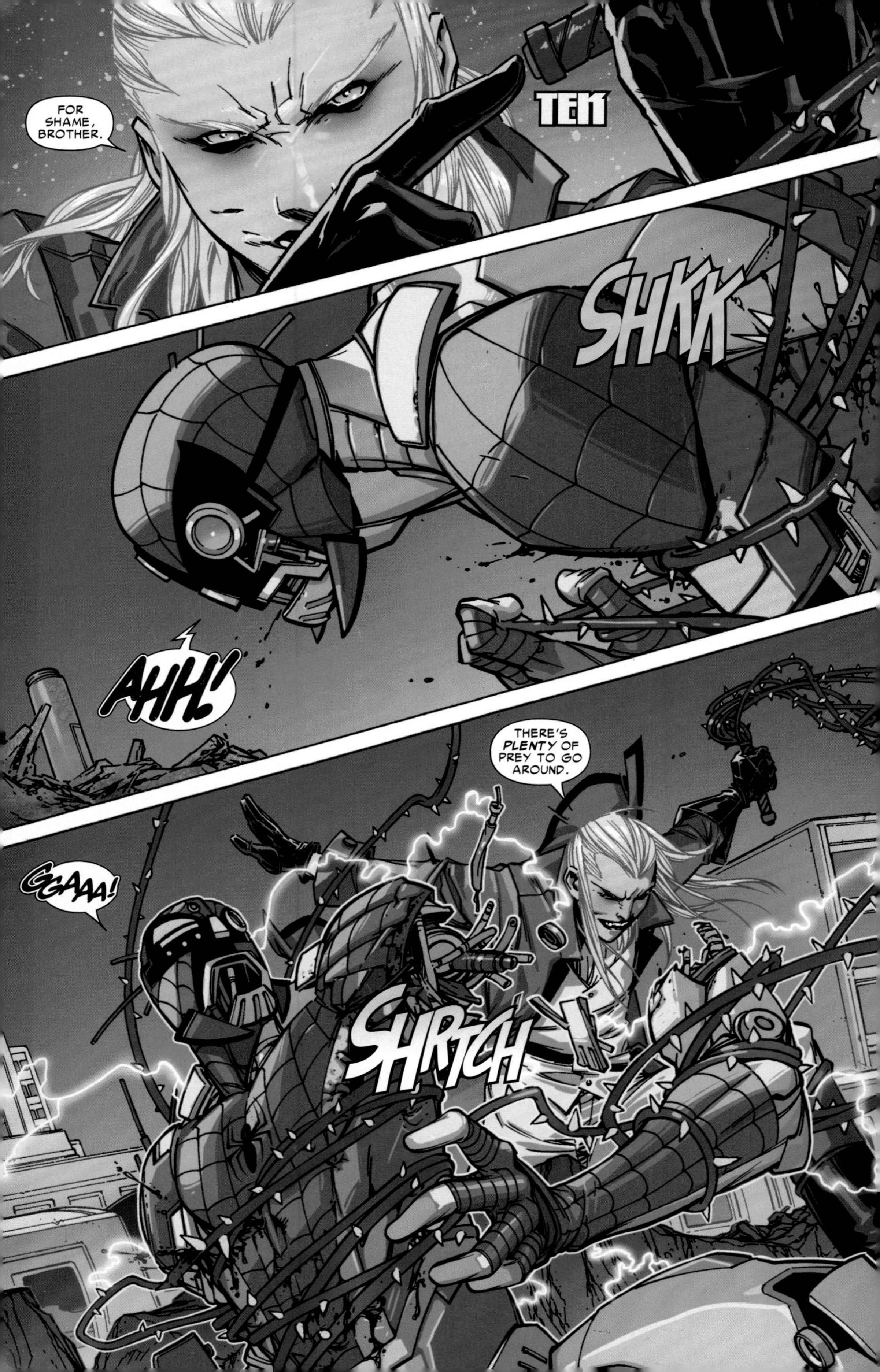
FOR SHAME, BROTHER.
TEK
SHKK
AHH!
THERE'S PLENTY OF PREY TO GO AROUND.
GGAAA!
SHRTCH

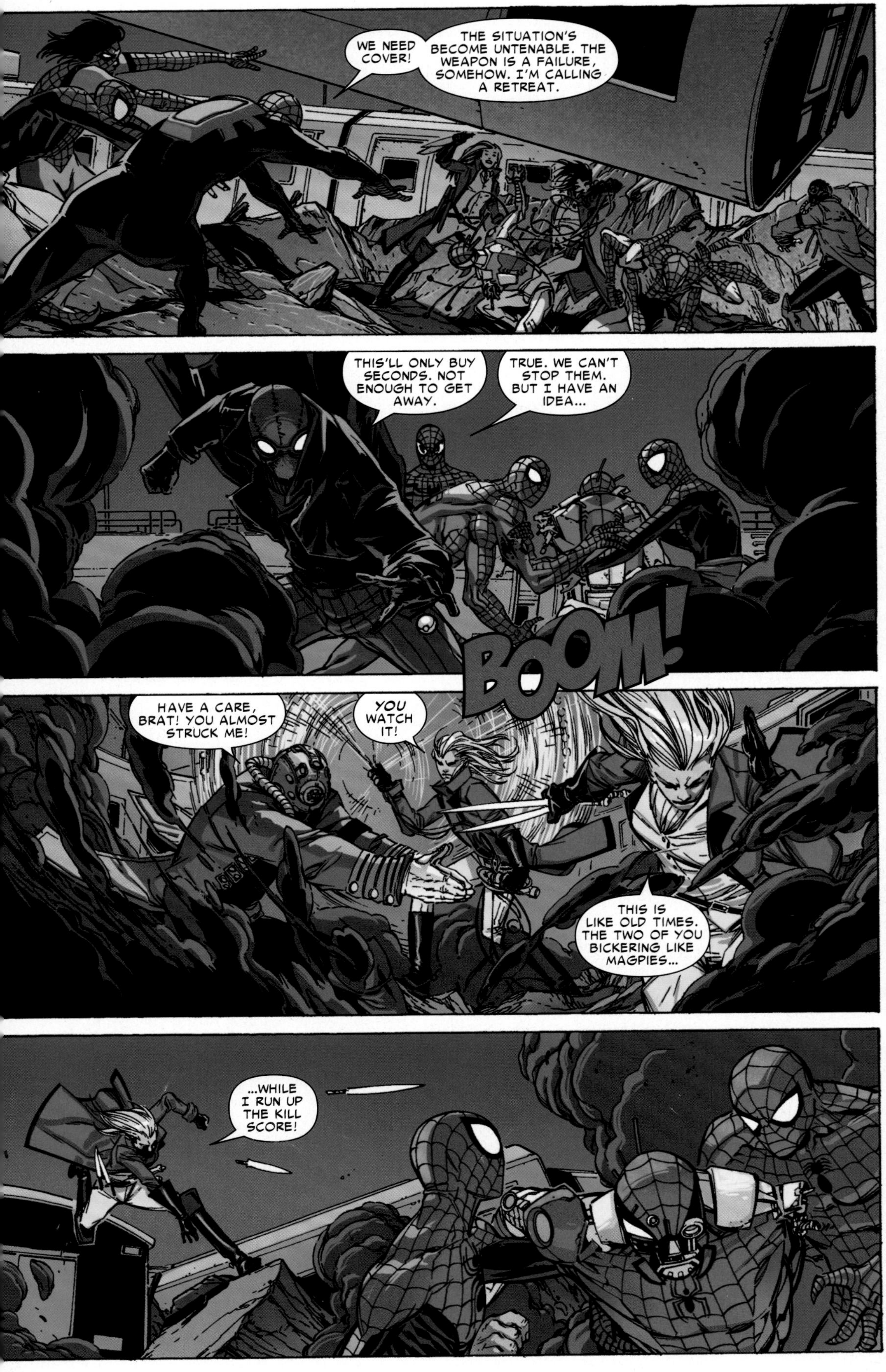
WE NEED COVER!
THE SITUATION'S BECOME UNTENABLE. THE WEAPON IS A FAILURE, SOMEHOW. I'M CALLING A RETREAT.
THIS'LL ONLY BUY SECONDS. NOT ENOUGH TO GET AWAY.
TRUE. WE CAN'T STOP THEM. BUT I HAVE AN IDEA...
BOOM!
HAVE A CARE, BRAT! YOU ALMOST STRUCK ME!
YOU WATCH IT!
THIS IS LIKE OLD TIMES. THE TWO OF YOU BICKERING LIKE MAGPIES...
...WHILE I RUN UP THE KILL SCORE!

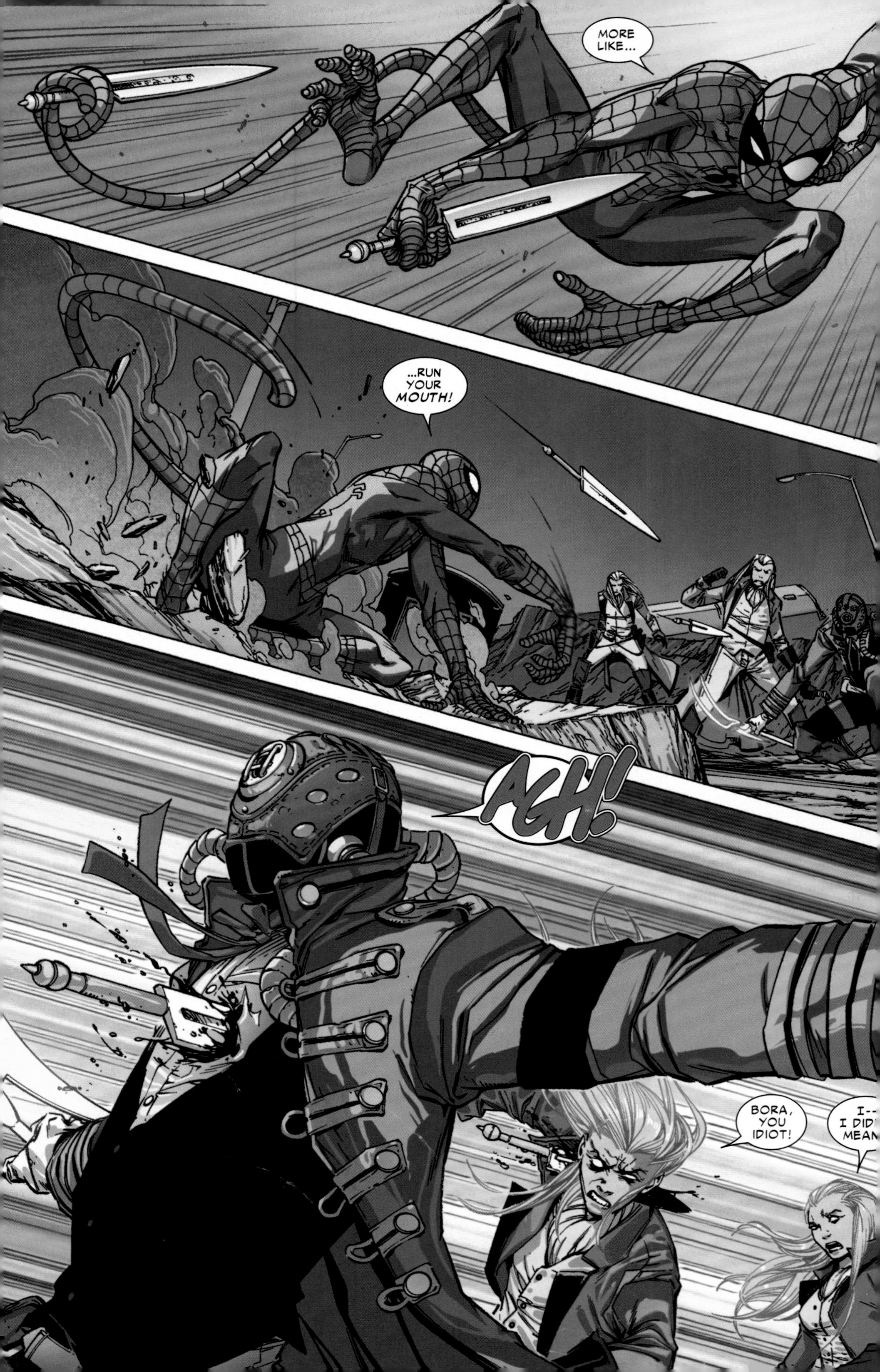

MORE LIKE...
...RUN YOUR MOUTH!
AGH!
BORA, YOU IDIOT!
I-- I DID MEAN

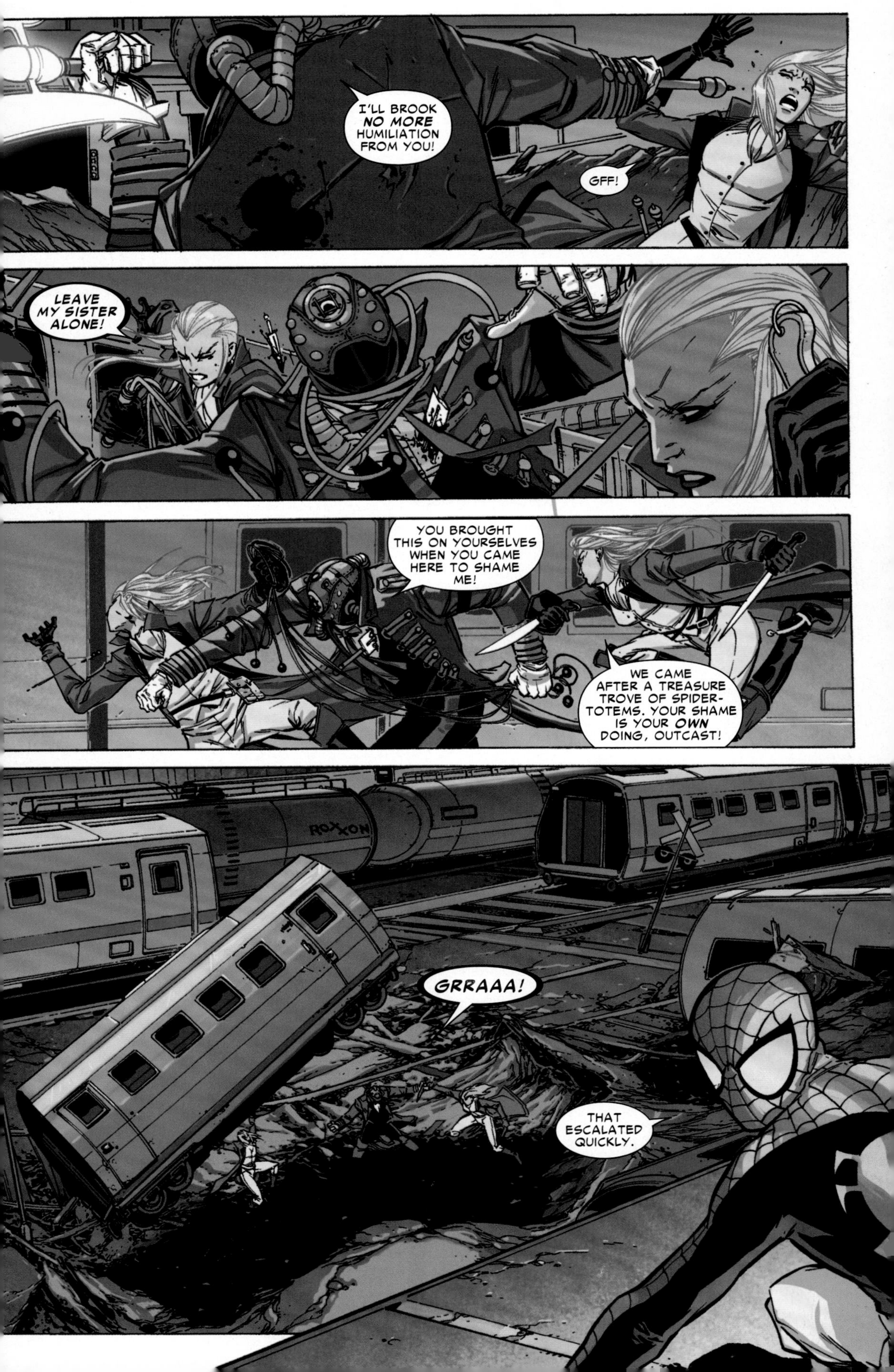
I'LL BROOK NO MORE HUMILIATION FROM YOU!
GFF!
LEAVE MY SISTER ALONE!
YOU BROUGHT THIS ON YOURSELVES WHEN YOU CAME HERE TO SHAME ME!
WE CAME AFTER A TREASURE TROVE OF SPIDER-TOTEMS. YOUR SHAME IS YOUR OWN DOING, OUTCAST!
ROXXON
GRRAAA!
THAT ESCALATED QUICKLY.

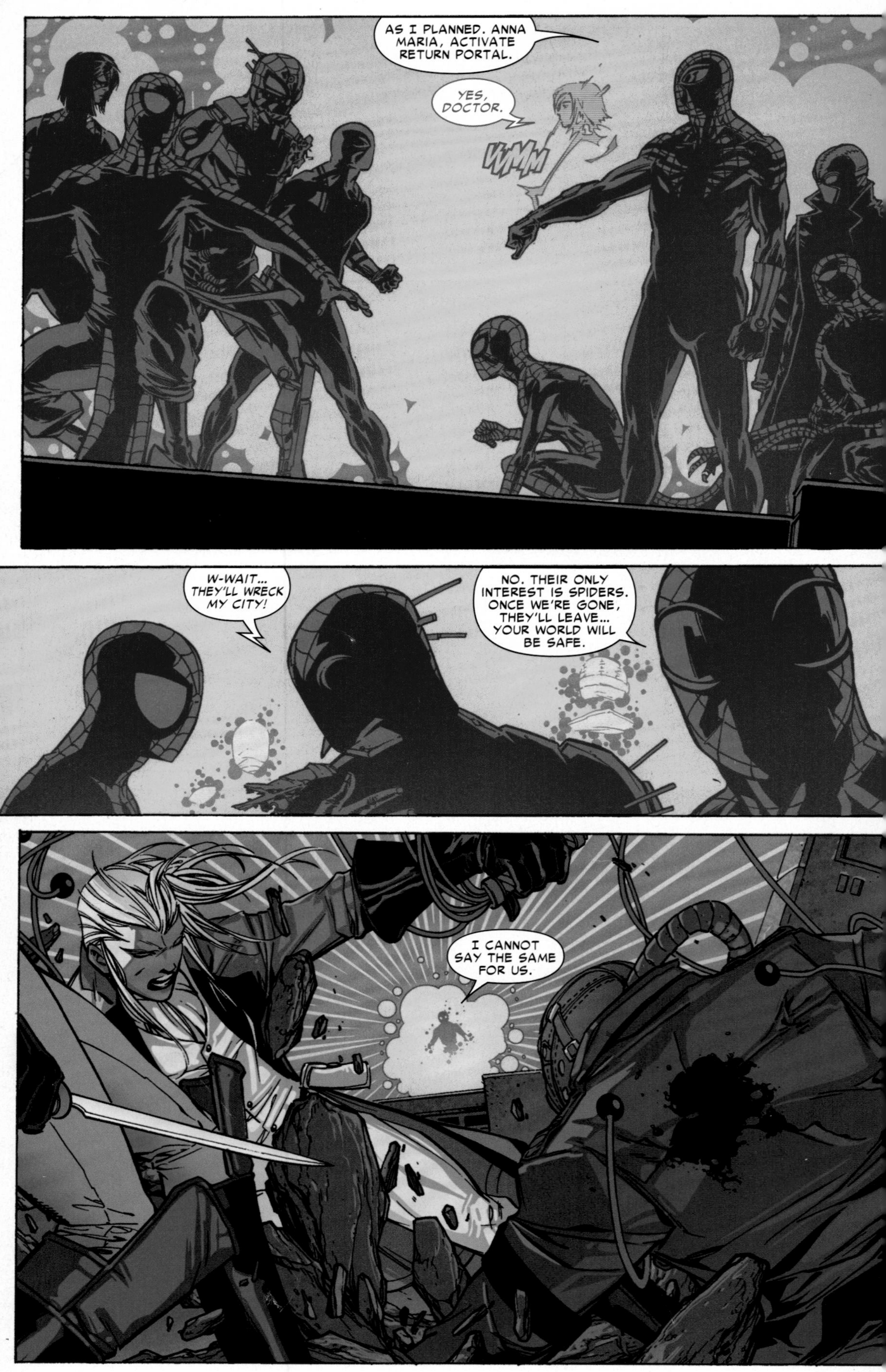
AS I PLANNED. ANNA MARIA, ACTIVATE RETURN PORTAL.
YES, DOCTOR.
VWMM
W-WAIT... THEY'LL WRECK MY CITY!
NO. THEIR ONLY INTEREST IS SPIDERS. ONCE WE'RE GONE, THEY'LL LEAVE... YOUR WORLD WILL BE SAFE.
I CANNOT SAY THE SAME FOR US.

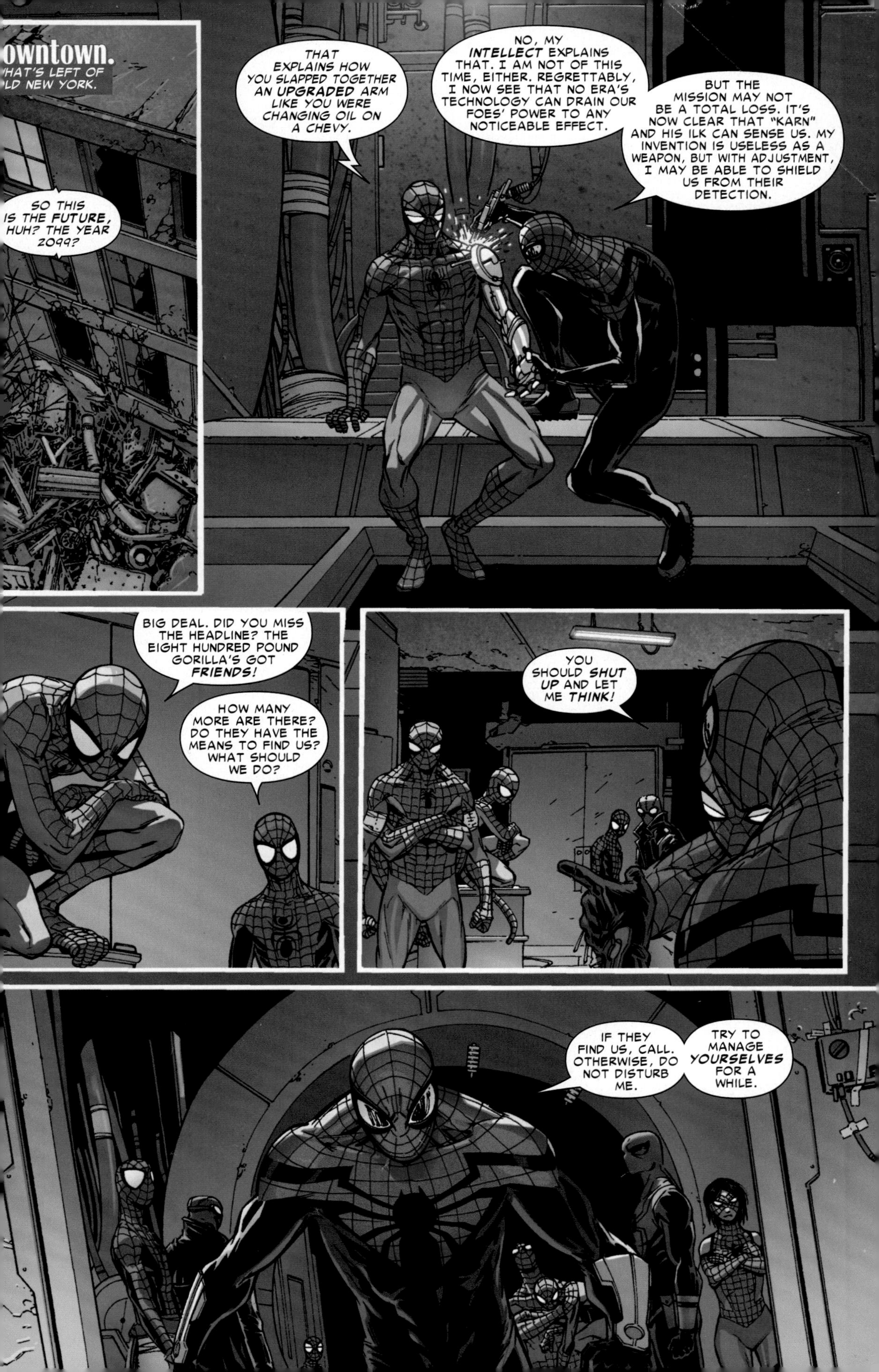

...OWNTOWN.
...HAT'S LEFT OF
...LD NEW YORK.
SO THIS IS THE FUTURE, HUH? THE YEAR 2099?
THAT EXPLAINS HOW YOU SLAPPED TOGETHER AN UPGRADED ARM LIKE YOU WERE CHANGING OIL ON A CHEVY.
NO, MY INTELLECT EXPLAINS THAT. I AM NOT OF THIS TIME, EITHER. REGRETTABLY, I NOW SEE THAT NO ERA'S TECHNOLOGY CAN DRAIN OUR FOES' POWER TO ANY NOTICEABLE EFFECT.
BUT THE MISSION MAY NOT BE A TOTAL LOSS. IT'S NOW CLEAR THAT "KARN" AND HIS ILK CAN SENSE US. MY INVENTION IS USELESS AS A WEAPON, BUT WITH ADJUSTMENT, I MAY BE ABLE TO SHIELD US FROM THEIR DETECTION.
BIG DEAL. DID YOU MISS THE HEADLINE? THE EIGHT HUNDRED POUND GORILLA'S GOT FRIENDS!
HOW MANY MORE ARE THERE? DO THEY HAVE THE MEANS TO FIND US? WHAT SHOULD WE DO?
YOU SHOULD SHUT UP AND LET ME THINK!
IF THEY FIND US, CALL. OTHERWISE, DO NOT DISTURB ME.
TRY TO MANAGE YOURSELVES FOR A WHILE.

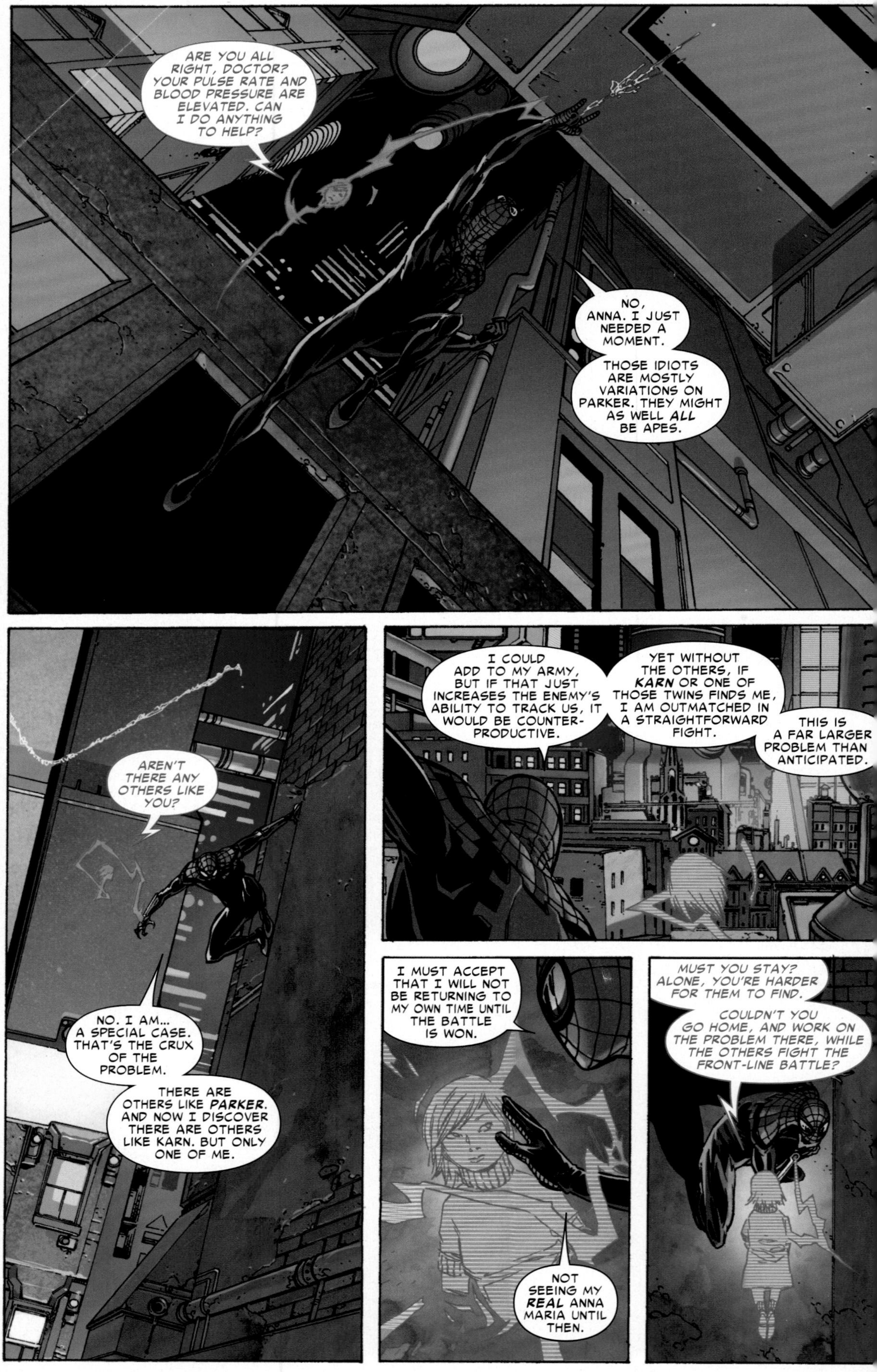
ARE YOU ALL RIGHT, DOCTOR? YOUR PULSE RATE AND BLOOD PRESSURE ARE ELEVATED. CAN I DO ANYTHING TO HELP?
NO, ANNA. I JUST NEEDED A MOMENT.
THOSE IDIOTS ARE MOSTLY VARIATIONS ON PARKER. THEY MIGHT AS WELL ALL BE APES.
AREN'T THERE ANY OTHERS LIKE YOU?
NO. I AM... A SPECIAL CASE. THAT'S THE CRUX OF THE PROBLEM.
THERE ARE OTHERS LIKE PARKER. AND NOW I DISCOVER THERE ARE OTHERS LIKE KARN. BUT ONLY ONE OF ME.
I COULD ADD TO MY ARMY, BUT IF THAT JUST INCREASES THE ENEMY'S ABILITY TO TRACK US, IT WOULD BE COUNTER-PRODUCTIVE.
YET WITHOUT THE OTHERS, IF KARN OR ONE OF THOSE TWINS FINDS ME, I AM OUTMATCHED IN A STRAIGHTFORWARD FIGHT.
THIS IS A FAR LARGER PROBLEM THAN ANTICIPATED.
I MUST ACCEPT THAT I WILL NOT BE RETURNING TO MY OWN TIME UNTIL THE BATTLE IS WON.
NOT SEEING MY REAL ANNA MARIA UNTIL THEN.
MUST YOU STAY? ALONE, YOU'RE HARDER FOR THEM TO FIND.
COULDN'T YOU GO HOME, AND WORK ON THE PROBLEM THERE, WHILE THE OTHERS FIGHT THE FRONT-LINE BATTLE?

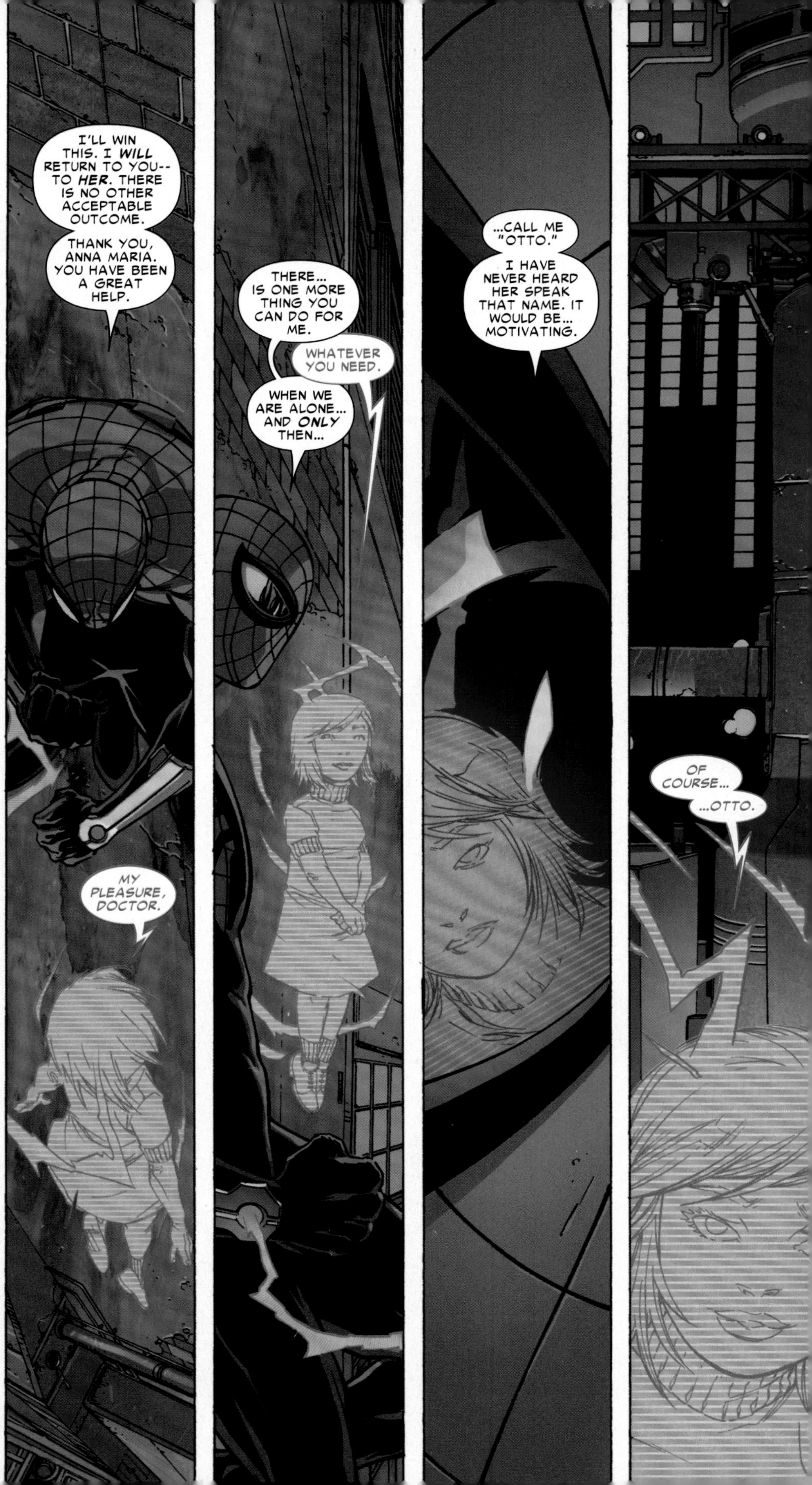
I'LL WIN THIS. I WILL RETURN TO YOU-- TO HER. THERE IS NO OTHER ACCEPTABLE OUTCOME.
THANK YOU, ANNA MARIA. YOU HAVE BEEN A GREAT HELP.
MY PLEASURE, DOCTOR.
THERE... IS ONE MORE THING YOU CAN DO FOR ME.
WHATEVER YOU NEED.
WHEN WE ARE ALONE... AND ONLY THEN...
...CALL ME "OTTO."
I HAVE NEVER HEARD HER SPEAK THAT NAME. IT WOULD BE... MOTIVATING.
OF COURSE...
...OTTO.

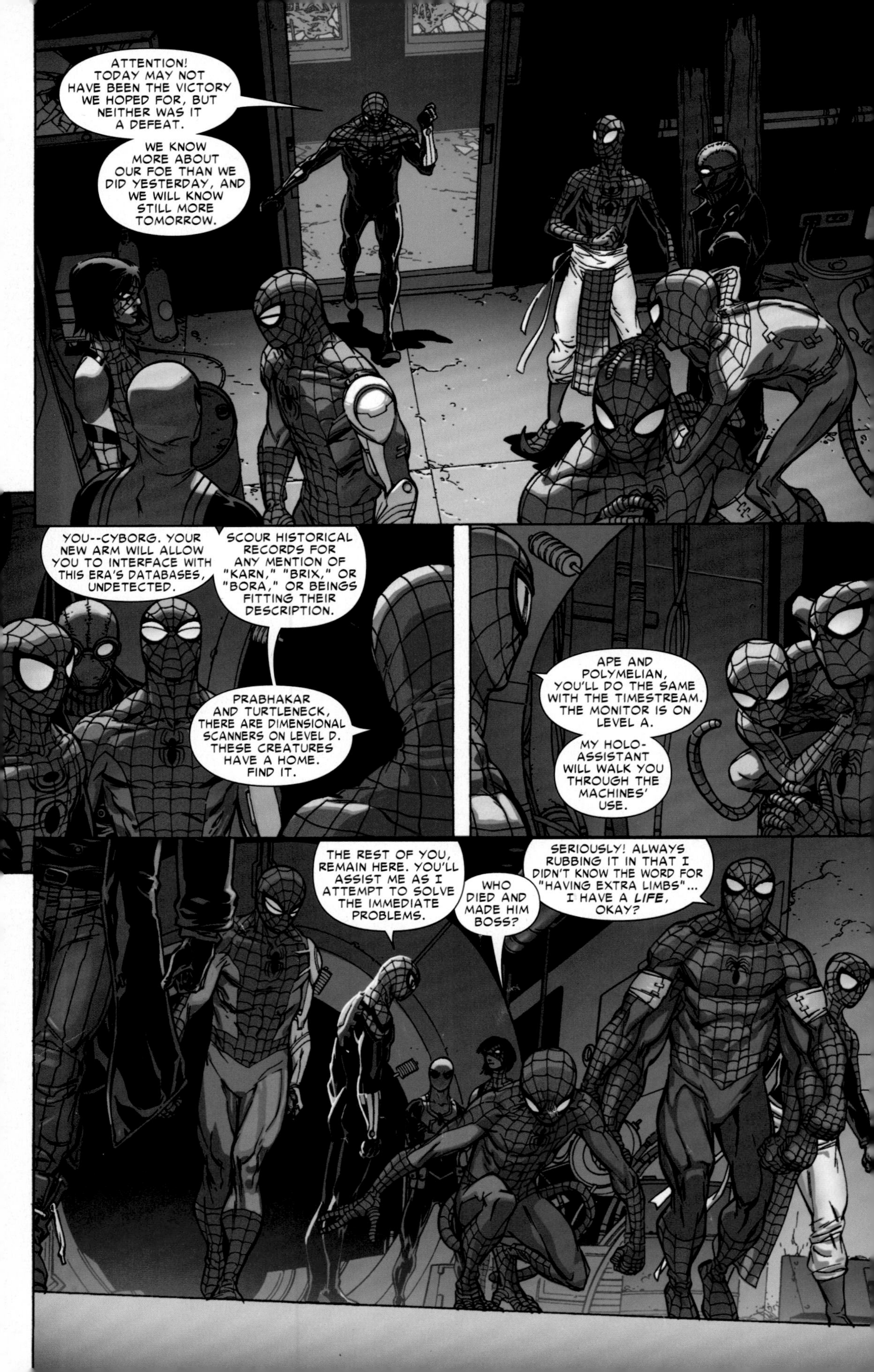
ATTENTION! TODAY MAY NOT HAVE BEEN THE VICTORY WE HOPED FOR, BUT NEITHER WAS IT A DEFEAT.
WE KNOW MORE ABOUT OUR FOE THAN WE DID YESTERDAY, AND WE WILL KNOW STILL MORE TOMORROW.
YOU--CYBORG. YOUR NEW ARM WILL ALLOW YOU TO INTERFACE WITH THIS ERA'S DATABASES, UNDETECTED.
SCOUR HISTORICAL RECORDS FOR ANY MENTION OF "KARN," "BRIX," OR "BORA," OR BEINGS FITTING THEIR DESCRIPTION.
PRABHAKAR AND TURTLENECK, THERE ARE DIMENSIONAL SCANNERS ON LEVEL D. THESE CREATURES HAVE A HOME. FIND IT.
APE AND POLYMELIAN, YOU'LL DO THE SAME WITH THE TIMESTREAM. THE MONITOR IS ON LEVEL A.
MY HOLO-ASSISTANT WILL WALK YOU THROUGH THE MACHINES' USE.
THE REST OF YOU, REMAIN HERE. YOU'LL ASSIST ME AS I ATTEMPT TO SOLVE THE IMMEDIATE PROBLEMS.
WHO DIED AND MADE HIM BOSS?
SERIOUSLY! ALWAYS RUBBING IT IN THAT I DIDN'T KNOW THE WORD FOR "HAVING EXTRA LIMBS"... I HAVE A LIFE, OKAY?

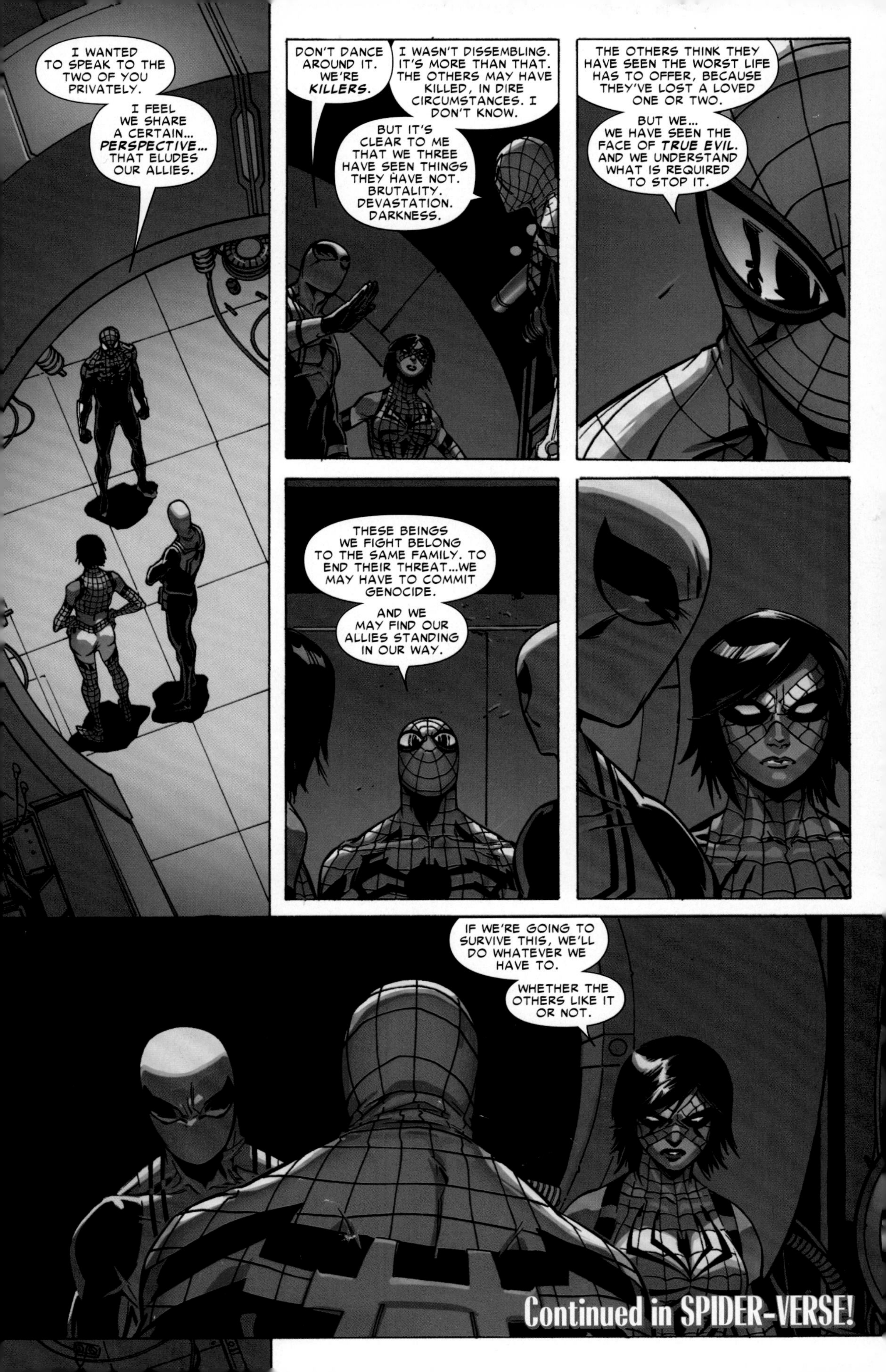
I WANTED TO SPEAK TO THE TWO OF YOU PRIVATELY.
I FEEL WE SHARE A CERTAIN... PERSPECTIVE... THAT ELUDES OUR ALLIES.
DON'T DANCE AROUND IT. WE'RE KILLERS.
I WASN'T DISSEMBLING. IT'S MORE THAN THAT. THE OTHERS MAY HAVE KILLED, IN DIRE CIRCUMSTANCES. I DON'T KNOW.
BUT IT'S CLEAR TO ME THAT WE THREE HAVE SEEN THINGS THEY HAVE NOT. BRUTALITY. DEVASTATION. DARKNESS.
THE OTHERS THINK THEY HAVE SEEN THE WORST LIFE HAS TO OFFER, BECAUSE THEY'VE LOST A LOVED ONE OR TWO.
BUT WE... WE HAVE SEEN THE FACE OF TRUE EVIL. AND WE UNDERSTAND WHAT IS REQUIRED TO STOP IT.
THESE BEINGS WE FIGHT BELONG TO THE SAME FAMILY. TO END THEIR THREAT...WE MAY HAVE TO COMMIT GENOCIDE.
AND WE MAY FIND OUR ALLIES STANDING IN OUR WAY.
IF WE'RE GOING TO SURVIVE THIS, WE'LL DO WHATEVER WE HAVE TO.
WHETHER THE OTHERS LIKE IT OR NOT.
Continued in SPIDER-VERSE!

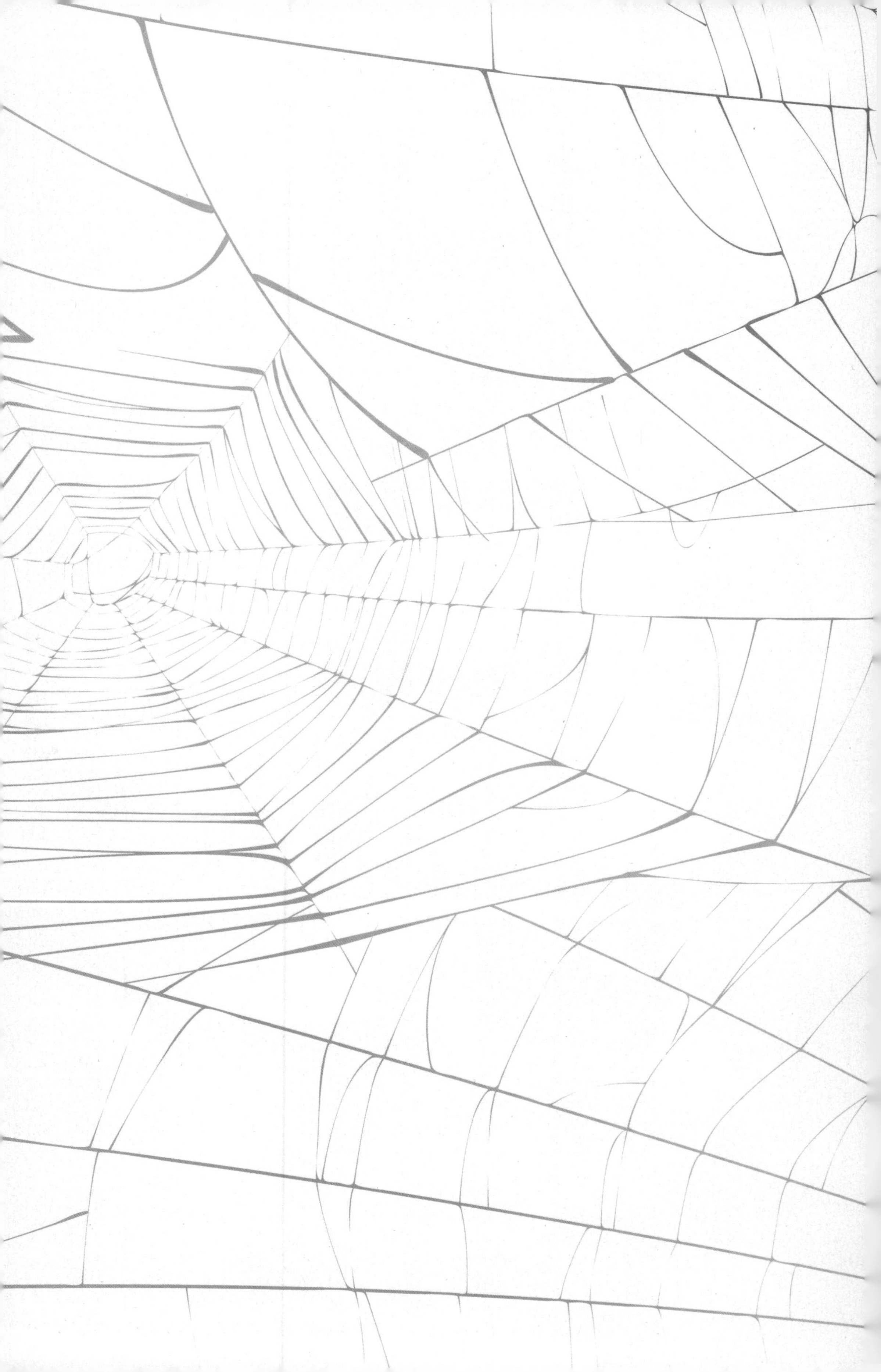

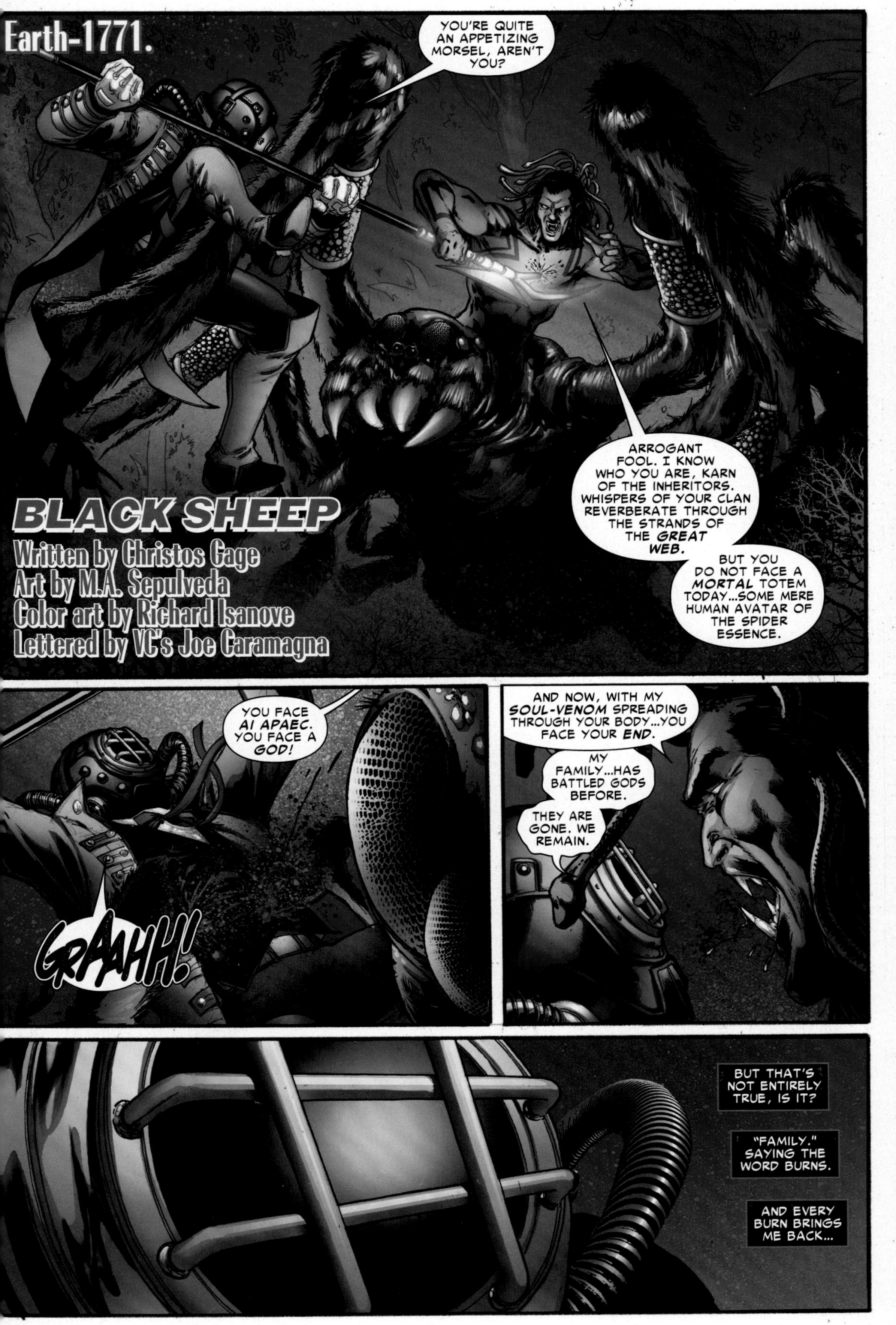
Earth-1771.
YOU'RE QUITE AN APPETIZING MORSEL, AREN'T YOU?
ARROGANT FOOL. I KNOW WHO YOU ARE, KARN OF THE INHERITORS. WHISPERS OF YOUR CLAN REVERBERATE THROUGH THE STRANDS OF THE GREAT WEB.
BUT YOU DO NOT FACE A MORTAL TOTEM TODAY...SOME MERE HUMAN AVATAR OF THE SPIDER ESSENCE.
BLACK SHEEP
Written by Christos Gage
Art by M.A. Sepulveda
Color art by Richard Isanove
Lettered by VC's Joe Caramagna
YOU FACE AI APAEC. YOU FACE A GOD!
GRAAHH!
AND NOW, WITH MY SOUL-VENOM SPREADING THROUGH YOUR BODY...YOU FACE YOUR END.
MY FAMILY...HAS BATTLED GODS BEFORE.
THEY ARE GONE. WE REMAIN.
BUT THAT'S NOT ENTIRELY TRUE, IS IT?
"FAMILY." SAYING THE WORD BURNS.
AND EVERY BURN BRINGS ME BACK...

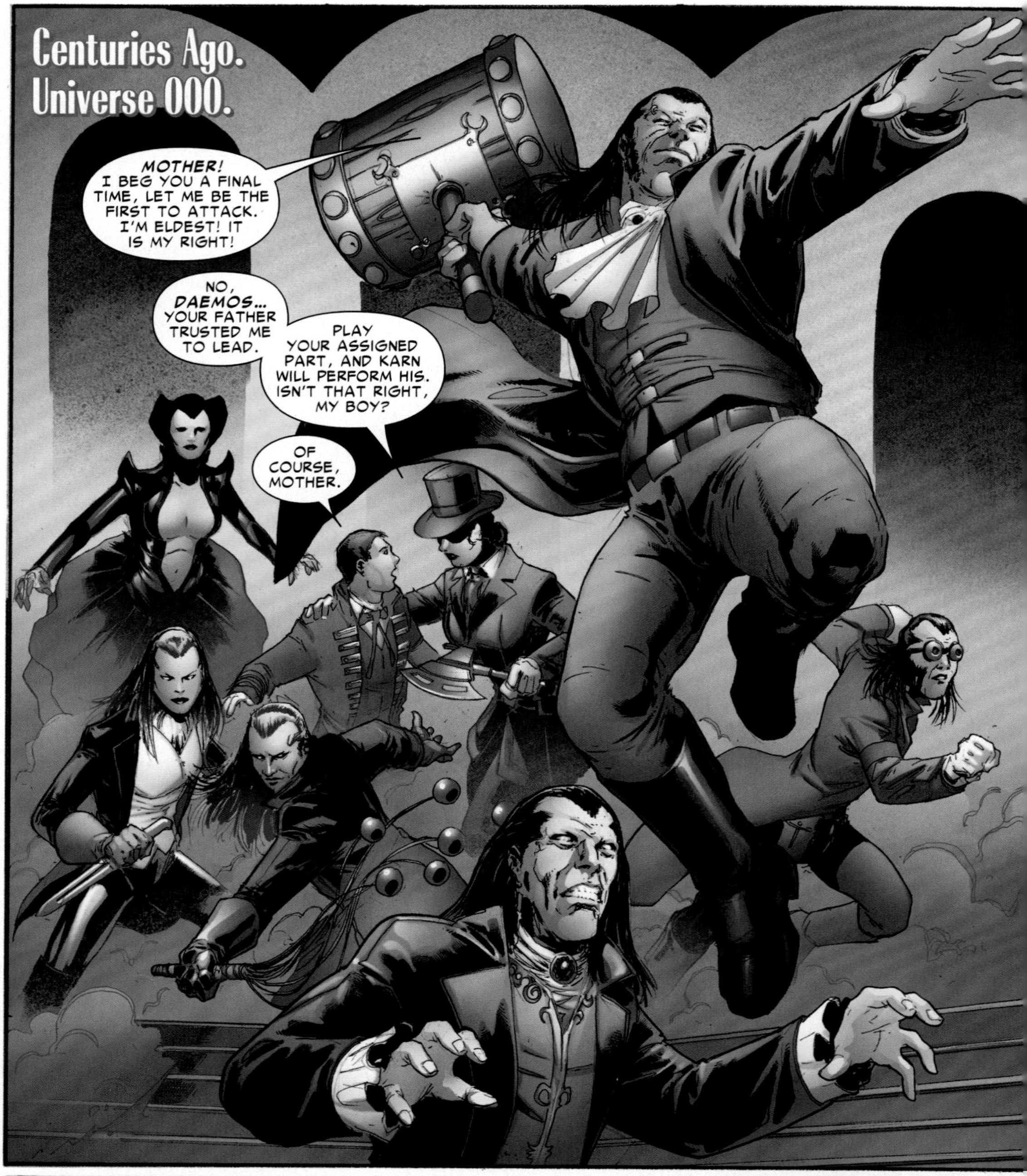
Centuries Ago.
Universe 000.
MOTHER! I BEG YOU A FINAL TIME, LET ME BE THE FIRST TO ATTACK. I'M ELDEST! IT IS MY RIGHT!
NO, DAEMOS... YOUR FATHER TRUSTED ME TO LEAD.
PLAY YOUR ASSIGNED PART, AND KARN WILL PERFORM HIS. ISN'T THAT RIGHT, MY BOY?
OF COURSE, MOTHER.

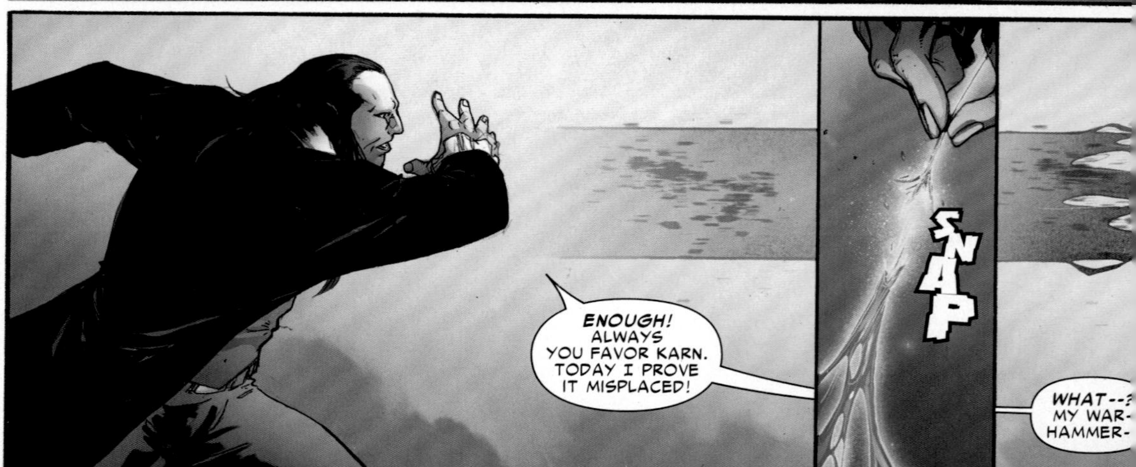
ENOUGH! ALWAYS YOU FAVOR KARN. TODAY I PROVE IT MISPLACED!
SNAP
WHAT--? MY WAR-HAMMER-

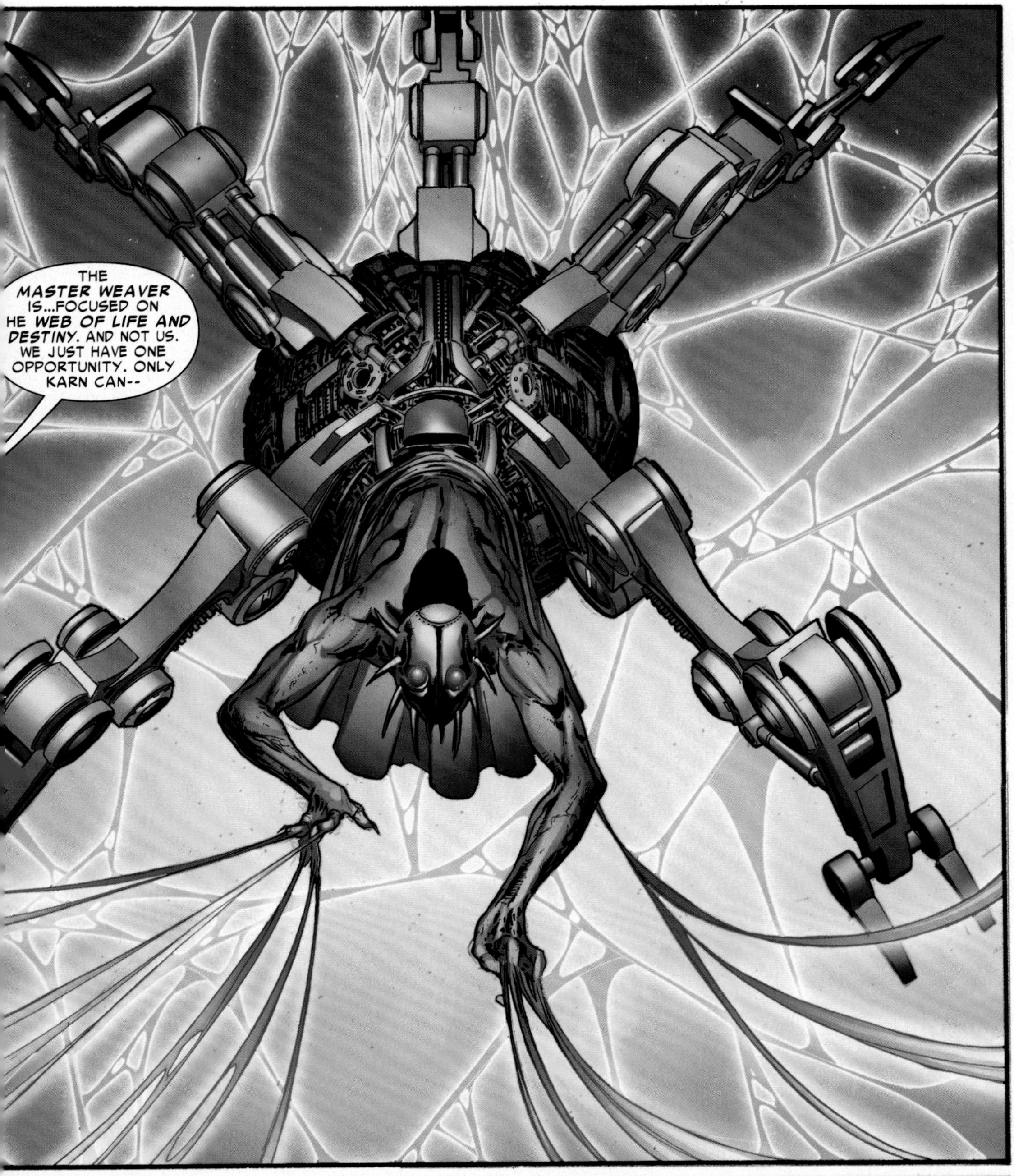
THE MASTER WEAVER IS...FOCUSED ON HE WEB OF LIFE AND DESTINY. AND NOT US. WE JUST HAVE ONE OPPORTUNITY. ONLY KARN CAN--

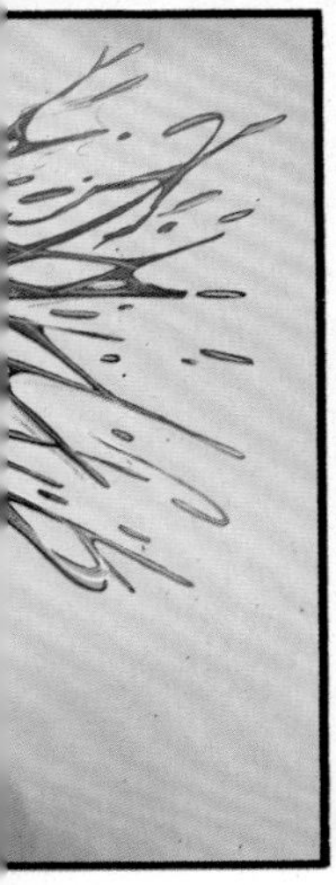

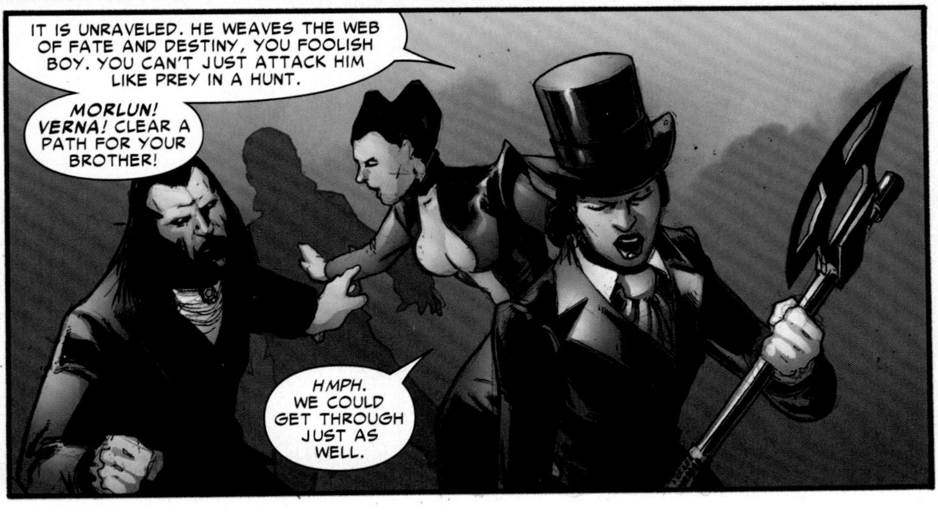
IT IS UNRAVELED. HE WEAVES THE WEB OF FATE AND DESTINY, YOU FOOLISH BOY. YOU CAN'T JUST ATTACK HIM LIKE PREY IN A HUNT.
MORLUN! VERNA! CLEAR A PATH FOR YOUR BROTHER!
HMPH. WE COULD GET THROUGH JUST AS WELL.

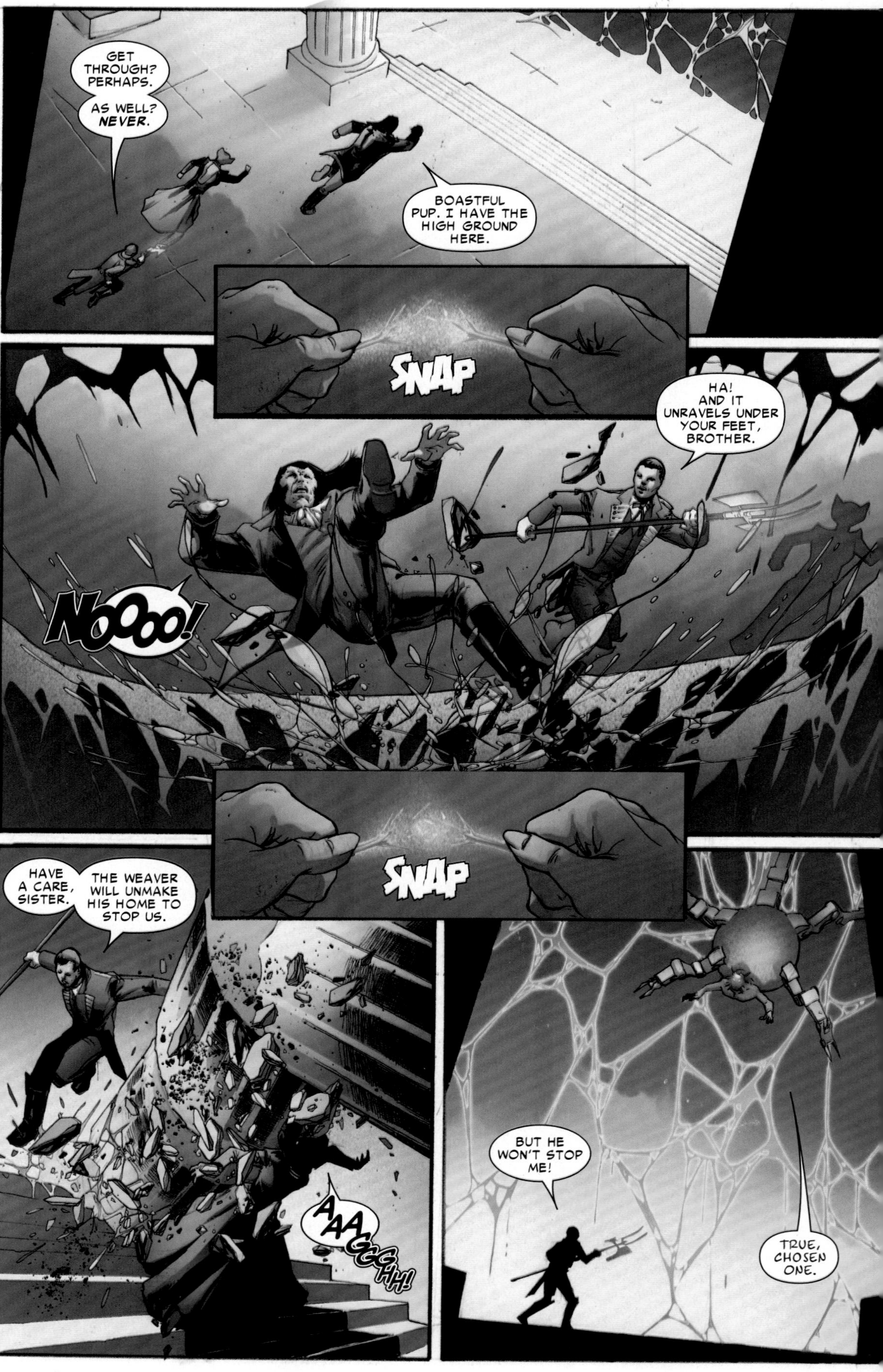
GET THROUGH? PERHAPS.
AS WELL? NEVER.
BOASTFUL PUP. I HAVE THE HIGH GROUND HERE.
SNAP
HA! AND IT UNRAVELS UNDER YOUR FEET, BROTHER.
NOOOO!
SNAP
HAVE A CARE, SISTER.
THE WEAVER WILL UNMAKE HIS HOME TO STOP US.
AAAGGGHH!
BUT HE WON'T STOP ME!
TRUE, CHOSEN ONE.

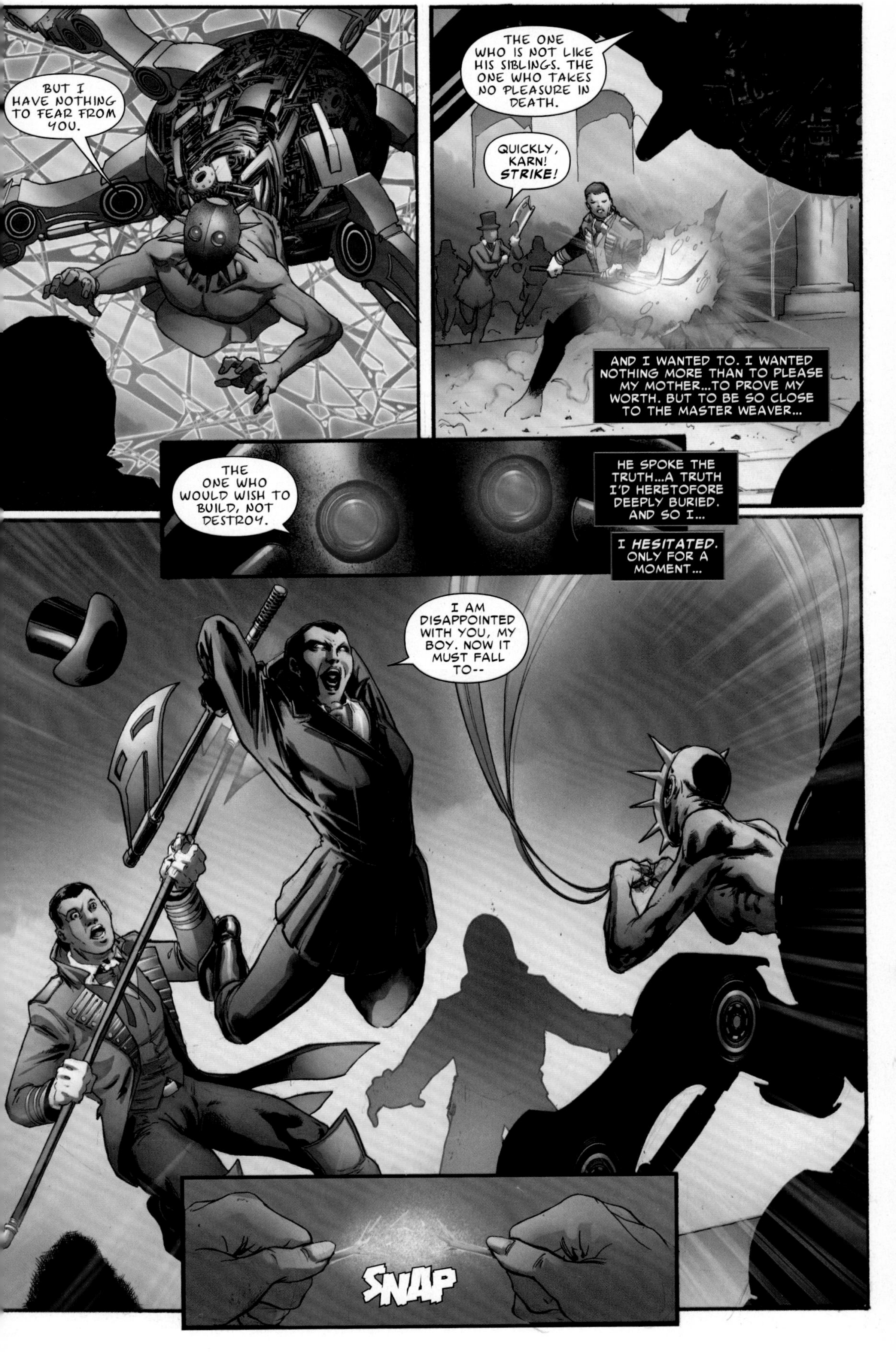
BUT I HAVE NOTHING TO FEAR FROM YOU.
THE ONE WHO IS NOT LIKE HIS SIBLINGS. THE ONE WHO TAKES NO PLEASURE IN DEATH.
QUICKLY, KARN! STRIKE!
AND I WANTED TO. I WANTED NOTHING MORE THAN TO PLEASE MY MOTHER...TO PROVE MY WORTH. BUT TO BE SO CLOSE TO THE MASTER WEAVER...
THE ONE WHO WOULD WISH TO BUILD, NOT DESTROY.
HE SPOKE THE TRUTH...A TRUTH I'D HERETOFORE DEEPLY BURIED. AND SO I...
I HESITATED. ONLY FOR A MOMENT...
I AM DISAPPOINTED WITH YOU, MY BOY. NOW IT MUST FALL TO--
SNAP

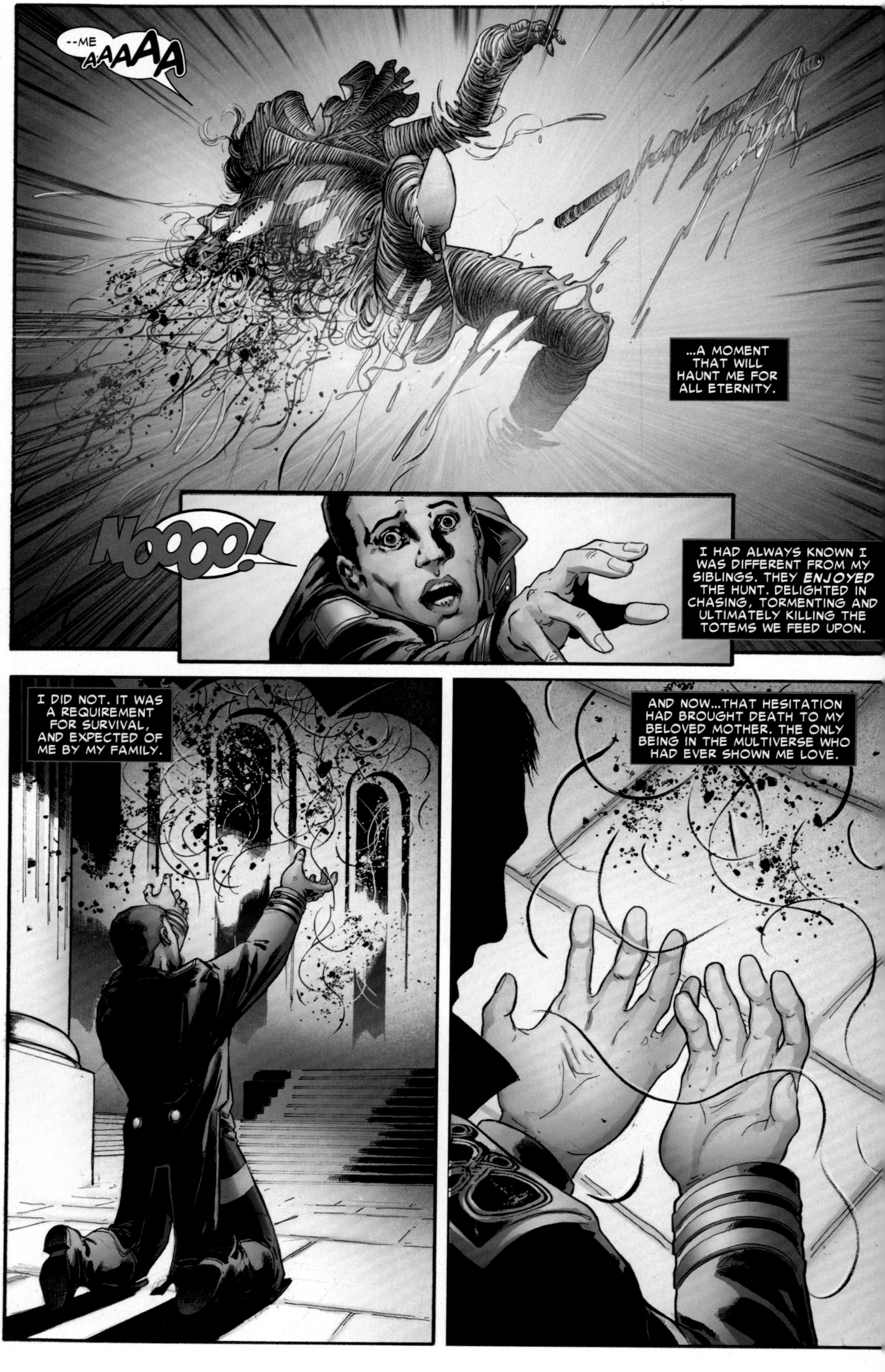

--ME AAAAA
...A MOMENT THAT WILL HAUNT ME FOR ALL ETERNITY.
NOOOO!
I HAD ALWAYS KNOWN I WAS DIFFERENT FROM MY SIBLINGS. THEY ENJOYED THE HUNT. DELIGHTED IN CHASING, TORMENTING AND ULTIMATELY KILLING THE TOTEMS WE FEED UPON.
I DID NOT. IT WAS A REQUIREMENT FOR SURVIVAL, AND EXPECTED OF ME BY MY FAMILY.
AND NOW...THAT HESITATION HAD BROUGHT DEATH TO MY BELOVED MOTHER. THE ONLY BEING IN THE MULTIVERSE WHO HAD EVER SHOWN ME LOVE.

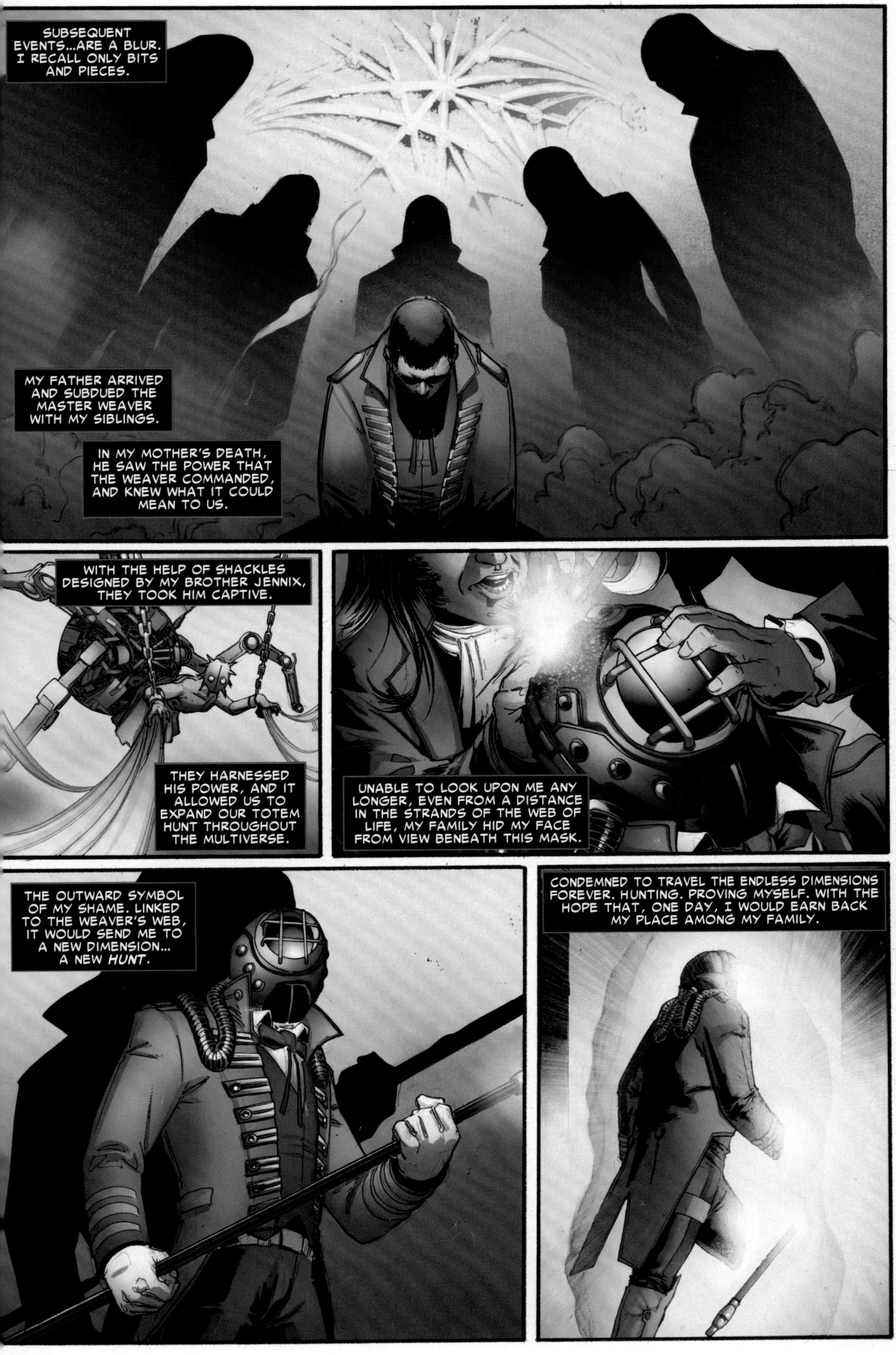
SUBSEQUENT EVENTS...ARE A BLUR. I RECALL ONLY BITS AND PIECES.
MY FATHER ARRIVED AND SUBDUED THE MASTER WEAVER WITH MY SIBLINGS.
IN MY MOTHER'S DEATH, HE SAW THE POWER THAT THE WEAVER COMMANDED, AND KNEW WHAT IT COULD MEAN TO US.
WITH THE HELP OF SHACKLES DESIGNED BY MY BROTHER JENNIX, THEY TOOK HIM CAPTIVE.
THEY HARNESSED HIS POWER, AND IT ALLOWED US TO EXPAND OUR TOTEM HUNT THROUGHOUT THE MULTIVERSE.
UNABLE TO LOOK UPON ME ANY LONGER, EVEN FROM A DISTANCE IN THE STRANDS OF THE WEB OF LIFE, MY FAMILY HID MY FACE FROM VIEW BENEATH THIS MASK.
THE OUTWARD SYMBOL OF MY SHAME. LINKED TO THE WEAVER'S WEB, IT WOULD SEND ME TO A NEW DIMENSION... A NEW HUNT.
CONDEMNED TO TRAVEL THE ENDLESS DIMENSIONS FOREVER. HUNTING. PROVING MYSELF. WITH THE HOPE THAT, ONE DAY, I WOULD EARN BACK MY PLACE AMONG MY FAMILY.

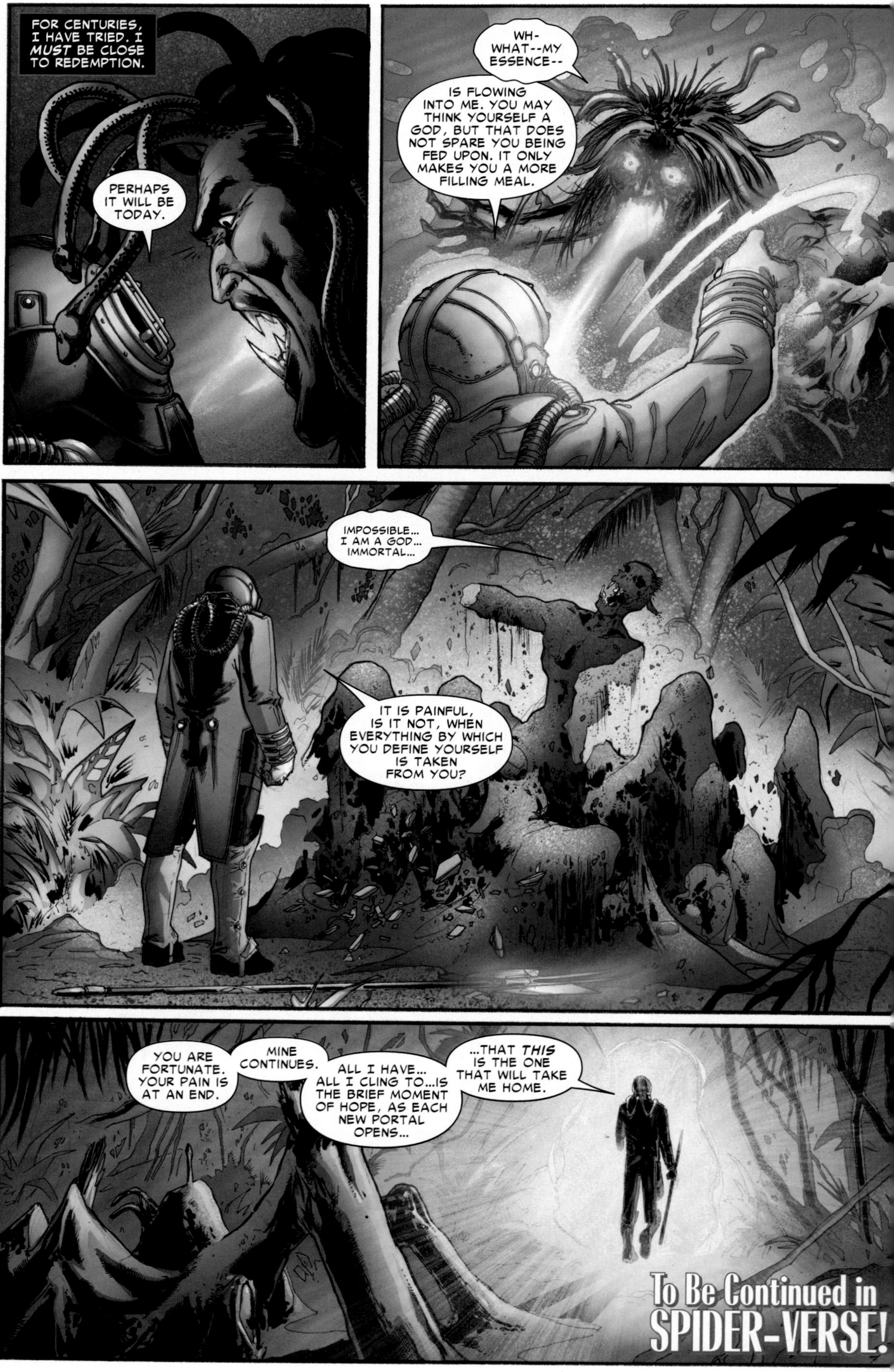
FOR CENTURIES, I HAVE TRIED. I *MUST* BE CLOSE TO REDEMPTION.
PERHAPS IT WILL BE TODAY.
WH- WHAT--MY ESSENCE--
IS FLOWING INTO ME. YOU MAY THINK YOURSELF A GOD, BUT THAT DOES NOT SPARE YOU BEING FED UPON. IT ONLY MAKES YOU A MORE FILLING MEAL.
IMPOSSIBLE... I AM A GOD... IMMORTAL...
IT IS PAINFUL, IS IT NOT, WHEN EVERYTHING BY WHICH YOU DEFINE YOURSELF IS TAKEN FROM YOU?
YOU ARE FORTUNATE. YOUR PAIN IS AT AN END.
MINE CONTINUES.
ALL I HAVE... ALL I CLING TO...IS THE BRIEF MOMENT OF HOPE, AS EACH NEW PORTAL OPENS...
...THAT *THIS* IS THE ONE THAT WILL TAKE ME HOME.
To Be Continued in SPIDER-VERSE!

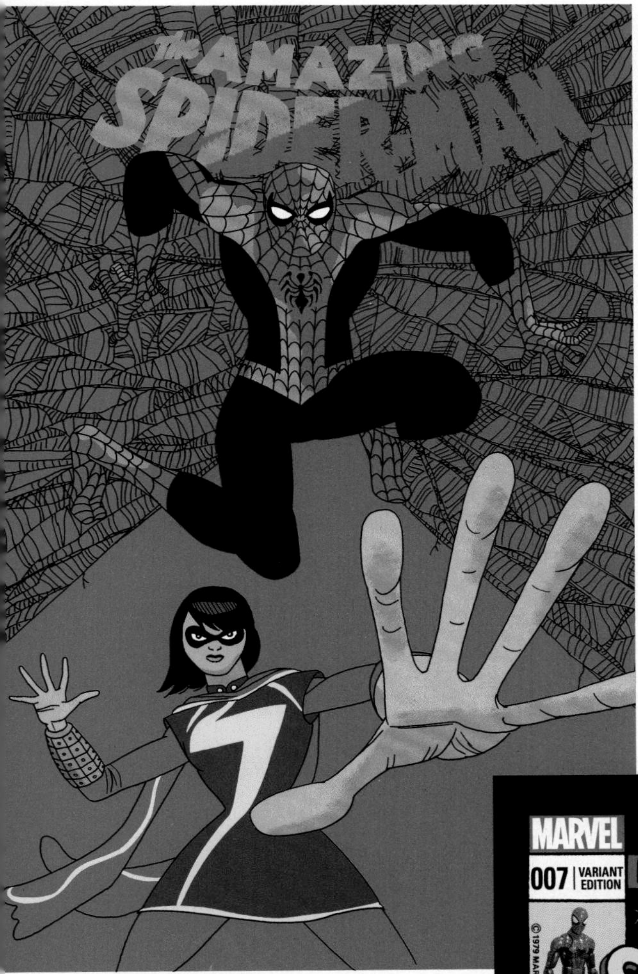
the AMAZING
SPIDER-MAN

AMAZING SPIDER-MAN #7 VARIANT
JAVIER PULIDO

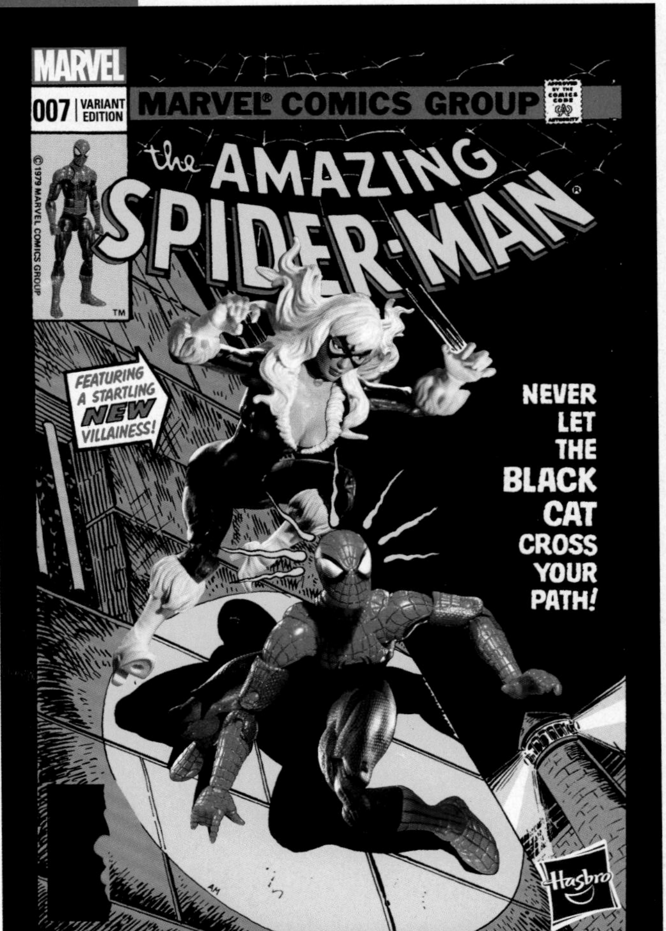
MARVEL
007 VARIANT EDITION
MARVEL® COMICS GROUP
the AMAZING
SPIDER-MAN®
© 1979 MARVEL COMICS GROUP
TM
FEATURING A STARTLING NEW VILLAINESS!
NEVER LET THE BLACK CAT CROSS YOUR PATH!
Hasbro

AMAZING SPIDER-MAN #7 HASBRO VARIANT

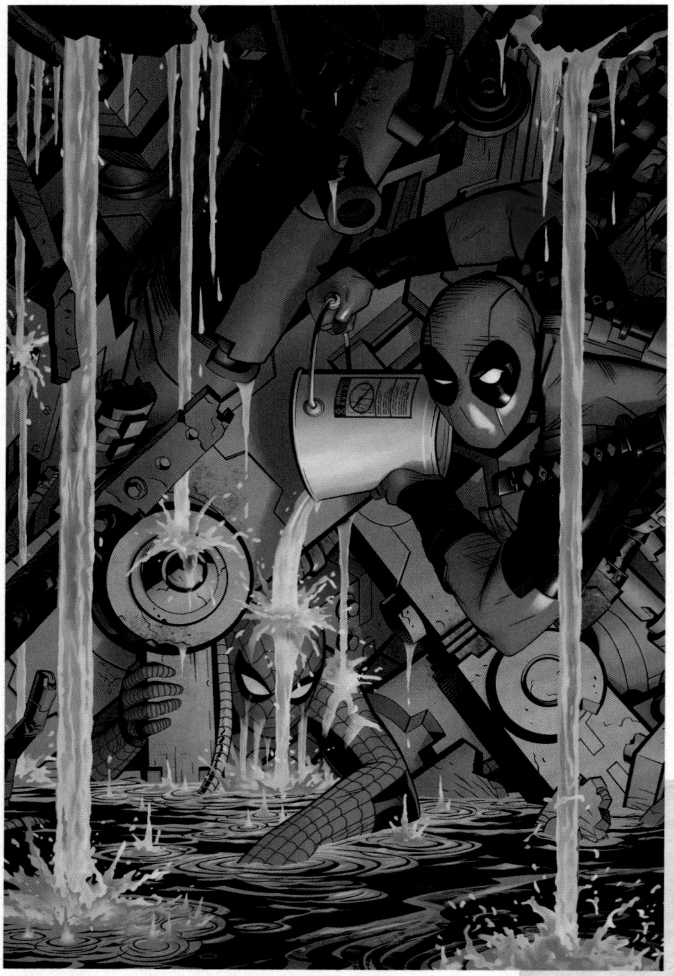

AMAZING SPIDER-MAN #7 DEADPOOL 75TH ANNIVERSARY VARIANT
BY MICHAEL GOLDEN

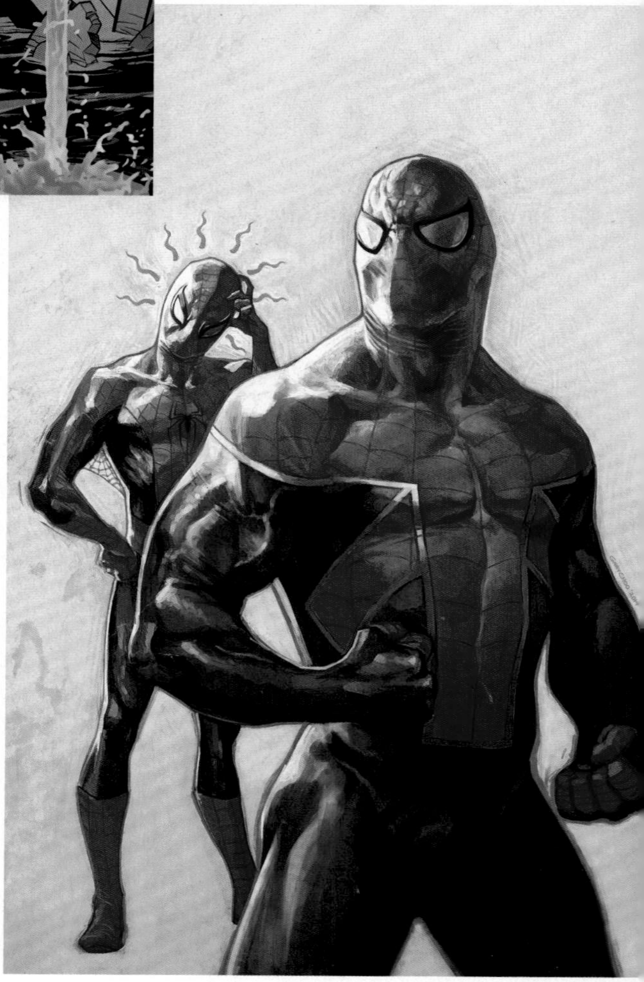

AMAZING SPIDER-MAN #7 VARIAN
BY CHOO YIHANG GA

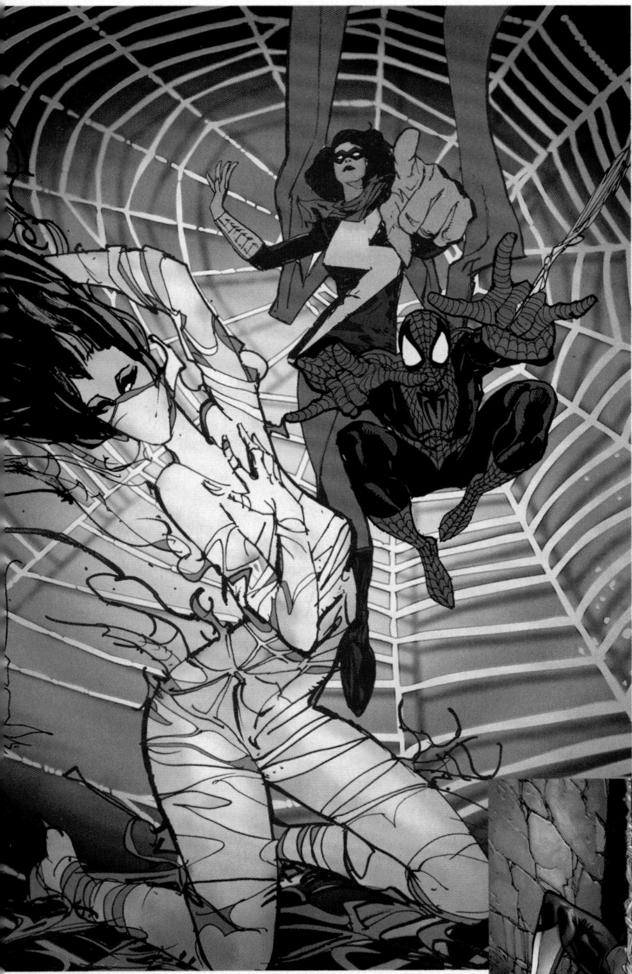

AZING SPIDER-MAN #7 VARIANT
BILL SIENKIEWICZ

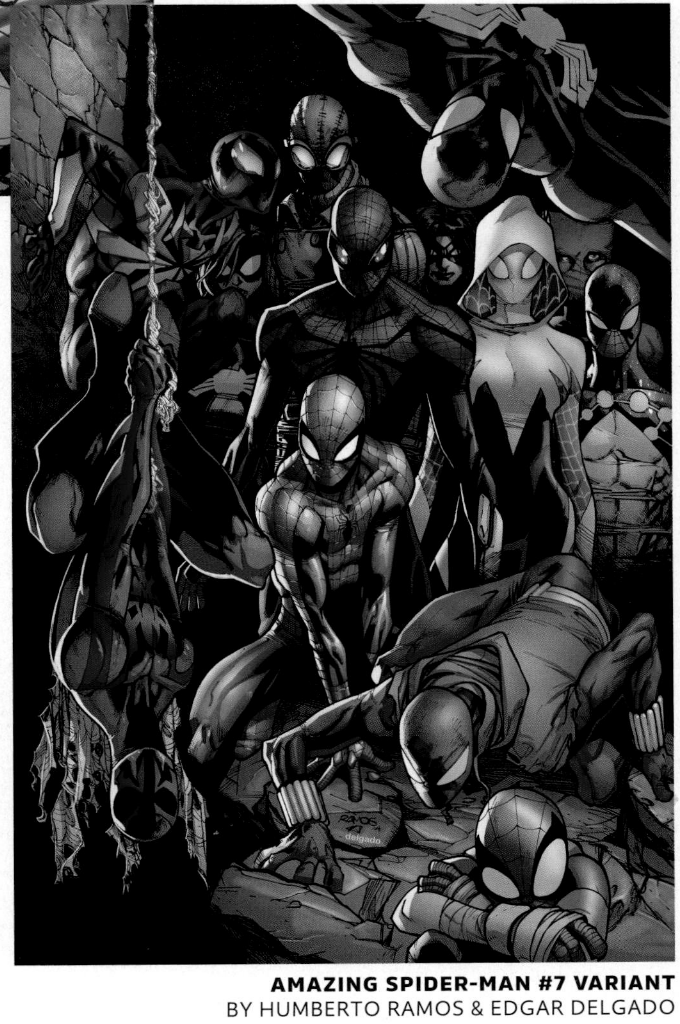
RAMOS
delgado

AMAZING SPIDER-MAN #7 VARIANT
BY HUMBERTO RAMOS & EDGAR DELGADO

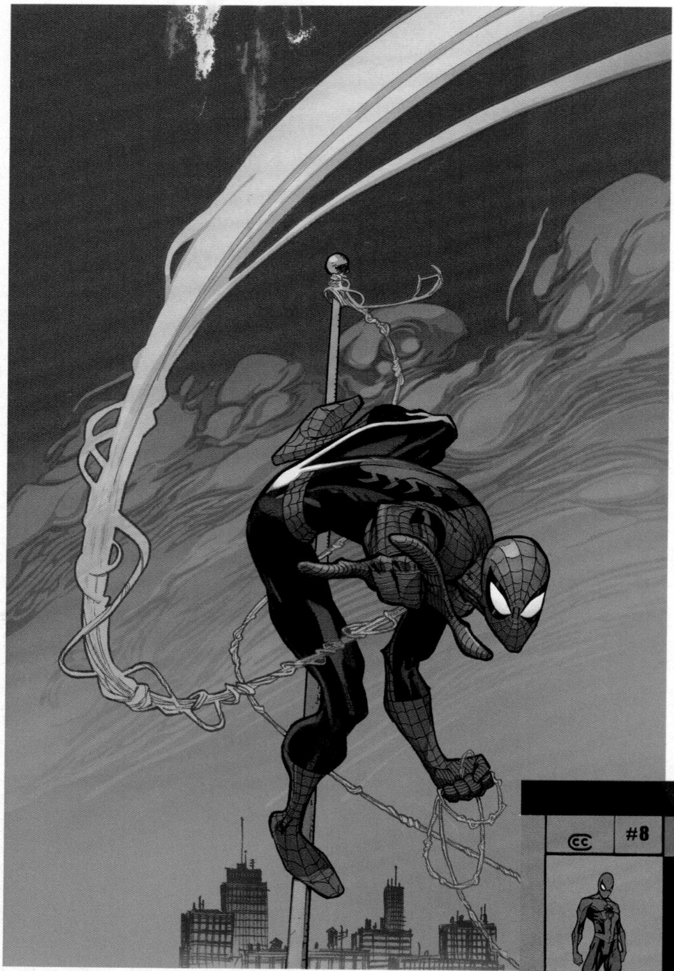

AMAZING SPIDER-MAN #8 VARIANT
BY RYAN OTTLEY & MARTE GRACIA

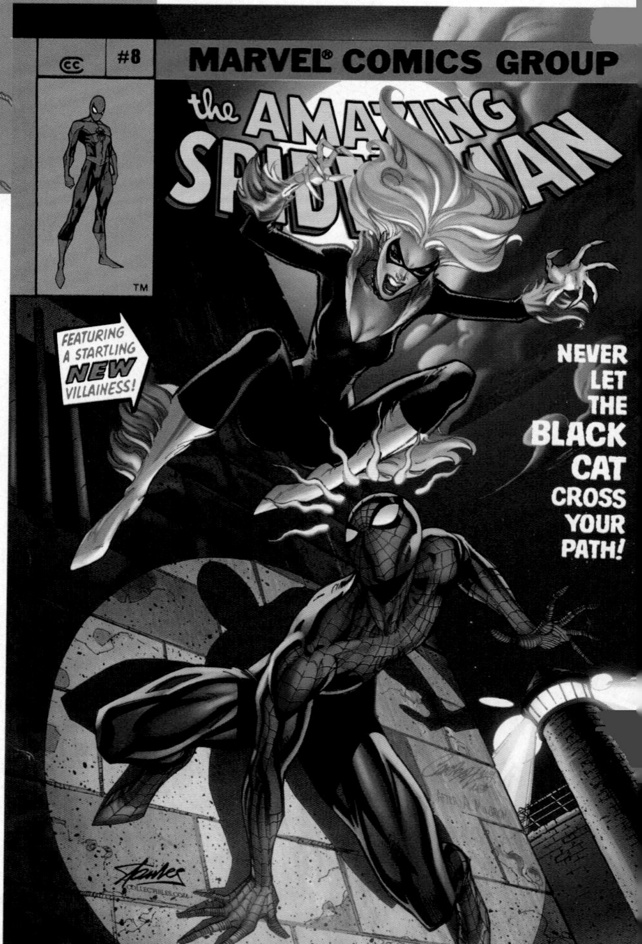
#8
MARVEL® COMICS GROUP
the AMAZING SPIDER-MAN
TM
FEATURING A STARTLING NEW VILLAINESS!
NEVER LET THE BLACK CAT CROSS YOUR PATH!

AMAZING SPIDER-MAN #8 VARIA
BY J. SCOTT CAMPBELL & NEI RUFFI

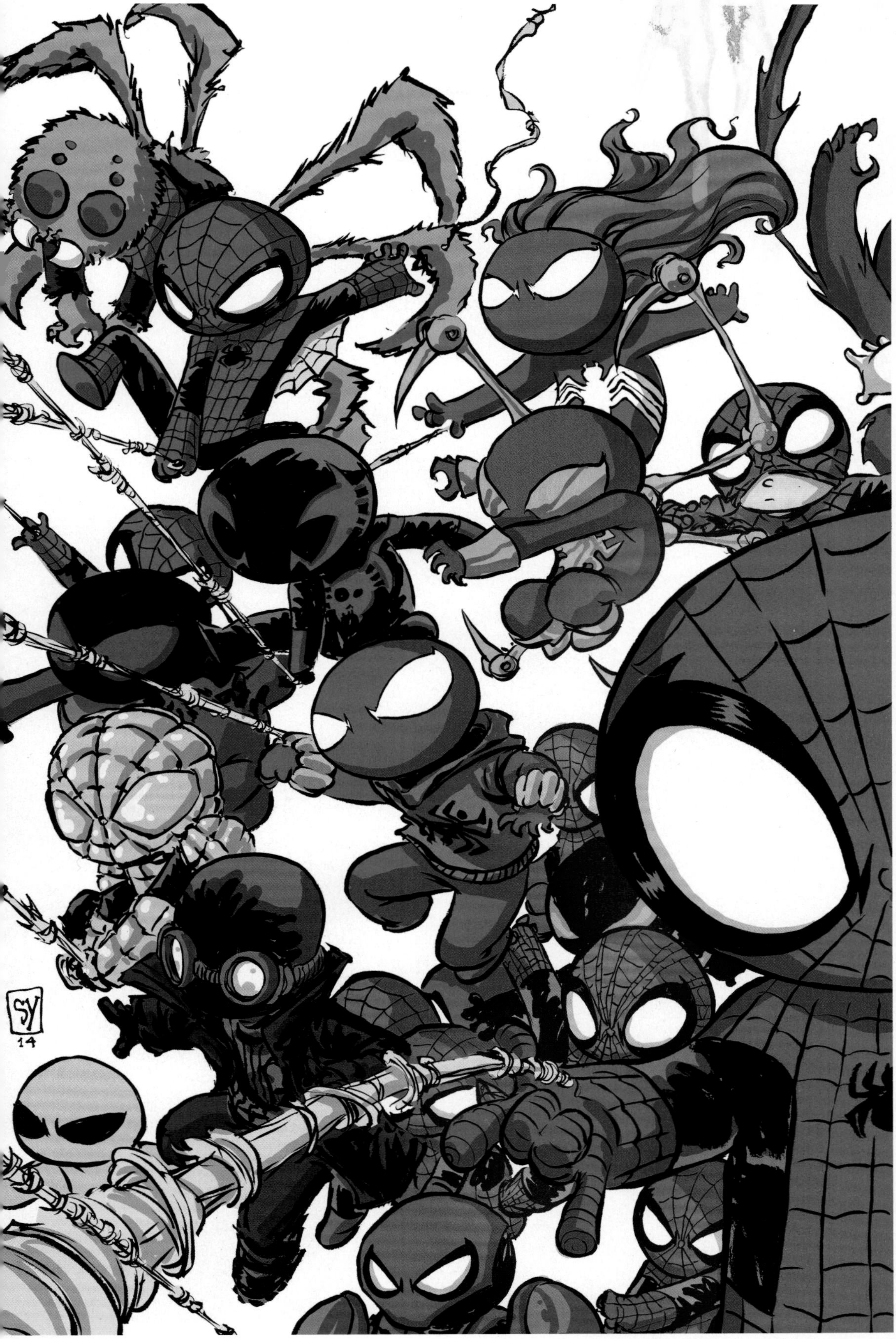
SY
14

SUPERIOR SPIDER-MAN #32 VARIANT
BY SKOTTIE YOUNG

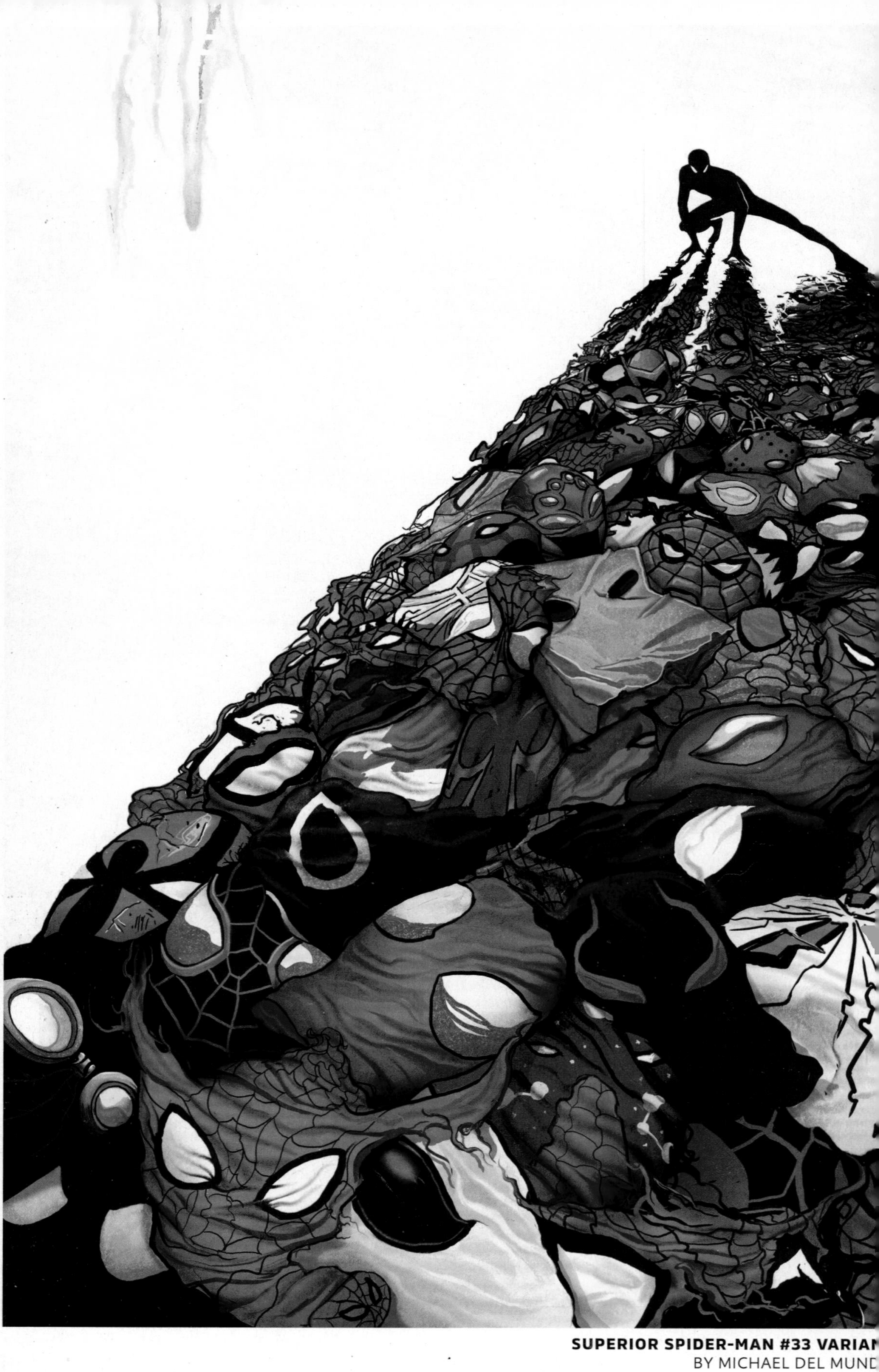

SUPERIOR SPIDER-MAN #33 VARIAN
BY MICHAEL DEL MUND